The Wages of Motherhood

Also by Gwendolyn Mink—

*Old Labor and New Immigrants in American Political
Development: Union, Party, and State, 1875–1920*

The Wages of Motherhood INEQUALITY

IN THE WELFARE STATE, 1917–1942

GWENDOLYN MINK

Cornell University Press

ITHACA AND LONDON

First published 1995 by Cornell University Press.

Printed in the United States of America

⊗ The paper in this book meets the minimum requirements
of the American National Standard for Information Sciences—
Permanence of Paper for Printed Library Materials, ANSI Z39.48–1984.

Library of Congress Cataloging-in-Publication Data

Mink, Gwendolyn, 1952–
    The wages of motherhood : inequality in the welfare state, 1917–
1942 / Gwendolyn Mink.
        p.   cm.
    Includes bibliographical references and index.
    ISBN 0-8014-2234-5
    1. Maternal and infant welfare—Government policy—United States.
2. Motherhood—Government policy—United States. 3. Poor women—
Government policy—United States. 4. New Deal, 1933–39. 5. United
States—Economic conditions—1918–1945. I. Title.
HV699.M525   1995
362.83'0973—dc20   94-39190

C · O · N · T · E · N · T · S

P · R · E · F · A · C · E

How did welfare—a policy once celebrated as a break-through for social provision—become a metonym for women's inequality? Why are some citizens stigmatized for depending on the state while others enjoy richer benefits with social approval? How did a policy once praised for honoring motherhood become the icon of the race-coded politics of the late twentieth century? This book examines the racial and cultural regulation of women in welfare policy and politics between the two World Wars in a search for answers to these questions.

I start from a now-familiar observation: that Anglo American women policy activists cleared a place for women in the state and won policies to mitigate the effects of other women's poverty. My aim is to define how Anglo American women reformers interwove their own racial and cultural perspectives with their genuine concern for poor women. Along with gender prescriptions, women welfare reformers imposed cultural rules and admonitions through social policies designed to promote Anglo Americanized domestic motherhood.

Gender and culture were the axes of early twentieth-century welfare policies. These policies were won by privileged women and applied to poor women. Although the reformers made a principled claim for social support for motherhood in general, they developed proposals primarily affecting poor, immigrant mothers from southern and eastern Europe—policies that conflated social support for motherhood with expectations about how mothers ought to perform their role.

A mighty body of scholarship now details the gender ideological framework of the U.S. welfare state. During the 1980s, feminist scholars identified the codification of gender inequality in the welfare state as a major theme in welfare history and an enduring problem for women's citizenship. I am indebted to the work of Mimi Abramovitz, Eileen Boris, Barbara Nelson, and Diana Pearce showing the gender bias in the structure of social policy. Linda Gordon has tracked the gendered intellectual and philosophical roots of welfare thought as well as their implications for women's relationship to the state. Twenty years ago, J. Stanley Lemons described the policy commitments and social activism of Anglo American women reformers during the 1920s. More recently, Robyn Muncy, Ellen Fitzpatrick, Molly Ladd-Taylor, and Theda Skocpol have examined the policy contributions of this network of reformers, establishing their decisive influence in the development of mother-directed child welfare policy.

Feminist scholarship has established that political decisions about women's proper place ran to the core of stratification, conflict, and power in the welfare state. In this book I build on existing work but shift the emphasis, adding a cultural and racial focus to the gender analysis. Also, in addition to bringing the cultural dynamics behind maternalist reform into sharper view, I shift the traditional time frame for analysis, and trace the implications of maternalist reform through the interwar years to determine how the initiatives of the Progressive Era became the reflexes of the New Deal. I have organized the book around policy topics, but the discussion proceeds more or less chronologically. Part One sets out the political context of reform and examines mothers' pensions and maternity policy, tracing the stress both policies placed on supervision and education to maternalist ideas about cultural poverty. Part Two explores maternalist interventions in education politics during the 1920s, showing the centrality of cultural reform to the maternalist agenda, articulating nuances of maternalist cultural politics, and charting the lineage from cultural reform to racial liberalism. Part Three tracks maternalist continuities in welfare policy and politics during the New Deal, mapping out the various ways maternalists resisted wage work as an alternative to welfare.

The book ends at the beginning of World War II because in many respects that war opened a new era for women. White, married women entered the wage labor force in unprecedented numbers, many to stay. A new generation of political women came of age, many of whom subordinated the politics of motherhood to a new politics of opportunity. These and other developments arguably complicated the map of racialized gender politics. As early as 1948, for example, legislative discussions led by Congresswomen and clubwomen about war widows' benefits explicitly rejected income supplements for war widows with children, instead favoring a GI Bill for widowed mothers to prepare them for employment. This inchoate expectation that poor single mothers should seek economic security through self-sufficiency and jobs developed over succeeding decades into a fundamental axiom of welfare politics.

I ruminate about some of these changes in the Afterword. But I also point out continuities in the racial and cultural construction of motherhood. Although welfare lost some of its most intrusive aspects as it became an entitlement during the 1960s, the requirements for cultural conformity have turned social opinion against the welfare mothers of today. If anything, racialized gender images have become even more powerful determinants of social policy and politics, even as the principles of women's citizenship have diverged from the single ideal of domestic motherhood.

Late twentieth-century feminists face the challenge of putting our evolving agendas to work for all women. To do so requires shifting our thinking about equality and difference beyond male-female dualisms. As we work for gender equality, we must not forget that "men" and "women" are not homogeneous categories. Ideas about race and culture have always invigorated notions of "American" manhood and womanhood; racism has always entangled ideas about gender. To move beyond the constraints and inequalities of gender we must understand and contest the racial and cultural underpinnings of the gender system itself. Equality for women means equality among women, as well as with men. It means affirming women's many different paths, and recognizing that differences of race, culture, class, and sexuality among us are constitutive of how we each live our womanhood.

Questions directed my research, but my grandmothers and parents inspired me. Their lives and ideas sparked my interest in the welfare state, revealed to me the intersection of women's inequality and cultural politics, and encouraged me to live my own race, culture, and gender unapologetically and in my own way.

Helen Hlavaty Mink became a widow in 1930. A World War I veteran and union organizer in the coal mines of eastern Pennsylvania, my grandfather died of opportunistic pneumonia that his war-damaged lungs could not resist. In the midst of the Great Depression, my grandmother was unable to provide for all of her six children in her own home. My father and three siblings were placed in a Ukrainian Catholic orphanage for six years, until their oldest brother and mother were able to pool an income on which the family could survive. How different things would have been had my grandfather died a decade later. And, as my father often reminds me, how different things would have been for him and his siblings had welfare agencies and courts made my grandmother's decision for her.

Mitama Tateyama Takemoto was the third of eleven children born to Gojiro and Tsuru Tateyama, emigrés from Japan during the great migration of sugar plantation contract laborers to Hawaii in the late nineteenth century. An Anglo American benefactor sent Mitama and her sisters to a missionary school, where she completed the eighth grade. At the Maunaolu Seminary on Maui, Hawaii, my grandmother absorbed Americanizing education. She learned to read and write English, cook oatmeal and other "American" dishes, use doilies—in short, to move confidently among Anglo American ladies. She and my mother accommodated the dominant culture by understanding it, and they showed me how to thrive by choosing our own degree of assimilation and, more important, by cherishing and upholding our own cultural integrity.

If my family inspired me, friends and associates helped me organize, discard, and craft arguments to make that inspiration a book. Dana Frank, Sandra Meucci, and Bill Tetreault read the entire manuscript, boosting my confidence and providing crucial editorial and analytic insights during its final stages of development. Christine Wong, Jeremiah Riemer, Robert Moeller, Carole McCann, Wally Goldfrank, Michael Brown, and Sonia Alvarez responded to various chapters with wildly differing but uniformly helpful criticism. During the most difficult phases of the project, Michael's prodigious avocado harvest kept me fed, Wally's endless supply of mots justes rescued me from frustration, and Chris's theories about the cultural origins of gyoza and ketchup kept me entertained.

Students have been an important part of this project—even those unhappy souls who weren't pleased to find race, culture, and gender at the forefront of a course on American political development. My seminar students patiently allowed me to test ideas about equality and difference, work and motherhood, and the often conflicted affinities of race, culture, and gender. They expanded my thinking by challenging my assumptions and conclusions and by offering their own sophisticated insights.

Julie Andrijeski, Sandra Meucci, Kereth Ami Frankel, Siri Vaeth, Naomi Goldfrank, Melody Rose, and Suzanne Reading were irreplaceable research assistants. Keri Frankel's technical assistance greatly eased the process of checking footnotes, proofreading, and preparing an index.

At Cornell University Press, Peter Agree's early interest in this project stirred my energy and resolution to proceed. His cheerful support and prodding over the years has bailed me out of many a writer's doldrum. Anonymous reviewers offered thorough feedback and provided clear instructions for revision. Barbara Dinneen policed my prose strictly but with generous respect for my voice. Carol Betsch ushered me toward production with firm advice about how to use my last chance for manuscript repair to my best advantage.

Funding from the Rockefeller Foundation and the University of California, Santa Cruz, made my work feasible. The Rockefeller Foundation gave me a year to ponder, read, and write. The university's committee on Faculty Research and the Social Sciences Divisional Research Committee funded incidental expenses as well as travel and research assistance.

GWENDOLYN MINK

Santa Cruz, California

P · A · R · T   O · N · E

THE PROMISE OF MOTHERHOOD
Maternalist Social Policy between the Wars

Miss Abbott focused her principal effort upon the neglected portion of the population. She befriended the mothers of the United States because she realized as few other sociologists did that they hold the fate of the republic in their hands. With similar comprehension she strove for every conceivable advantage for children, appreciating the fact that democracy can survive only with the support of a loyal younger generation.
— *The Washington Evening Star*, June 21, 1939

Throughout the twentieth century, race, culture, and gender have run to the core of welfare policy and politics. "Welfare" began eighty years ago in state-level mothers' pension programs designed to mitigate the poverty of worthy mothers without husbands to depend on. In the Aid to Dependent Children program, the New Deal nationalized the mothers' pension concept, carrying into the modern welfare state its premises and prescriptions. Welfare asked society to honor women's side of the sexual division of labor while naturalizing that division. It supported poor, single women's mother-work while enforcing women's domesticity. It offered political tribute to motherhood while requiring poor women to earn their tribute through cultural assimilation. Welfare's premises were that the health of the polity depended on the quality of its children; that the preparation of the child for citizenship depended on the quality of home life; that mother care was the linchpin of the family; that cultural and individual differences among

I first explored many of the themes developed in this chapter in "The Lady and the Tramp: Gender, Race, and the Origins of the Welfare State," in Linda Gordon, ed., *Women, the State, and Welfare* (Madison, 1990).

3

mothers were differences of quality and not of kind; and that, therefore, the needs of poor mothers were not strictly economic but behavioral, moral, and cultural as well.

Welfare policy was forged between the world wars by educated, middle-class women reformers who worked simultaneously to soften racism and to win political recognition for women. Of northern European stock primarily, these reformers advanced social policies to offset both the social costs of capitalism for mothers and children and the political costs of diversity for the Anglo American order. Until the 1930s, the principal subjects of welfare policy activists were poor, usually southern and eastern European immigrants in cities such as Chicago, New York, and Philadelphia. Along with most of Anglo America, welfare activists understood the cultural practices and individual choices of immigrants in racial terms—terms given scientific validity by Teutonic and Nordic theories of racial hierarchy and backed up by the new science of intelligence testing. Moreover, like most Anglo Americans, they assigned social significance to the spread of unmanaged cultural difference. But where racist hereditarians insisted on the irreversibility of racialized cultural difference, welfare activists believed that culture was the product of environment and therefore amenable to change. During the New Deal, they applied this analysis to African Americans, hoping to win for African American women an equal share in women's welfare state.

Prescribing democratic harmony through the social incorporation of immigrants and African Americans, the reformers drove a wedge into the politics of cultural and racial subordination and exclusion. Tying poverty to culture, they contested the strict separation of public affairs and private life. Pinning the health of the polity to the quality of motherhood, they called upon government to provide economic and educational assistance to poor women and their children. Thus the reformers deployed gender ideology against the strict proscriptions of laissez-faire capitalism, voluntarist trade unionism, and racial essentialism.[1]

---

[1] Some class-premised policies for social provision were debated by progressives, labor, and business during the Progressive Era—in the National Civic Federation, in the American Association for Labor Legislation, and in the Progressive Party. The Progressive Party, for example, included a health plank on its platform in 1912, and Congress considered health provision along with other proposals for social insurance in 1916. But the ambivalence of business toward socializing risks other than those already borne in tort liability (workmen's compensation), the interest of union labor

MATERNALIST SOCIAL POLICY AND WOMEN'S INEQUALITY IN THE WELFARE STATE

If welfare policy served cultural purposes, the primary concern of the middle-class, Anglo American social innovators I discuss in this book was the welfare of the child. The reformers measured child welfare by the home conditions and educational opportunities that either fostered or retarded the child's healthy development. Central to the reformers' definition of healthy development was the degree and speed of the child's assimilation of the conventions of "American" society. The reformers identified mothers as crucial to child welfare, developing a policy template to inspire a "higher," more "American" quality of motherhood.

Called "maternalists" because they targeted mothers in social policy and asserted the social and political significance of the maternal role, these policy activists—Florence Kelley, Julia Lathrop, Grace Abbott, Edith Abbott, Sophonisba Breckinridge, and many others—identified the public interest with private values and so charted women's path into the state. For middle class, Anglo American women, their place in the state included having the vote. For the most privileged among them, it included having a direct role in government—women claimed such policy arenas as the U.S. Children's Bureau and U.S. Women's Bureau. For the least privileged women—southern and eastern European immigrants and women of color—their relationship to the state was limited to their condition as subjects of maternalist social policy.

Women policy innovators drew from a broad tradition of maternalist thinking. It traced its roots from the republican ideology of gendered citizenships to the separate spheres ideology of the Victorian period to the mothers' politics of the late nineteenth and early twentieth centuries which asserted women's political significance to "the race" and the nation. Maternalist thinking perme-

---

in providing for its own constituency, and the concern of the middle class about using public benefits for patronage purposes (e.g., Civil War pensions and outdoor relief) generated powerful resistance to social provision. Daniel Nelson, *Unemployment Insurance: The American Experience* (Madison, 1969), chaps.2 and 3; Roy Lubove, *The Struggle for Social Security* (Pittsburgh, 1986); Jill Quadagno, *The Transformation of Old Age Security* (Chicago, 1988); Gwendolyn Mink, *Old Labor and New Immigrants in American Political Development* (Ithaca, 1986); Michael Rogin, "Voluntarism: The Political Functions of an Anti-Political Doctrine," *Industrial and Labor Relations Review* 15 (1962): 521–535.

ated many women's organizations and crossed racial lines. All maternalists subscribed to the ideal of domestic motherhood, but they did not all share identical political instincts, nor did they reach identical political conclusions.[2] Some Anglo American maternalists—in the National Congress of Mothers, for example— were politically conservative, resistant to the idea of government intervention into family and social affairs. African American maternalists, denied government solutions because of racism and disfranchisement, treated the domestic ideal less as a behavioral prescription for women outside their culture than as a means for women within it to claim respect and justice in Anglo American society.[3]

The Anglo American maternalist reformers considered here played a distinctive role both within maternalism and within the politics of social reform. In directing their innovations toward women less fortunate than themselves and outside the Anglo

---

[2]   On the ideological variations within maternalism, see Sonya Michel, "The Limits of Maternalism: Policies toward American Wage-Earning Mothers during the Progressive Era," in Seth Koven and Sonya Michel, eds., *Mothers of a New World: Maternalist Politics and the Origins of Welfare States* (New York, 1993), pp. 277–321. On women's distinctive relationship to the welfare state more generally, see Barbara Nelson, "The Origins of the Two-Channel Welfare State: Workmen's Compensation and Mothers' Aid," in Linda Gordon, ed., *Women, the State, and Welfare* (Madison, 1990), pp. 123–152; Virginia Sapiro, "The Gender Basis of American Social Policy," in ibid., pp. 36–55; Mimi Abramovitz, *Regulating the Lives of Women: Social Welfare Policy from Colonial Times to the Present* (Boston, 1988); Linda Gordon, "Social Insurance and Public Assistance: The Influence of Gender in Welfare Thought in the United States, 1890–1935," *American Historical Review* 97 (February 1992): 19–54; Stanley Lemons, *The Woman Citizen: Social Feminism in the 1920s* (Urbana, 1973); Robyn Muncy, *Creating a Female Dominion in American Reform, 1890–1935* (New York, 1991); Ellen Fitzpatrick, *Endless Crusade: Women Social Scientists and Progressive Reform* (New York, 1990); Molly Ladd-Taylor, *Mother-Work: Women, Child Welfare, and the State, 1890–1930* (Urbana, 1994); Theda Skocpol, *Protecting Soldiers and Mothers: The Political Origins of Social Policy in the United States* (Cambridge, Mass., 1992).
[3]   Eileen Boris, "The Power of Motherhood: Black and White Activist Women Redefine the Political," in Koven and Michel, *Mothers of a New World*, pp. 213–246; Deborah Gray White, "The Cost of Club Work, the Price of Black Feminism," in Nancy Hewitt and Suzanne Lebsock, eds., *Visible Women: New Essays on American Activism* (Urbana, 1993), pp. 247–270; Evelyn Brooks Higginbotham, "African-American Women's History and the Metalanguage of Race," *Signs* 17 (Winter 1992): 271; Darlene Clark Hine, "Rape and the Inner Lives of Black Women in the Middle West," *Signs* 14 (Summer 1989): 915; Linda Gordon, "Black and White Visions of Welfare: Women's Welfare Activism, 1890–1945," *Journal of American History* 78 (September, 1991): 559–590.

American mainstream, maternalist policy activists acted as the social mothers of poor women. In directing their claims toward the state, these maternalists were agents of Progressive Era reform.

"Progressive maternalists," to borrow Molly Ladd-Taylor's term, made three claims that helped change the political landscape. First, they articulated the public, political significance of woman's role, a significance that not only required women's enfranchisement but governmental recognition of its reciprocal obligations to female citizens. Second, they domesticated anxieties about cultural diversity by linking incentives to cultural conformity with their social innovations. Third, they insisted on the possibility of cultural conformity, even by people widely viewed as members of "lesser races," and thus they strengthened the emerging discourse of racial liberalism.

Progressive maternalist thinking was by no means uniformly "liberating." It called for the social mediation of women's poverty but defined the "needs" of poor, mostly immigrant, women in terms of the gender and cultural interests of the polity. It claimed social and political respect for women's work but confined women to a separate and dependent citizenship. And though it demanded the civic integration of southern and eastern European immigrants and people of color it required in exchange their assimilation to a common, dominant culture.

Progressive maternalists claimed universal political rights for women but did not write universalistic social policies for them. Rather, they crafted homogenizing policies to enhance the quality and conditions of motherhood among women of lower social rank. Maternalists derived their notion of woman's social responsibility from her biological assignment and measured woman's needs by her distance from the dominant culture's family configurations, home customs, and gender norms. Maternalists interwove woman's responsibility with woman's needs in social policies that affirmed the social and political significance of differences between women and men while also addressing cultural and class differences among women. Through separate, gendered provisions tailored to woman's social location, role, and responsibility, then, maternalists claimed policy equity for women in relation to men. But they also sought to establish assimilating, integrative policies intended to nurture similarity among women. The problem with maternalist reform was not that it noticed, and responded to, social and political differences between women and men. Rather, the problem was that it required women to be different from men each in the same way, by accepting their gender role assignment and by approximating a uniform cultural standard of motherhood and family life. Nor was the problem with maternalist cultural reform that it shared the secrets of the dominant class and culture with the "other" America; the problem was that it required the assimilation of those secrets as a precondition for equality. First to European immigrants, then to people of color, maternalists offered the tools of cultural conformity—literacy and language instruction, vocational training, civics lessons, health services—and they became important weapons for subordinated groups. But they also required individuals to earn equality and acquitted society of its responsibilities to treat people as created equal by respecting differences among them. For women, the principle subjects of maternalist social policy, the dual requirements of cultural and gender role conformity prescribed not only our separate incorporation into the welfare state but also our subordination within it.

The prescriptive premises of maternalist policy help explain women's persistent inequality in the welfare state. The progressive maternalist answer to the economic and political effects of patriarchy, capitalism, racism, and masculine democracy on women's lives were child-centered, woman-directed, culturally remedial social policies: mothers' pensions, maternity policy, gendered schooling, protective labor standards. Maternalist prescriptions for women—principally domestic "American" motherhood—modernized gender inequality by politicizing and codifying social roles and relations. Maternalist prescriptions fastened worthy woman's citizenship to the maternal ideal, disparaged and regulated the role of paid labor in women's lives, and legitimated gender segregation in the labor market. Withholding the tools of independent citizenship from most poor women, maternalist prescriptions impaired women's ability to maintain a household outside of marriage and without assistance from the state. And withholding the presumption of equality from women in "lower" cultural castes, maternalist prescriptions inscribed debates about women and welfare with the idiom of culture and character.

THE CULTURAL POLITICS OF MATERNALIST REFORM

The maternalists' social program arose from the politics of political reproduction. Industrialism, immigration, and emancipation simultaneously bred diversity and spread poverty within the citizenry. The movement of new peoples into the political community excited cultural anxieties among settled Americans. These anxieties fired popular and scientific racial ideologies that defined cultural differences as inherited, essential characteristics of groups, that ranked cultures on a hierarchy dominated by Anglo Saxons, and that treated poverty as an index of cultural inferiority.[4] Many settled, "old-stock" Americans felt that cultural differentiation corrupted citizenship and degraded democracy.[5] During the late nineteenth and early twentieth centuries, the forces of exclusion mobilized to defend democracy against diversity through immigration restriction, segregation, disfranchisement, and compulsory monoculturalism. White, middle-class, women reformers countered the clamor for exclusion with an agenda for the social incorporation of new groups through cultural assimilation and the socialization of motherhood.

The reformers shared broad concerns about the quality of the citizenry and the future of democracy. In their writings and in their activities they explored the cultural conditions of poverty and the cultural impediments to good citizenship. Julia Lathrop, for example, warned of the tendency of immigrant men to become "in-

[4] For an excellent intellectual history of race that treats both the culture and color components of racist thinking in the United States, see Thomas Gossett, *Race: The History of an Idea in America* (Dallas, 1965). For a discussion of the changing discourse about race between the wars, see Elazar Barkan, *The Retreat of Scientific Racism: Changing Concepts of Race in Britain and the United States between the World Wars* (Cambridge, 1992).

[5] American thinking about race divided whites, counterposing "old-stock" settled Americans of English, Welsh, Scots, Irish, and German extraction to "new" immigrants from Italy, the Balkans, Slovakia, Lithuania, Russia, and so forth, most of whom were Jewish or Catholic. By artifice of late-nineteenth-century scientific racism, the former groups were assigned the inherent democratic character of Teutonic peoples.

termittent husbands" as a "masculine expediency . . . in the face of non-employment or domestic complexity or both."[6] Writing of the new immigrants serviced by Hull House, which she founded, Jane Addams lamented: "Their ideas and resources are cramped. The desire for higher social pleasure is extinct. They have no share in the traditions and social energy which make for progress. Too often their only place of meeting is a saloon, their only host a bartender; a local demagogue forms their public opinion."[7] But where exclusionist politics took these observations as proof of inferiority and therefore as reasons to resist the incorporation of new peoples, Anglo American women reformers worked to nurture a higher quality of citizenship through education and social interaction.

The maternalists' faith in the nurturing potential of women produced a gendered angle of vision into industrial America's demographic crisis. The underlying assumption was that men and women inhabited separate, but equally significant, political spheres. The manly citizen waged war and engaged in productive labor; the woman citizen raised children and thereby promoted political reproduction. The reformers believed that all women shared the maternal vocation and that therefore all women controlled the future of the republic. Given that the "prime function of woman must ever be the perpetuation of the race," the reformers sought to create one motherhood from diversely situated women.[8] Viewing woman's role as social and political as well as biological, the reformers proposed to nurture mothers in their maternal vocation in order to ensure in turn that children would be nurtured to worthy citizenship.

Industrial America's race challenge heightened the political significance of motherhood and socialized woman's work. The old-stock women reformers who took up this challenge accepted woman's gender assignment even while transforming it. They claimed political rights on the basis of woman's domestic role and values, bringing political visibility to woman's sphere, and they staked out a political role on the basis of women's common identity as nurturers and common gift for caring. "Woman's place is Home,"

---

[6] Quoted by Jane Addams, "Julia Lathrop and Outdoor Relief in Chicago: 1893-94," *Social Service Review* 9 (March 1935): 29.

[7] Jane Addams, *A Centennial Reader* (New York, 1960), p. 11.

[8] Annie Marion MacLean, *Wage-Earning Women* (New York, 1910), p. 177.

wrote suffragist Rheta Childe Dorr. "But Home is not contained within the four walls of an individual home. Home is the community. The city full of people is the Family. The public school is the real Nursery. And badly do the Home and the Family and the Nursery need their mother. . . . Woman's place is Home, and she must not be forbidden to dwell there. . . . For woman's work is race preservation, race improvement, and who opposes her, or interferes with her, simply fights nature, and nature never loses her battles."[9]

If the reformers pinned their case for political rights on the universality of the maternal vocation, they tied their claims for social innovations to the need to universalize the conditions of motherhood. The generic woman regenerated politics "in the service of the family."[10] She brought a "gentler side" to city life and applied domestic skills to "civic housekeeping."[11] She drew attention to the "inherent differences" between men and women and improved the polity through laws that recognized and rewarded those differences.[12] But real women experienced gender differently, depending on class and culture, and accordingly—from the reformers' point of view—did not contribute equally to the task of political reproduction. Recognizing variation in women's gender experiences, reformers aimed to minimize differences among women, especially among women with children.

Staking woman's citizenship on her maternal role, Anglo American women reformers politicized their own domestic values of nurturing and caring. Staking future citizenship on the quality of motherhood, they directed their initiatives at mothers and through mothers to children. Mother-directed, maternalist reform worked to mitigate the effects of poverty on home life and thus to safeguard child welfare. For example, it countered poor mothers' need to work outside the home with income support for families that had lost

---

[9]   Rheta Childe Dorr, *What Eight Million Women Want* (Boston, 1910), pp. 327, 330.
[10]   Florence Kelley, *Modern Industry in Relation to the Family, Health, Education, Morality* (New York, 1914), p. 36.
[11]   Jane Addams, "Why Women Should Vote," *Ladies' Home Journal*, January 1910; Jane Addams, "Utilization of Women in City Government," in *Newer Ideals of Peace* (New York, 1907).
[12]   Florence Kelley, "Should Women Be Treated Identically with Men by the Law?" *American Review* 3 (May–June 1923): 277.

their breadwinner. It taught poor mothers how better to manage family resources through household budgeting and more efficient food selection and preparation. These initiatives promoted domestic motherhood. They also provided venues for the cultural remediation of immigrant family life.

From the universality of the maternal vocation, progressive maternalists drew faith in the individual mother's ability to transcend her social and cultural station. From women's universal role as natural educators, they derived not only women's crucial role in creating the citizenry but an educational strategy for reforming mothers. Maternalists accordingly eschewed the dominant racial discourse and substituted the promise of assimilation for the ideology of subordination and exclusion. The maternalists' gendered perspective led them to contest the invidious racial distinctions that negated the possibility of universal motherhood. Although they generally accepted the view that "new" European immigrants from southern and eastern Europe, along with Latinos, Asians, and Africans, were socially inferior to Anglo Saxons, progressive maternalists rejected the claim that the inferiority was biological, inherent, and immutable. Instead, they traced the social position of groups to the cultures they practiced. A part of Anglo Saxon America, maternalists agreed that cultural diversity heralded the political and moral decay of the American democratic order. But cultural diversity, in the progressive maternalist view, could be managed: culture was neither fixed nor essential. The biological analysis of culture and race embraced by jingoists, nativists, and white supremacists supported segregation, separation, and subordination. The progressive maternalist analysis, by contrast, inspired efforts to bring new cultural groups into the "American" mainstream.

The maternalist commitment to assimilation expressed an emergent racial liberalism, one that stressed the possibility of becoming "American." But the maternalist insistence on conformity—to woman's gender role and to an Americanized family life—exacted a heavy toll for political and social incorporation: new immigrant women had to accept cultural interventions by maternalist policy administrators in exchange for the material benefits of those policies. The interventions did not always require immigrant mothers to eschew their cultures, but they did put policy administrators in charge of deciding what to salvage, modify, or expunge from immigrant traditions. Always, the index of maternalist cultural management was the child's welfare and upbringing as a citizen. Child-centered mothers' policies made the mother the medium for political regeneration but did not invest her with rights and resources for her own sake. The mother's status as a citizen and as a beneficiary of maternalist policies was thus conditional, dependent on her willingness to approximate the maternalists' universal, maternal ideal.

GENDER AND CULTURE IN WORLD WAR I

The Anglo American, progressive maternalist policy leaders whose ideas and innovations are the focus of this study drew their inspiration from their work with immigrants in the settlement houses of New York and Chicago. They were social activists and social researchers legendary for their ardor in improving the lot of the urban poor: Jane Addams, Florence Kelley, Julia Lathrop, Sophonisba Breckinridge, Grace Abbott, Edith Abbott, Mary Anderson, Lillian Wald. They worked with women's organizations—the National Consumers' League, the General Federation of Women's Clubs, the Young Women's Christian Association, the National Congress of Mothers, to name a few—to attract political attention to their ideas and to win policy victories for their specific proposals. An early triumph came in 1912, with the creation of the U.S. Children's Bureau, the brainchild of Florence Kelley and Lillian Wald. The bureau was housed in the Department of Labor and headed by Julia Lathrop. A maternalist place in national government, the Children's Bureau used its investigative authority to monitor child welfare, to assess the progress of local maternalist reforms, and to formulate policy recommendations for mothers and children.

Though maternalist reform made steady progress between 1900 and 1916—judicial approval of protective labor legislation in 1908, wildfire adoption of mothers' aid programs by the states beginning in 1911, and the establishment of the Children's Bureau—World War I provided the definitive boost to the maternalist policy drive. Ironically, when wartime anxieties about the deterioration of

American *manhood* erupted, they catapulted maternalist Americanization initiatives to the forefront of social reform.[13]

Race-conscious monoculturalism, deeply inscribed in American political thinking after sixty years of emancipation and immigration, was inflamed by the wartime draft. For the first time, the American armed forces reflected the ethnic and racial diversity of American society: the army certified 367,000 Black soldiers, for example—some 13 percent of the draftees.[14] This apparent democratization of the American military developed from the contradictions of caste and citizenship, not from widespread affirmation of the equality of male citizens. Though the soldier was the citizen par excellence, many whites objected to the idea that their sons might be drafted to fight and die while young African American men stayed at home. Draft boards were accordingly pressured to recruit universally and thus to create a heterogeneous army.

An army including Blacks and immigrants presented a dilemma for Anglo America. In the South, many whites feared the consequences of a combat-trained Black male population for the southern racial order.[15] In the North, many old-stock whites worried that the presence of immigrants and their children in the army imperiled a competent and patriotic war effort. In both North and South, many Anglo Americans recoiled at the idea that military service would support legitimate claims to equality from people who were not really "American." Although segregation and discrimination limited the mobility of Blacks within the armed forces, for example, commentators predicted that "out of the war would come . . . a 'new negro'," "proud of having been picked by the Army, exposed to social equality while in France, and mobilized by the ideals of freedom, democracy and equality for which he was asked to fight."[16] These fears of social proximity and political equality were height-

---

[13]   John F. McClymer, "Gender and the 'American Way of Life': Women in the Americanization Movement," *Journal of American Ethnic History* 10 (Spring 1991): 3–5.
[14]   Bernard C. Nalty, *Strength for the Fight: A History of Black Americans in the Military* (New York, 1986), p. 108.
[15]   Walter Wilson, "Old Jim Crow in Uniform," *Crisis*, February 1939, p. 44.
[16]   "The American Negro as a Fighting Man," *American Review of Reviews*, August 1918, p. 210; Glenn Frank, "The Clash of Color: The Negro in American Democracy," *Century Magazine*, November–April, 1919–1920, pp. 86–98; W. E. Burghardt Du Bois, "An Essay toward a History of the Black Man in the Great War," *Crisis*, June 1919, p. 79.

ened and seemingly vindicated by the results of mass mental testing of the draftees. Indeed, for white supremacist and assimilationist alike, Army mental test results underscored the corrupting effects of diversity on democratic citizenship.

Though they arrived at different conclusions, commentators from across the political spectrum agreed that the "enlistment records . . . [were] at once a warning and a national disgrace."[17] Army recruitment data showing high rates of illiteracy, mental deficiency, and ill-health among draftees suggested a decline in the quality of American manhood. More important, the army made culture and race the categories of analysis for its data and assigned scientific validity to its findings. Screening tests conducted for the army by hereditarian scientist R.M. Yerkes attributed "low intelligence" among draftees to their race/ethnicity: according to Yerkes' data, the average mental age of Italians was 11.01 years, of Poles 10.74 years, of Blacks 10.41 years.[18]

The highly publicized discovery of mass "feeble-mindedness" in Black and new immigrant America fired racial hostilities but did not halt the demographic diversification of the army. In fact, Blacks were inducted at higher rates than were whites, and even illiterate immigrants were called into service.[19] Thus one observer complained: "Many of [the draftees] could not understand English, and yet they were, of course, compelled to drill in response to orders spoken in English. One officer is said to have placed a foreign-born and an American in line, so that when orders were given the American could tweak the trousers of his neighbor and thus convey the contents of the order."[20]

The army managed diversity—and allayed anxiety about America's defective warriors—by sifting, ranking, and segregating troops by race and culture. The mental tests were useful in this

[17]   George Creel, "Melting Pot or Dumping Ground?" *Collier's*, September 3, 1921, p. 26; Mary White Ovington, "Reconstruction and the Negro," *Crisis*, February 1919, p. 171; S. Josephine Baker, "Lessons from the Draft," American Association for Study and Prevention of Infant Mortality, *Transactions* of the Ninth Annual Meeting (December 5–7, 1918), pp. 181, 187–188.
[18]   Stephen Jay Gould, *Mismeasure of Man* (New York, 1981), chap. 5. Paula Fass provides an excellent discussion of intelligence testing in *Outside In: Minorities and the Transformation of American Education* (New York, 1989), pp. 44–47.
[19]   Walter Wilson, "Old Jim Crow in Uniform," p. 43
[20]   Winthrop D. Lane, "The National Conference of Social Work," *Survey*, June 1, 1918, p. 251.

regard as they graded and grouped mental ability. Beyond the tests were such military personnel policies as racial segregation and combat restrictions for most Black and many new immigrant soldiers. Austro-Hungarian non-citizen recruits, for example, were assigned to menial labor and were barred from certain military theaters. Most Black recruits were classified in support roles, as stevedores and laborers: of the 200,000 Black soldiers sent to France, only 42,000 were combat troops. The army furthermore limited officer training for Blacks, resisted commissioning Black officers and excluded Blacks from artillery units, the air corps, and the navy. The few Black combat units that were assembled for war duty were deployed without combat training; and the four Black regiments in the ninety-third division of the American Expeditionary Force were farmed over to the French.[21]

Indeed, when ranking, separation, and subordination could not be accomplished by army policy alone, the United States sought international cooperation. Unsuccessfully, the army asked the British to take on the Black regiments of the 92nd division and thus to relieve it of all Black combat units.[22] The army urged the French to impose American racial restrictions on the Black American troops under their command. French military authorities thus cautioned their units: "Although a citizen of the United States, the black man is regarded by the white American as an inferior being with whom relations of business or service only are possible. The black is constantly being censured for his want of intelligence and discretion, his lack of civic and professional conscience, and for his tendency toward undue familiarity." The directive concluded:

[21]   Walter Wilson, "Old Jim Crow in Uniform—Part II," *Crisis*, March 1939, p. 73; Du Bois, "An Essay toward a History," pp. 63–87; Nalty, *Strength for the Fight*, pp. 108–109. The decision not to train Black combat troops before sending them to Europe—and the decision to assign most Blacks to labor battalions—was intended to mollify white Americans who worried that combat-ready Blacks would bring disorder to their communities. *The Literary Digest* reported on April 21, 1917, that "Among southern Congressmen . . . we find opposition to universal service on the ground that it would be inadvisable to give thousands of Negroes training in the use of arms." See also, "The Houston Mutiny," *Outlook*, September 5, 1917; "The Houston Horror," *Crisis*, February 1918, pp. 187–188; "Where to Encamp the Negro Troops," *Literary Digest*, September 29, 1917, pp. 14–15; Mary White Ovington, *The Walls Came Tumbling Down* (New York, 1947), pp. 134–139.
[22]   Wilson, "Old Jim Crow in Uniform—Part II."

We must prevent the rise of any pronounced degree of intimacy between French officers and black officers . . . we cannot deal with them on the same plane as with the white American officers without deeply wounding the latter. We must not eat with them, must not shake hands or seek to talk or meet with them outside of the requirements of military service. We must not commend too highly the black American troops, particularly in the presence of [white] Americans. . . . [We must] make a point of keeping the native cantonment population from "spoiling" the Negroes. [White] Americans become greatly incensed at any public expression of intimacy between white and black men.[23]

Despite efforts of the American Army to export Jim Crow and race prejudice, African American soldiers in France were generally welcomed by host communities, which treated them as "white men with black skin." The exposure of several hundred thousand Blacks to different white attitudes portended a change in the Black soldiers' expectations of white America. The decision by the French government to decorate three African American regiments for bravery raised fears that Black soldiers would demand the freedom, equality, and recognition long associated with battlefield heroism.[24]

At the nub of old-stock America's race anxiety was the clash between the masculine ideal of the citizen-soldier and the World War I reality of a culturally plural, polyglot army that included Black men considered to be inferior and immigrant men considered to be un-American. According to the American political tradition, martial sacrifice was the sine qua non of fearless, disinterested, and virtuous manly citizenship. In prerevolutionary America, martial sacrifice was so central to notions of manly virtue that it established a right to freedom: thus in some colonies, slaves who took prisoners in battle were rewarded with emancipation. Political education had been preoccupied with this ethic during the nineteenth century; schoolbooks treated American history as a sequence of military heroics.[25] Public policy affirmed this ethic after the Civil

---

[23] "A French Directive on the Treatment of American Negro Troops in World War I," in Martin Duberman, *In White America* (Boston, 1964), pp. 110–112.
[24] *Survey*, May 13, 1919, p. 207; *Survey*, September 13, 1919, p. 858.
[25] Jean H. Baker, *Affairs of Party: The Political Culture of Northern Democrats in the Mid-Nineteenth Century* (Ithaca, 1983), pp. 84–85.

War, when the pension system for Union Army veterans tied America's first experiment with social provision to military service for the republic.[26] Having sacrificed life, limb, and lungs in the trenches of Europe, would Black and immigrant veterans now assert equality?

The specter of feeble-minded troops and "rapist divisions" combined with the fear of immigrant radicalism to ensure that immigrant and Black men could not easily claim citizen equality after the war. Notwithstanding the performance of Black soldiers and the eager response of resident aliens to America's call to arms, homecoming Black and white ethnic veterans encountered an acrimonious race politics. For race essentialists, the army test data made the idea of equality laughable ("it is as absurd as it would be to insist that every laborer should receive a graduate fellowship") and spurred political eugenics through immigration restriction, forced sterilization, a carefully controlled franchise, and lynching.[27] For many sectors of the Anglo American public, the enlistment records sharpened old prejudices and kindled new ones, not only in the South, where white supremacy ruled, but also in the North, where hundreds of thousands of Blacks had migrated by 1920 and where the majority of new immigrants had settled.[28] Racism, monoculturalism, xenophobia, and violence greeted returning new immigrant and Black soldiers: seventy-six Blacks died by lynching in 1919; the Ku Klux Klan nationalized its activities and

[26]   Heywood Sanders, "Paying for the 'Bloody Shirt': The Politics of Civil War Pensions," in Barry Rundquist, ed., *Political Benefits* (Lexington, Mass., 1980), pp. 137–159; Richard Bensel, *Sectionalism and American Political Development* (Madison, 1984), pp. 60–73; Theda Skocpol, *Protecting Soldiers and Mothers*, chap. 2.
[27]   R. M. Yerkes quoted in Gould, *Mismeasure of Man*, p. 197. For examples of race essentialist analyses of and prescriptions for safeguarding the citizenry and the republic, see, e.g., H. H. Goddard, *Psychology of the Normal and Subnormal* (New York, 1919), pp. 237–246; Lothrop Stoddard, *The Rising Tide of Color* (New York, 1920); Madison Grant, *The Passing of the Great Race* (New York, 1921); C. C. Brigham, *A Study of American Intelligence* (Princeton, 1923).
[28]   Professor Kelly Miller of Howard University warned that "the feeling of the white race against the Negro varies directly as the square of the distance of removal from the mass." Quoted in the *Survey*, June 1, 1918, p. 257. By 1923, it was widely believed that "the negroes attracted to the North in this and recent years are largely from the lowest classes. They are illiterate, happy-go-lucky, highly emotional, highly gregarious, and grossly ignorant. They have been fed up on wild tales of equality, and they enter the cities of the North wild to experience hitherto unknown freedom and social privilege." W. O. Saunders, "Why Jim Crow Is Flying North," *Collier's*, December 8, 1923, p. 16.

broadened its hateful creed to include Jews and Catholics, along with Blacks; "Americanization" became the watchword for the schools, industry, and the American Legion; and race riots erupted in Chicago, Washington, and other cities.[29]

New immigrant and African American members of the American Expeditionary Force returned to a country intent on criminalizing their leisure habits (Prohibition), expelling the least "American" among them (deportation of anarchists), bleaching their cultures (Americanization), limiting their numbers (the National Origins Quota and eugenics), and fixing them to their place through terror and intimidation. In Georgia and Mississippi, whites lynched Black soldiers for appearing in public in uniform. In industrial communities, white workers harassed Black migrants. In Chicago, white mobs rioted against the expanding Black community. In Washington, D.C. white soldiers incited a three-day riot against Blacks for their "crimes against white women" and other "outrages" (including honors received from the French government). In factories, employers such as Henry Ford marched immigrants into melting pots and fished them out waving flags, wearing "American" clothes, and speaking English.[30]

The federal government, too, disparaged the martial contributions of Black soldiers, in particular. In an act emblematic of white supremacy, the U.S. Army excluded African American troops from the victory parade in Paris. The Congress later tabled a proposal for universal military service, partly in deference to southern objections to the idea of a standing army that included armed or combat-trained Black troops. Beginning in 1919, the War Department severely curtailed new African American enlistments in the army. Thereafter, very few Black men could achieve the full manly citizenship associated with military service: by the end of the 1930s, Blacks accounted for less than 2 percent of the combined strength of the army and the National Guard.[31]

In addition, the federal government was slow and stingy in

[29] Mary White Ovington, "The Gunpowder of Race Antagonism," *American City* (September 1919): 248–251; "Our Own Subject Race Rebels," *Literary Digest*, August 2, 1919, p. 25; Wilson, "Old Jim Crow in Uniform," p. 42.

[30] McClymer, "Gender and the 'American Way of Life,' " p. 9; Guichard Parris and Lester Brooks, *Blacks in the City: A History of the National Urban League* (Boston, 1971), chap. 16; W. E. B. Du Bois, *Dusk of Dawn* (New York, 1940), pp. 263–265.

[31] Nalty, *Strength for the Fight*, pp. 128–133.

awarding social benefits to veterans. During the nineteenth century, government had steadily developed rewards for veterans of wars. Veterans of the Revolutionary War and of the War of 1812 received land grants and cash bonuses. Needy veterans received pensions. During the 1830s, all veterans and their widows became categorically eligible for pensions. Union Army veterans enjoyed preference in the Homestead Act, received free prosthetics and incidental medical care at thirteen branches of the National Home for Disabled Volunteer Soldiers, experienced preference in federal employment; and collected pensions for the disabled and their dependents until 1890, when pensions were offered to aging and unemployable veterans, as well. Veterans of the Indian Wars and the Spanish American War and their dependents received similar compensation.[32] Veterans of the first twentieth-century war, by contrast, had to engage in considerable political combat to indemnify their sacrifices and secure rewards for service. Reluctant to extend new benefits to World War I veterans qua veterans, the government's policy towards World War I veterans created distinctions among soldiers—distinctions based in part on the nature of the soldier's sacrifice, but also, in practice, on inequalities in political status and social relations.

To be sure, the federal government promised treatment and compensation to war-injured or war-disabled soldiers, but these benefits were not always adequate or reliable. Also, when the United States entered the war, Congress offered contributory life insurance to veterans and guaranteed hospitalization, vocational rehabilitation, and pension benefits to service-disabled soldiers.[33] In a reaction against the corruption of the Civil War pension system by patronage politics, World War I veterans' policy was both more strictly and more bureaucratically administered than its predecessors, which meant that legitimate benefits could be difficult to collect. The army medical records needed to prove injury or disability, for example, were typically sketchy and incomplete. Furthermore,

---

[32]   Dixon Wecter, *When Johnny Comes Marching Home* (Cambridge, Mass., 1944), pp. 205–206, 211–216, 250–253; William Graebner, *A History of Retirement: The Meaning and Function of an American Institution* (New Haven, 1980), pp. 58–62.
[33]   *The Provision of Federal Benefits for Veterans: An Historical Analysis of Major Veterans' Legislation, 1862-1954*, U.S. House of Representatives, Committee on Veterans' Affairs (Washington, D.C., 1955), pp. 198–199.

"service-disability" was narrowly construed, so that veterans who had been exposed to diseases, trauma, or gasses during the war but whose illnesses did not develop until afterward, were not extended medical benefits until the mid-1920s. Even disabled veterans who met the policy's criteria often found medical services difficult to obtain, for nonmilitary public hospital facilities were scarce generally and, in the South, Jim Crow hospital policies were enforced.[34] Meanwhile, the broadly accessible veterans' pension system of the late nineteenth century was now directed only at the service-disabled.

Equally important, World War I veterans' policy did not provide readjustment programs and benefits akin to the land grants and public jobs offered to nineteenth-century veterans.[35] Readjustment bonuses to compensate veterans for enduring the risks of war and for missing out on wartime prosperity were refused by Congressional majorities. Readjustment training was likewise refused for the non-service-disabled. Despite the salience of education policy on the national agenda—as a result of the educational deficit revealed by the draft—no education or training provisions were developed for the healthy veterans. And though the service-disabled were promised vocational training, this training was channeled through business and trade schools and through colleges. Illiterate or "feeble-minded" disabled veterans who had not completed elementary school before the war—75 percent of all Black soldiers—thus were not beneficiaries of the program.[36]

The leaner restrictions of World War I veterans' policy owed in part to the fact that veteran's programs had been poisoned by the patronage politics of the Civil War pension system and in part to public resistance to the expansion of the federal role following the war, as well as to the political effects of later scandals in the Veterans' Bureau under Warren Harding. But the relative stinginess

---

[34]   W. E. B. Du Bois, "The Tuskegee Hospital," *Crisis*, July 1923, p. 106; "The Tuskegee Hospital Muddle," *Crisis*, September 1923, pp. 216–218; Statement of Charles H. Houston, National Association for the Advancement of Colored People, U.S. Senate, Committee on Finance, Economic Security Act *Hearings* (S.1130) 74th Congress, 1st session (Washington, D.C., 1935), pp. 646–647.

[35]   Sar A. Levitan and Karen A. Cleary, *Old Wars Remain Unfinished: The Veteran's Benefit System* (Baltimore, 1973), p. 9.

[36]   Wilson, "Old Jim Crow in Uniform," p. 42; Wecter, *When Johnny Comes Marching Home*, pp. 396–402.

of the federal response to World War I veterans also reflected a decline of the martial ethic: the citizen-soldier was no longer presumed to be morally worthy. The decline of the martial ethic coincided with the rise of a culturally heterogeneous army, held in suspicion because of a diversity that had been "scientifically" correlated with a lower caliber of soldier. The outbreak of virulent racism, anti-radicalism, and jingoism in 1919 focused racial and cultural suspicions and gelled the view that not all soldiers were *deserving* veterans. Anglo American veterans' groups (the American Legion and Veterans of Foreign Wars) affirmed the new cultural and racial ratcheting of martial citizenship in their anti-alien campaigns and hyperpatriotic crusades.

While many returning soldiers were greeted with parades, confetti, training, jobs, hospitalization, and pensions, many others were not. World War I veterans were admonished that patriotic virtue required selfless sacrifice, which meant risks without remuneration. Under pressure from the American Legion and VFW, Congress finally granted general bonus certificates to veterans in 1925, but the certificates could not be redeemed until 1945. Congress also extended veterans a preference in federal employment —a preference not easily put to use by poorly educated new immigrant veterans and not available at all to Black veterans in a segregated government. For the most part, then, able-bodied veterans were denied the rewards extended in one form or another to their predecessors. Yet, into the 1930s, they were denounced as "malingerers," as "mercenaries of patriotism," and as a menace to citizenship.[37]

The war did not inspire national interest in supporting and uplifting American manhood. In fact, it intensified suspicion of diversely situated men and reinforced opposition to social provision for "unfit" men. As American Federation of Labor chief Samuel Gompers explained before the war, social provision for men would reward "the weak, the defective, the ineffective, the ignorant, and

[37]   Harold M. Hyman, *American Singularity: The 1787 Northwest Ordinance, the 1862 Homestead and Morrill Acts, and the 1944 G.I. Bill* (Athens, Ga., 1986), chaps. 1 and 2; Ralph Roberts, *The Veteran's Guide to Benefits* (New York, 1989), pp. 7–11; Davis R. B. Ross, *Preparing for Ulysses: Politics and Veterans during World War II* (New York, 1969), chap. 1; Donald J. Lisio, *The War Generation* (Port Washington, N.Y., 1975), pp. 38–58; "Bonus Raid," *Nation*, February 18, 1931, p. 170; "Mercenaries of Patriotism," *New Republic*, February 25, 1931, pp. 30–31.

the incorrigible"; it would validate "servile," "slavish," debased
manhood by servicing it.[38] This view resounded in many quarters
after the war, producing calls for "the eventual elimination of the
unfit stock which produced the unfit individual," as well as efforts
to spread the ethic of manly independence and paternal responsibility.[39]

Meanwhile, the domestic politics of the draft, of industrial mobilization, and of women's war effort actually strengthened maternalist claims for social policies aimed at mothers and children, to
whom the ethic of independence did not apply. Defining maternal
dependency—on unfit, absent, or unassimilated men—as a problem of long-term social and political significance, maternalists appealed to the state to mediate women's dependency. And, taking
the position that the mental and physical deficiencies revealed by
the draft were social rather than biological, maternalist reformers
pushed the goal of creating fit citizens through the uplift of mothers to the top of the reform agenda.

Joined by the National Conference on Child Labor, the National
Conference on Social Work, the League of Women Voters, the General Federation of Women's Clubs, the National Consumers'
League, settlements, and local child welfare agencies, maternalist
leaders in government extracted from the army's draft experience
evidence for more generous and more systematic social investment
in motherhood and child health. Where hereditarian scientists
read the army data as confirming scientific racial typologies, progressive maternalists read it as proof of the social and human costs
of ignorance, illiteracy, poverty, and cultural isolation. Deciding
"that something like half the unfitness was of a character that
could have been prevented by treatment or training during youth,"
maternalists sought to develop preventive policies.[40]

While much of Anglo America pursued a punitive monoculturalism during the years following World War I, progressive Anglo

[38] Samuel Gompers in the *American Federationist* 22 (1915): 113.
[39] Joseph K. Hart, "Public Welfare and Our Democratic Institutions," American
Academy of Political and Social Science *Annals* 105 (January 1923): 34; Allen F.
Davis, *Spearheads of Reform: The Social Settlements and the Progressive Movement*
(New York, 1967).
[40] Lilian Brandt, "A Program for Child Protection," *Survey*, December 14, 1918, pp.
338–342; William Harper Dean, "Safe Motherhood," *Ladies' Home Journal*, December 1920, p. 42.

American maternalists worked to defend the culture by assimilating women and children within it. Reprising their prewar strategies—rooted in settlements, social work, and schools—for moral, physical, and mental uplift through social interaction and cultural remediation, maternalists called for government policies linking mother and state in the reproduction of American democracy.[41]

MATERNALIST REFORM AND THE WELFARE STATE

Springing from the maternalists' gender ideology, welfare politics and policy during the 1920s forwarded cultural reform. Whereas the assimilationist impulse propelled maternalist efforts throughout the Progressive Era, World War I drove assimilation to the core of maternalist efforts and raised those efforts to the arena of social policy.[42] The wartime draft and wartime nationalism stoked concerns about the relationship of new immigrants and African Americans to the political community. The universal manhood draft carried with it the implication of manhood equality and thus threatened to unravel the racial organization of American society. Meanwhile, the draft screening scheme seemed to confirm the popular assumption that the quality of manhood varied by race and culture, vindicating prewar calls either to manage diversity or to expunge it.

Red-baiting, alien-bating, and white supremacist campaigns waged on during the 1920s, alongside programs to compel Americanism among immigrants in industry. In women's sphere of social policy and the state, however, maternalists domesticated Americanization and worked to induce cultural conformity among mothers and children through education and conditional social benefits. Holding that "Americanization comes from within," maternalists counseled that assimilation could best be achieved by example and interaction.[43] They implemented this strategy in policies that piggybacked cultural reform onto social and educational provision.

[41]   Allen T. Burns, "Uniting Native and Foreign Born," *Survey*, June 21, 1919, p. 453; "Uniting Native and Foreign Born in America," *Survey*, May 8, 1920. p. 8.
[42]   Graham Taylor, *Pioneering on Social Frontiers* (Chicago, 1930), pp. 215–216.
[43]   Mrs. G. V. Simkhovitch, "The Relation of the Foreign Born to His Home and Neighborhood," Americanization Conference *Proceedings*, Bureau of Education, Department of the Interior (Washington, D.C., 1919), pp. 277–284.

As Frances Kellor, a settlement veteran and vice-chair of the Committee for Immigrants and of the National Americanization Committee, explained, the race problem was a problem of social adjustment, not evidence of immigrants' inability to conform: "Americans have perhaps too readily assumed that all immigrants can be assimilated with equal ease. We now realize . . . that some races, unfamiliar with our language, form of government, industrial organization, financial institutions, and standards of living require much more aggressive efforts toward assimilation."[44] Reformers like Kellor drew from wartime experience the lesson that "the real problem of reconstruction was not in industrial and financial fields, which had greatly prospered and expanded during the war; but . . . in the field of race relations which had greatly suffered during the war."[45] Others identified the home as a place for social adjustment and improved race relations. Edith Terry Bremer of the YWCA's International Institutes reasoned that "to men it may appear that America's great concern is over the immigrants who could be citizens and soldiers. . . . [But] to America the 'immigration problem' is a great 'problem' of homes. . . . When it comes to homes, women and not men become the important factors."[46]

Maternalists answered wartime cultural anxieties with policies aimed at bringing immigrant mothers into conformity with Anglo American standards of childraising. Schooled in a tradition that tied cultural uplift to social reform, armed with new political weapons at the ballot box and in government, and left alone in woman's sphere of public policy, progressive maternalists pursued a program of social protection—income subsidies, health education, and schooling—that promised to safeguard society against unmediated diversity while protecting women and families against the degradations of poverty. The reformers' premise was that racial and cultural differences could be transcended and that good citizens could thereby be made. Recognizing "the inviolability of the relation of mother and child, [the state's] stake in the preservation of the home, and the unique social value of the service rendered by mothers," maternalists monitored mothers' pension programs, won a

---

[44] Frances Kellor, *Immigration and the Future* (New York, 1920), p. 65.
[45] Ibid., p. 59.
[46] Quoted in McClymer, "Gender and the 'American Way of Life,' " p. 10.

federal maternity and infancy policy, and promoted school reform to uplift home life and train citizens, all to enhance democracy's future.[47]

The relationship between women and the state charted by maternalist reform in the second and third decades of the century yielded women's distinctive position in the modern American welfare state. Maternalists won affirmation of their assumptions and innovations during the New Deal, when mothers' pensions were grafted onto the work-based welfare state. The reformers extended their innovations into the New Deal when they carved out space in employment programs and labor policy to instill domesticity among mothers.

Maternalist social welfare initiatives between the wars tackled problems of poverty by focussing on dependent motherhood and sought solutions to dilemmas of cultural and racial diversity by regulating mothers. Although these initiatives produced social supports and cultural tools that benefited some women, the interweaving of culture, race, and gender during the formation of the welfare state hindered the development of social rights for women. Measuring woman's welfare against the quality of her motherhood, maternalist initiatives stopped short of valuing motherhood on the terms of mothers themselves. Measuring a mothers' quality by her proximity to an Anglo American, middle-class norm, maternalist policies bred a sticky racial liberalism that conditioned equality on similarity and hardened American ambivalence toward the possibility of difference among equals.

[47]   Mary Bogue, *Administration of Mothers' Aid in Ten Localities*, U.S. Department of Labor, Children's Bureau Publication no.184 (Washington, D.C., 1928), p. 5; Gwendolyn Salisbury Hughes, *Mothers in Industry: Wage-Earning by Mothers in Philadelphia* (New York, 1925), pp. xvii–xviii.

WAGES FOR MOTHERHOOD
Mothers' Pensions and Cultural Reform

> We are fighting to make the world safe for democracy; we must also
> fight to make our children fit to perpetuate this democracy.
> —Dr. S. Josephine Baker, 1918

The wartime preoccupation with unassimilated new immigrants reinforced the belief that the social consequences of poverty were as much a product of home life as of economic condition.
The seat of maternalist policy activism, the U.S. Children's Bureau
took the lead in developing measures that would simultaneously
answer the cultural anxieties of society and mute the economic
hardship of needy families. The bureau's researchers repeated the
method of army draft analysts, interpreting problems of infant
mortality, delinquency, and truancy in terms of the racial and cultural composition of the communities studied. Meanwhile, studies
by maternalist scholar-activists like Sophonisba Breckinridge and
Edith Abbott further associated these social problems with the
structure of families and the quality of family habits, paying special attention to mothers' ability to fulfill family responsibilities.[1]
The fruits of maternalist social policy research were policies designed to improve motherhood through cultural reform. The beneficiary of these policies was the child, the conduit her mother, the
social goal the fully Americanized citizen.

Child-centered maternal reform provided a principle for mothers' pensions. Like other maternalist policies, the pension program
articulated the social and political stakes of woman's proper performance of her gender role by offering public support to needy

---

[1] Sophonisba Breckinridge and Edith Abbott, *The Delinquent Child and the Home*
(New York, 1917).

27

women in exchange for public regulation and supervision of both potential and actual motherhood. As Molly Ladd-Taylor has pointed out, the progressive maternalist aim for mothers' pensions was less to dignify motherhood than to strengthen standards of child welfare.[2] Accordingly, the value maternalists assigned to the work of motherhood depended on the reproduction of biologically, culturally, and ideologically "fit" citizens. Behind public intervention into the practice of motherhood lurked the fear that ethnic, racial, and class deviations from Anglo American, middle-class maternal norms imperiled the cultural and ideological reproduction of a distinctively American citizenry. Maternalist reformers fashioned universalizing policies, building a welfare state that linked the uplift of women's material conditions through social provision to the uplift of mothers' character and quality through Americanization.

Maternalist policies defined ethnic motherhood in opposition to "American" childhood and thereby in opposition to the best interests of the polity. Immigrant children, who were exposed to "American" values and customs in schools, were the motor of assimilation for their family, whereas the mother was isolated in the home and "ignorant of the true American spirit." She nonetheless "exerts more influence over the lives of others than does anyone else."[3] In urban and industrial America, child-focused, mother-directed social policies gave maternalists the opportunity to promote "habit reformation" among mothers so that they might "keep up with their children as they adopt American standards."[4] As one child welfare advocate explained, mother-directed social policies guided "the colonized women in perhaps the line of least resistance and perhaps with least cost."[5] Cultural reformers elaborated this view, arguing that although the individual instruction of mothers—by

[2] Molly Ladd-Taylor, *Mother Work: Women, Child Welfare, and the State, 1890–1930* (Urbana, 1994), p. 138.

[3] Elmer K. Sexton, Assistant Superintendent of Schools, Newark, N.J., to the National Education Association, *Proceedings* (Oakland, Calif., August 1915), p. 442.

[4] Bradley Buell, Secretary, Council on Immigrant Education, New York, "The Immigrant in the Community," National Conference of Social Work *Proceedings*, 52d annual session (June 10–17, 1925), p. 618; L. R. Alderman, "Helps for Teachers of Adult Immigrants and Native Illiterates," Department of the Interior, Bureau of Education, Bulletin no.27 (Washington, D.C., 1928), pp. 35–36.

[5] Sexton to the National Education Association, p. 443.

home visitors, social workers, nurses, and dietitians—was "a continued tedious process because the habits of years have to be overcome; yet the children are the future citizens and it is not right that they should suffer."[6] For the sake of the children and of the republic, motherhood became a cultural project.

When maternalist policy linked social provision to Americanization, it insinuated into social policy discourse the idea that poverty and culture were part of the same problem, the solution to which lay in uplift through conformity. More than any other single policy, mothers' pensions—available in principle in most states by World War I—linked poverty to culture and the welfare of families to assimilation of the "American" way of life. In the philosophy of mothers' pensions articulated by maternalists, in the eligibility criteria applied to recipients, and in the supervision recipients received in exchange for benefits, maternalists conditioned social benefits on the behavior of mothers.

THE CULTURAL DIMENSIONS OF MOTHERS' PENSIONS

In settlement houses, women's organizations, and social agencies, maternalist reformers defined the family as the crucible of Americanism and emphasized the special responsibilities of motherhood to democracy.[7] Though they viewed motherhood as woman's natural vocation, maternalists did not believe that the quality of motherhood was either natural or automatic. As Grace Abbott explained to the House Ways and Means Committee in 1935, in testimony reviewing the history of the mother-directed provisions of the Economic Security Act, "Mothers do not know, just because they are mothers, how to care for children in a sci-

---

[6] Velma Phillips and Laura Howell, "Racial and Other Differences in Dietary Customs," *Journal of Home Economics* 12 (September 1920): 411.

[7] Contesting the masculine bias of many Americanizers, Edith Terry Bremer of the YWCA's International Institutes wrote: "To men it may appear that America's great concern is over the immigrants who could be citizens and soldiers . . . [But] to America the 'Immigration Problem' is a great 'problem' of homes . . . . When it comes to homes, women and not men become important factors." Quoted in John F. McClymer, "Gender and the 'American Way of Life': Women in the Americanization Movement," *Journal of American Ethnic History* 10 (Spring 1991): 10.

entific way, and if they get that supervision, they do know it."[8] The "supervision" entailed visits to poor homes by social workers, nurses, and home teachers who offered instructions on homemaking, childbearing, and child raising.

Though intrusive and condescending in their view that poor women were *culturally* needy, maternalists did assume that all mothers were capable of "development under proper guidance." Indeed, against the hysteria of race essentialism and xenophobia of the World War I period, maternalist reformers insisted that the universality of the maternal vocation was at least as powerful a force for political and social order as cultural differentiation was a force for political and social decay. While Anglo American supremacists preached jingoism, immigration restriction, eugenics, and political repression, maternalists worked to domesticate Americanization in both location and style. To the reformers, Americanization meant the assimilation of common moral, physical, and mental standards established by the dominant Anglo American culture. Maternalists did not mean to erase cultural differences altogether but simply to eliminate their political significance. Frances Kellor, settlement veteran, immigrant reformer, and Americanization chief for the federal Bureau of Education, explained: "For the immigrant the test is whether in a strange country and in the midst of native born Americans and many other races he shows, without sacrifice of racial qualities for which America has no substitute, a capacity to adjust himself to new conditions, to acquire new standards, to follow American trends of thought, and to accept American ideals and ideas."[9]

Maternalists domesticated Americanization through such policies as mothers' pensions and maternity and infancy protection. These mother-directed policies traveled through women to children, standardizing the behavior of one in order to universalize the citizenship of the other. As the director of Pennsylvania's Mothers' Assistance Fund observed in a Children's Bureau study: "Mothers' aid is given in the interest of future citizenship and . . . the test of

---

8   Statement of Miss Grace Abbott, Chicago, Illinois, Editor, *Social Service Review*, and Professor of Public Welfare, University of Chicago, *Economic Security Act Hearings* (HR4120), Committee on Ways and Means, United States House of Representatives, 74th Congress, 1st session (Washington, D.C., 1935), p. 1087.

9   Frances Kellor, *Immigration and the Future* (New York, 1920), p. 257.

its worth and efficacy is not wholly and primarily the alleviation of material distress but also the well-being of the children under supervision, as expressed in terms of adequate mother care, health, both physical and mental, school progress, and preparation for effective manhood and womanhood."[10]

Although mother-directed policies aimed to universalize the quality of motherhood, they did not create universal entitlements for mothers. They claimed only certain kinds of women as their subjects and the management of cultural diversity as a major objective, targeting poor, single mothers and offering means-tested benefits to compensate for an absent paternal wage, thereby to reduce the single mother's need to work outside the home.[11] In northern cities like Chicago, which was a laboratory for maternalist reform, recipients were drawn primarily from the foreign-born population. Though immigrants comprised less than a third of Chicago's population in 1920, they accounted for more than two-thirds of mothers' pension beneficiaries. The demographics of the recipient population was reflected in the moral and cultural philosophy of the program. Furthermore, mothers' pension programs typically distinguished between deserving and undeserving mothers, restricting benefits to morally worthy, assimilable mothers who bore no blame for the plights of their families.[12] This course reflected a consensus achieved at the watershed White House Conference on the Care of Dependent Children in 1909. When the conference endorsed the mothers' aid concept, it added specific caveats regarding the character of recipients: "Children of parents of worthy character, suffering from temporary misfortune, and children

---

[10] Mary Bogue, *Administration of Mothers' Aid in Ten Localities*, U.S. Department of Labor, Children's Bureau Publication no.184 (Washington, D.C., 1928), p. 5. See also Sherman C. Kingsley, "The Theory and Development of the Mothers' Pension Movement," *Proceedings* of the Conference on Social Insurance, U.S. Department of Labor, Bureau of Labor Statistics Bulletin no.212 (Washington, D.C., 1917), pp. 794–803.

[11] According to Joanne Goodwin, 40 percent of women in mother-only families in Chicago worked outside the home. Joanne L. Goodwin, "An American Experiment in Paid Motherhood: The Implementation of Mothers' Pensions in Early Twentieth Century Chicago," *Gender and History* 4 (Autumn 1992): 330.

[12] Winifred Bell provides a good general treatment of distinctions among mothers in early social policy in *Aid to Dependent Children* (New York, 1965), chap. 1. See also Mark Leff, "Consensus for Reform: The Mothers' Pension Movement in the Progressive Era," *Social Service Review* 47 (September 1973): 397–417.

of reasonably efficient and deserving mothers who are without the support of the normal breadwinner, should, as a rule, be kept with their parents, such aid being given as may be necessary to maintain suitable homes for the rearing of children. . . . Except in unusual circumstances, the home should not be broken up for reasons of poverty, but only for considerations of inefficiency and immorality."[13]

Maternalist policy activists welcomed the finding of the White House Conference, for it strengthened their policy claim for poor mothers. This claim had been advanced in 1908 by Julia Lathrop, future director of the U.S. Children's Bureau, when she called for income subsidies for poor mothers. Sophonisba Breckinridge and Jane Addams, both Hull House workers and social thinkers, presented similar proposals at state and national Conferences of Charities and Corrections in 1910. In the same year, Breckinridge published a piece in the *American Journal of Sociology* calling for aid to single mothers "sufficient in amount, regular in payment, dignifying in its assurance of the community's concern for the well-being of her group."[14] Beginning in Illinois in 1911, women mobilized across the spectrum of maternalist politics—local mothers' clubs, the National Congress of Mothers, the General Federation of Women's Clubs, the National Consumers' League, and progressive policy activists from the settlement movement—to win passage of state-level mothers' pension programs. [15]

From the start, these programs conditioned provisions for mothers and children on the quality of mothers and home life. The Massachusetts Commission on Mothers' Pensions, for example, recommended aid "only where there are young children in a good family." Most states' pension statutes required that mothers "meet certain standards as to character" to establish pension eligibility. Most states also required investigation to determine not only whether a mother was a "proper" person but whether her

---

[13]   Quoted in Kingsley, "Theory and Development of the Mothers' Pension Movement," p. 796.

[14]   Sophonisba P. Breckinridge, "Neglected Widowhood in the Juvenile Court," *American Journal of Sociology* 16 (July 1910): 55.

[15]   On the role of women's organizations in the campaign for government-provided benefits for mother-only families, see Theda Skocpol, *Protecting Soldiers and Mothers: The Political Origins of Social Policy in the United States* (Cambridge, Mass., 1992), chap. 8.

home was "a satisfactory place for the training and rearing of the child."[16]

Though the criteria for propriety varied among states, a single mother's conjugal status was a typical index of maternal quality and hence of eligibility. Deserted women were eligible for benefits in some states; divorced women most often were not.[17] Never-married mothers were usually treated as morally suspect and therefore ineligible. Widowed mothers received priority in all state programs; in a few states, they were the only program beneficiaries. Still, widowhood did not establish categorical right to a pension. Even widows had to prove moral character—by showing intelligence, willingness to learn English, piety, celibacy, and full-time child-centered domesticity.[18]

In theory, at least, mothers' assistance eased the economic burden on worthy widowed mothers by regularly supplementing income.[19] It also provided an alternative to warehousing children from destitute families in orphanages and other institutions. As a Children's Bureau report reflected in 1931:

> Twenty years ago mothers' aid or mothers' assistance allowances or mothers' pensions as they were called, represented a new departure in public relief administration . . . . The progress in public provision for dependent children that enables mothers to care for them in their own homes has been one of the most significant developments in the field of public welfare during the last two decades . . . . Back of these developments lie recognition of the essential values of home life in the rearing of children and

[16]   Grace Abbott, *The Child and the State*, vol. 2 (Chicago, 1930), pp. 248–255.

[17]   Some states considered protecting deserted women and their children through "Lazy Husband" laws that required "men who wilfully desert their wives and children without good cause, or by reason of indolence" to financially support their dependents. "Indolent" fathers could be arrested and sentenced to public jobs, with a portion of their pay reserved for the support of dependents. See, e.g., Washingon State Federation of Labor *Proceedings* (1914), pp. 138–139.

[18]   For a discussion of eligibility criteria in one state, see Elizabeth Hall, *Mothers' Assistance in Philadelphia: Actual and Potential Costs* (Hanover, N.H., 1933), pp. 2–3, 25–29.

[19]   Grace Abbott, "Recent Trends in Mothers' Aid," *Social Service Review* 8 (June 1934): 194: "While they often present many health and personality problems and the mother frequently needs other assistance than financial support, the money for these families is the most important service rendered."

acceptance of the principle that no child should be separated from his family because of poverty alone.[20]

If mothers' assistance helped preserve family integrity, it also established the state's interest in the home, specifically in the quality of home conditions maintained by recipients. The very idea of mothers' pensions sprang from the premise that the home "is the great molding force of mind and of character." This concern to promote home life for children was not indiscriminate; rather, it fired interest in the quality of home life by linking family customs and conditions to the quality of children's minds and character. Reformers satisfied this interest by conditioning benefits on recipients' acceptance of instruction and supervision through home visits by dieticians and social workers.[21]

Some proponents likened a mother's pension to "a salary given her by the community as a child rearer".[22] Others compared mothers' pensions to the soldier's unconditional reward for military service under the Civil War Pension System. In fact, however, mothers' pensions were far more contingent benefits than were either a wage or a soldier's indemnity, for they were based on the character and need of the applicant and on the behavior and home conditions of the recipient. According to one commentator, "The expenditure of the large sums of money given by the counties in pensions can be justified only by definite improvement in the surroundings of the children's homes. If the home is degrading, if the mother shows herself unwilling or incapable of raising it to the level which we feel we have the right to expect it to reach, then the pension is not justified. The aim of the law is the benefit of the child, not the assistance of the mother."[23]

The view that assistance should be conditioned on maternal fit-

---

[20]   *Mothers' Aid*, U.S. Department of Labor, Children's Bureau Publication no.220 (Washington, D.C., 1931).
[21]   S. Josephine Baker, "Day Nursery Standards," *Standards of Child Welfare: Report of the Children's Bureau Conferences* (Washington, D.C., 1919) p. 223; S. P. Breckinridge, "Family Budgets," in *Standards*, p. 34; Agnes L. Petersen, "Mothers' Pensions," *Survey*, November 15, 1912, pp. 281–282.
[22]   "From Advocates of the Measure," *Woman Voter*, March 1915, p. 15.
[23]   Mrs. Otto Wittpenn, President, New Jersey State Board of Children's Guardians, "Experiences in Administration of Mothers' Pensions," *Proceedings* of the Conference on Social Insurance, p. 807.

ness dominated mother's pension debates after World War I. The educational aspect of mothers' pension programs took on added urgency in the climate of popular anxiety over the quality of citizens during and after World War I. Reformers transposed the educational deficit exposed by the army draft data into a cultural deficit and redoubled their efforts to "make our children fit to perpetuate this democracy." At the national Americanization Conference sponsored by the federal Bureau of Education in 1919, reformers challenged teachers, nurses, social workers, and industry to promote immigrant assimilation aggressively: "The Surgeon General's report shows that 24.9 per cent of those in the selective draft were unable to write a letter home or to read the newspapers. The conscious or unconscious assimilation of these into the language, ideals, and knowledge of American institutions constitute one of the gravest problems of the reconstruction period."[24] The Bureau of Naturalization accepted the challenge, developing a handbook for the Americanization of immigrant women. Asserting that "America is no better than its homes" and that "foreign-born mothers have much of the responsibility of determining what kind of citizens their children shall become," the pamphlet urged maternal reform through home visits and mothers' classes that taught and monitored domestic management and child welfare.[25]

The mother's influence over family values and family life made her assimilation key to the successful cultural and political integration of future citizens. Her isolation in the home, meanwhile, made the persistent separation of state and family, public and private, culturally and politically untenable. Maternalists worried that "of all the members of the immigrant family, the mother remains most untouched by American influences. The father gets out into the factory and shop, the children are absorbed into the life of the schools and the streets, but the mother lives at home with her old-world customs clinging to her in all that she does."[26]

By asserting the political significance of motherhood and home

[24] C. W. Smith, "Training Teachers for the Americanization Problem," Americanization Conference *Proceedings*, U.S. Department of the Interior, Bureau of Education (Washington, D.C., 1919) p 109.

[25] *Americanization Work among Foreign-Born Women*, U.S. Department of Labor, Bureau of Naturalization (Washington, D.C., 1921).

[26] Josephine Roche, "The Effect of the Cable Law on the Citizenship Status of Foreign Women," National Conference of Social Work *Proceedings* (1925), p. 614.

life, maternalists brought women and the family into public focus during the war years. After the war, armed with suffrage, two agencies in federal government (the Children's Bureau and the newly formed Women's Bureau), and a decade of experience with mothers' pension programs, maternalists worked to study, revise, and expand mothers' pensions in order to Americanize mothers and children.

MOTHERS' PENSIONS AND AMERICANIZATION

The reformers' review of mothers' pension programs during the 1920s generated two related sets of recommendations. The first set addressed problems in the administration of pension programs, and maternalists insisted that social provision be much more closely tied to administrative supervision of recipients' home lives. The second set of recommendations underlined the goal of keeping worthy mothers at home with their children. Here, maternalists argued for increased grant levels, as well as for enforcement of rules barring wage work. The maternalist goal of discouraging wage work by increasing pensions strengthened the call for sharper scrutiny of home life. Children's Bureau chief Julia Lathrop explained the findings of the 1919 Child Welfare Conferences:

The policy of assistance to mothers who are competent to care for their own children is now well established. It is generally recognized that the amount provided should be sufficient to enable the mother to maintain her children suitably in her own home, without resorting to such outside employment as will necessitate leaving her children without proper care and oversight; but in many states the allowances are still entirely inadequate to secure this result under present living costs. The amount required can be determined only by careful and competent case study, which must be renewed from time to time to meet changing conditions.[27]

[27]   Julia Lathrop, "Standards of Child Welfare," American Academy of Political and Social Sciences *Annals* 98 (November 1921): 7.

From the beginning, eligibility criteria for mothers' allowances distinguished deserving from undeserving mothers. But in the maternalist point of view, even deserving mothers required continuing direction and oversight. Mothers' pensions were designed not for angels, but for needy women of reasonably sturdy character who could be molded into mothers of good citizens. The premise was that pensioners were educable—competent, cooperative, and willing to transcend cultural practices reformers considered at odds with child welfare. The education of mothers—the reform of motherhood—was a process that required application of stringent home standards, regular home inspections, and incentives to full-time domesticity.[28]

The call for stricter standards and better enforcement was a reminder that the social policies developed by progressive maternalists were not simply offers of economic security or public services but promises of regulation and instruction as well. This association between mothers' pensions and cultural reform was not new. Prewar calls for public assistance for mothers highlighted the potential educative function of relief policy. According to one analyst, pension boards "recognize[d] that undoubtedly numbers of mothers are too unskilled in cooking, sewing, etc. to give the best home care." Where mothers were ignorant, or where "a large population are accustomed to food which may be ill-adapted to the American climate, the boards would like to see the localities themselves develop ways and means for instructing mothers of young families."[29]

During the twenties, reformers strengthened the educational role of pensions with proposals that made continued eligibility contingent on the assimilation of skills taught by home visitors. Ironically, women who had purchased their own independence—either by hiring domestic servants or by trading domestic motherhood for

---

[28] Edith Abbott and Sophonisba Breckinridge, *The Administration of the Aid-to-Mothers Law in Illinois*, U.S. Department of Labor, Children's Bureau Publication no.82, Legal Series no.7 (Washington, D.C., 1921); Emma O. Lundberg, "Aid to Mothers with Dependent Children," American Academy of Political and Social Science *Annals* 98 (November 1921): 97–105; Florence Nesbitt, *Standards of Public Aid to Children in Their Own Homes*, U.S. Department of Labor, Children's Bureau Publication no. 118 (Washington, D.C., 1923); Emma O. Lundberg, *Public Aid to Mothers with Dependent Children*, U.S. Department of Labor, Children's Bureau Publication no. 162 (Washington, D.C., 1926).

[29] A. E. Sheffield, "Administration of the Mothers' Aid Law in Massachusetts," *Survey*, February 21, 1914, pp. 644–645.

"city housekeeping"—argued for institutionalizing women's dependency through rules enforcing domesticity and regulating maternal behavior.[30]

Sexual activity was one reason some reformers argued for greater state involvement in dependent families' lives. One 1926 study revealed that nearly three-fifths of the working women reporting "conjugal conditions" in seventeen states were *unmarried*—a discovery that alarmed not only eugenicists but also reformers interested in transmitting Anglo American proprieties to working class and immigrant families. Stories about unrestrained breeding by the women least able to support large families elicited calls for tighter enforcement of "clearly and specifically worded" standards in the administration of mothers' pensions.[31]

For most maternalists, however, the impetus to regulate motherhood coincided with an impulse to Americanize it. They accordingly praised states whose pension policies clearly defined the "suitable" home, established regulations for continuing eligibility, and provided for monitoring home life. Some pension programs incorporated regular investigation of recipients to enforce moral and cultural dimensions of "Americanism": celibacy, temperance, English and citizenship training, "American" cooking, and maternal domesticity. Many of these programs also tied a mother's continuing eligibility to the satisfactory school progress of her children. Most pension programs, however, were loosely administered and highly decentralized; as a result, the degree of control varied

---

[30] I. M. Rubinow commented on how class determined woman's relationship to her gender role in an appeal for more generous mothers' aid: "The situation is only met halfway if, with such an allowance, the mother is still compelled to go out to work and neglect the very purpose for which widows' pensions have been established, namely, to devote herself to the care of her children. A woman's career is a possibility in the middle classes, where the earning capacity of the professional woman is sufficiently high to allow for employment of help." *Survey*, May 15, 1924, p. 235.

[31] Petersen, "Mother's Pensions." One such story involved a terminally ill man who produced several children with his wife even after being informed of his hopeless condition. Dependent on charity and various social services while the sick breadwinner was alive, the family would become eligible for a mother's pension upon his death. An angry essayist thus wondered: "Would not the social worker be justified in considering a family whose breadwinner is totally disabled or unable ever to support his family as one who should be referred to a clinic to receive proper contraceptive information? . . . Is it proper social policy to maintain a hands-off attitude while the family continues to multiply and to increase the burden the community is bearing?" Benjamin Glassberg, "What Should a Family Agency Do about It?" *Survey*, May 15, 1925, pp. 230–231.

greatly even within states. Even where clear standards for recipient behavior had been enumerated (for example, the bar on male boarders), enforcement was uneven due to the lack of regular supervision by social workers.[32] Nevertheless, though their efforts were impeded by the local funding and administration of mothers' pensions, maternalists in the Children's Bureau worked with women in welfare agencies and juvenile courts—caseworkers and administrators—to tighten pension standards and administration, thus to tighten the pension programs' mechanisms for assimilation.

Mothers' pensions were designed for moral and educable needy single mothers regardless of race. But the strong connection between racial/cultural status and economic need in urban America meant that a disproportionate number of pension beneficiaries in densely populated northern cities were from new immigrant groups. Meanwhile, strong prejudice against African Americans meant that Black mothers whose economic need established eligibility were disproportionately excluded from the program. According to Joanne Goodwin's data from Chicago in 1920, for example, although African American women heading mother-only families worked for wages to a greater extent than did European-born single mothers (72 percent of Black single mothers as compared with 40 percent of the general single-mother population) and although 50 percent of Black families on poor relief were headed by women, Black single mothers' participation in mothers' pension programs averaged only 3 percent of recipients.[33] Seventy-one percent of Chicago's pensioners, by contrast, were foreign-born; 60 percent came from "new" southern and eastern European immigrant groups. Two-thirds of Philadelphia's pensioners were either foreign-born or African American, and the former group was predominantly of Italian extraction. European immigrants had long been the target of maternalist outreach; their pension status offered maternalists a new opportunity to reform the cultural aspects of their poverty.[34]

In an effort to coordinate standards and administration across

[32] Edith Abbott, "The Administration of the Illinois 'Funds to Parents' Laws," *Proceedings* of the Conference on Social Insurance, pp. 819–834.

[33] Goodwin, "American Experiment," pp. 330, 336.

[34] Breckinridge and Abbott, *Delinquent Child*, p. 84; Elizabeth Hall, *Mothers' Assistance in Philadelphia*, pp. 27–29, 86.

the divisions of federalism, the National Conference on Social Work and the U.S. Children's Bureau convened a Conference on Mothers' Pensions in 1922. To better measure family needs, the conference recommended that administering agencies use budget schedules that itemized anticipated living costs. To better supervise home life, the conference also recommended that recipients be required to submit itemized household expense accounts. The conferees hoped that both budgeting and accounting would support arguments to raise the standard of relief above the meager levels typical in most localities. Just as important, they saw in budgets "carefully designated by the dietician, with the aid of the other workers having to do with family problems," a method of instructing mothers in how best to feed, clothe, and care for children.[35] Likewise, they saw in household accounting an "opportunity for instruction in food values, buying, and household management and thus . . . the basis of educational work."[36] This linking of benefits with instruction in and assimilation of "American" household techniques struck the keynote of maternal reform. Even though maternalists understood poverty as an evil in its own right, their prescriptions for treating the poverty of single mothers hinged on the assumption that poverty and culture were intertwined, and, therefore, Americanized homemaking would offset the effects of poverty.

Maternalists acknowledged the intrusiveness of regulation and supervision and recognized that such interventions could discourage some needy women from applying for assistance. But many reformers and pension administrators considered regulation and supervision to be necessary parts of the exchange between mother and state: "As a caretaker paid by the state, a widowed mother should be expected to manage her home comfortably, and to give care and training to her children."[37] As the employer, the state retained the prerogative to monitor and evaluate the performance of motherhood. As the worker, the mother bore the burden of coping with poverty. Thus Edith Abbott and Sophonisba Breckinridge

[35]   Breckinridge, "Family Budgets," p. 34.
[36]   Conference on Mothers' Pensions *Proceedings*, U.S. Department of Labor, Children's Bureau Publication no.109 (Washington, D.C., 1922), p. 14.
[37]   Evalyn T. Cavin, "Come, Let Us Reason Together," *Survey*, June 15, 1924, p. 347. Cavin headed the Mothers' Assistance Fund for Philadelphia.

pointed approvingly to the interventions of administrators in Chicago:

> The work of the field supervisor is a very important factor in maintaining the best possible care for the pensioned families. Under her direction methods have been worked out for improving the domestic skills of the pensioned mothers and for teaching them the household arts of cleaning, cooking, sewing, and skillful buying. The field supervisor discusses home conditions of the families with the officers in charge and suggests methods of improving the standards of the homes. The probation officer is then supposed to see that these suggestions of the field supervisor are adopted by the family.[38]

The Americanizing thrust of mothers' pension policy debates in the 1920s fastened the needy single mother's economic security to her cultural decisions. The cultural decisions of the single mother—what kind of food to buy, which way to prepare it, how many generations of family to live with, whether to run a child-centered family, what responsibilities to assign to older siblings—were in turn read as behavior. Most pensioners probably sifted and sorted advice from social workers and dieticians, following instructions that seemed most beneficial while rejecting others, but the more cooperative the mother the more worthy was her character judged and the more accessible was her benefit.[39]

MATERNAL REFORM AND WOMEN'S WELFARE

While moral, budgetary, dietary and other cultural instructions imposed an Anglo American model on immigrant home life, rules governing recipients' outside income inserted middle-class assumptions into the working-class home. During the mid-

---

[38] Breckinridge and Abbott, *Delinquent Child*, p. 28.
[39] Alice Hamilton recalls the frustrations of working with immigrant women who, though not unwilling recipients of maternalist interventions, nevertheless did not adopt middle-class, Anglo Saxon instructions wholesale. See Alice Hamilton, *Exploring the Dangerous Trades: The Autobiography of Alice Hamilton, MD* (Boston, 1943), pp. 69–70.

1920s, studies in Pennsylvania showed that less than half of recipients' income came from pensions: 56.5 percent of recipient families' incomes was raised by mothers' and children's wage work and by rent from lodgers: more than half of recipients worked outside the home to make ends meet.[40] Though paid for "the [full-time] care and training of the fatherless wards of the state," mothers were moonlighting. The prevalence of outside income contradicted "the very purpose of the mothers' pension philosophy," for mothers' outside wages (21 percent of recipients' total income) and children's contributions (23.4 percent) were earned "at the expense of time and energy that should have been put into education, or play, or rest, or care of the home."[41]

The maternalists' goal of paying poor single mothers to provide full-time care for their children was at odds with local realities. Pension programs were poorly funded and did not provide a survivable income for most families. Moreover, notwithstanding maternalist policy makers' expectations that local policies would subsidize domesticity, states permitted recipients to work outside the home under limited circumstances. In what was largely a budget-driven accommodation of women's wage work, Illinois, for example, factored women's potential earnings into determining eligibility and grant levels. In Chicago, between 1913 and 1915 two-thirds of recipients worked for wages.[42]

The disjuncture between the philosophy of mothers' pensions and local practice generated appeals for improved pension benefits. Just as the paternal wage should be sufficient to "enabl[e] the mother to specialize in the exercise of the maternal function," wrote Sophonisba Breckinridge, so the single mother's benefit should "enable the mother to maintain her children suitably in her own home, without resorting to such outside employment."[43] The extent of wage work by single mothers also supported proposals to disallow certain sources of supplemental income. The problem of nonpension income gnawed at reformers and administrators whose priority was to keep mothers at home but who nevertheless

[40] Florence Nesbitt, *Standards of Public Aid*, p. 17.
[41] "What Is Desirable Income?" *Survey*, February 17, 1927, p. 644.
[42] Goodwin, "American Experiment," p. 330.
[43] Breckinridge, "Family Budgets," p. 43; Lathrop, "Standards of Child Welfare," p. 7.

recognized that funding in most states was inadequate to support subsistence-level grants to single mothers and their families. In her 1926 study, Emma Lundberg compared the average mothers' assistance grant with the cost of living and found that in thirty-five of the forty-two states with mothers' pension programs, the maximum allowable annual grant to a mother with three children was $800, while their annual cost of living was estimated at $1,000. Worse, in twenty of these states the maximum actual annual grant was a meager $480.[44]

Differences in local political history and conflict over public spending accounted for variations in funding allocated to mothers' pension programs. Within local programs, differences in the moral rank of single mothers affected individual grant levels. Either by rule or as a result of administrative discretion, widows fared better than deserted mothers, for example. (Except in cases of spousal homicide, a widow could only be pitied for her loss, whereas a deserted mother might herself have been at fault. A dead husband can't come back, moreover, whereas a deserting father might be located and ordered to pay child support.) In any event, most recipients could not support their families—let alone assimilate them—on pensions alone.[45]

Though maternalists understood that dependent families could not live on their pensions, they nonetheless worked to restrict recipients' opportunities to augment their income. Working children were not being schooled for citizenship; therefore, reformers sought bars on wage-earning by recipients' children, except during school vacations. Working mothers jeopardized the integrity of the family ("the dependent mother cannot be father and mother both"); therefore, reformers advocated rules limiting wage work. The maternalists' rhetorical association between a mother's worthiness and her full-time, child-centered domesticity stigmatized mothers who worked outside the home even as local programs permitted or encouraged mothers to combine work with welfare.

Children's Bureau and related studies supported the reformers' concerns about wage-earning by mothers. Typical findings included higher infant mortality rates, high truancy rates, and poor

[44] Lundberg, *Public Aid to Mothers with Dependent Children*, p. 17.
[45] Goodwin, "American Experiment," pp. 332–334.

school performance among the children of wage-earning mothers. According to one 1919 study, 80 percent of the children of wage-earning women were in poor health, while "41.2 percent were found to be retarded, as compared with 25.4 percent retardation in all Philadelphia elementary school children."[46] A 1922 study also found "retardation" among wage-earning women's children in Chicago.[47] This retardation, defined as abnormal age-grade progress, was only minimally linked to low intelligence. Though many of the children studied (37 percent) were found to be "dull" and "backward," even more children were deemed retarded either because they came from first-generation immigrant families that spoke little English or because they did not attend school regularly.

Finding that 69 percent of the children of wage-earning mothers were between five and fifteen years of age, the 1919 study warned: "It is during these critical years when the influence of home standards begins to weaken, and the children look to their own numbers for their ideals of conduct, that mothers most frequently divide their attention between wage-earning and housekeeping."[48] Maternalists recommended that recipient mothers be barred from industrial home work, night work, half-time work where two or three children were young, and any work at all if there were five or more children under sixteen in the home.[49] These recommendations recognized the necessity of wage work for women in poor families—they allowed a recipient with only one young child to seek part-time employment, for example—but they clearly aimed to discourage work outside the home by most mothers of dependent children.

Maternalists acknowledged the contradiction between economic necessity and their view of children's interests. Attempting to rec-

---

[46]   Gwendolyn Salisbury Hughes, *Mothers in Industry: Wage Earning by Mothers in Philadelphia* (New York, 1925), p. 202; on wage-earning motherhood and infant mortality, see Emma Duke, *Infant Mortality: Results of a Field Study in Johnstown, Pa., Based on Births in One Calendar Year*, U.S. Department of Labor, Children's Bureau Publication no. 9 (Washington, D.C., 1915), p. 48, and Estelle B. Hunter, *Infant Mortality: Results of a Field Study in Waterbury, Conn.*, U.S. Department of Labor, Children's Bureau (Washington, D.C., 1918), p. 66.

[47]   Helen Russell Wright, *Children of Wage-Earning Mothers: A Study of A Selected Group in Chicago*, U.S. Department of Labor, Children's Bureau Publication no. 102 (Washington, D.C., 1922), p. 68.

[48]   Hughes, *Mothers in Industry*, p. 198.

[49]   Wright, *Children of Wage-Earning Mothers*, pp. 77–81.

oncile mother's work and children's welfare, some reformers suggested that "a visiting housekeeper should be employed to cook their food and keep their homes in order."[50] More to the point, they also called for more generous pensions to eliminate the need for wage earning by mothers altogether. Beginning with the 1919 Conferences on Child Welfare convened by the Children's Bureau, maternalists worked to reconcile grant levels with the cost of living. The 1922 conference of mothers' aid officials urged a more realistic definition of health, housing, and education standards. Meanwhile, the Children's Bureau published several studies that confirmed the view of pension administrators that allowances were generally too inadequate to support the policy's goals.[51]

Although maternalists won at least rhetorical recognition for motherhood in social policy, they were less successful in securing adequate funding. Administrators and social workers had the authority to experiment with rules during the 1920s, but the reformers' calls for more extensive public investment in mothers and future citizens depended on favorable political decisions. For the most part, these calls went unanswered. New York City spent $5 million to support 9,000 families in 1925—each at less than the annual thousand-dollar stipend required to meet the cost of living for a mother and three children. Toward the end of the 1920s, Pennsylvania offered an average stipend of only $37.16 per month while still strictly limiting supplemental income.[52] Political majorities of the 1920s refused dependent mothers of fatherless families an income commensurate with American maternal ideals while chastising them for their unAmerican behavior.

Notwithstanding the maternalists' genuine concern for mothers' poverty, the stinginess of political majorities reflected the maternalists' own ambivalence about the real solution to dependent motherhood. Although progressive maternalists affirmed the state's obligation to poor mother-only families, they also believed that breadwinning fatherhood was the best antidote to maternal

---

[50] *Standards of Child Welfare: Report of the Children's Bureau Conferences*, p. 232.
[51] In addition to studies already cited see Neva R. Deardorff, *Child Welfare Conditions and Resources in Seven Pennsylvania Counties*, U.S. Department of Labor, Children's Bureau Publication no.176 (Washington, D.C., 1927).
[52] Bailey B. Burritt, "Preventing Poverty," *Survey*, April 15, 1925, p. 81; *Survey*, December 15, 1916, p. 368; "What Is Desirable Income?," *Survey*, February 17, 1927, p. 644.

and child poverty. Aligning herself with Florence Kelley in testimony before the 1916 Conference on Social Insurance, Edith Abbott elaborated this view: Mothers' assistance "is a piece of relief machinery, and for this reason we should not accept this legislation as any final measure of social justice . . . . Mrs. Kelley warned a meeting at the National Conference of Charities and Correction a few years ago when the care of widows was being discussed that the proper way to provide for the widow and orphan was to abolish them by keeping the breadwinner alive. . . . the other remedy of course is such a lifting of the wage levels as shall make it possible for the wage earner to provide for his own wife and children."[53]

Florence Kelley, Sophonisba Breckinridge, Grace and Edith Abbott, and Julia Lathrop faced the fact that women worked outside the home and fought doggedly to secure labor standards for women. They also advocated wider professional opportunities for women, at least for women without the domestic responsibility of children. For women with children, however, the real solution to poverty and its consequences was a husband for every mother and a family wage for every father. As one California maternalist insisted, "every worker for children ought to join the fight for a living wage for men, and to see that the women do not go into industry."[54]

Maternalists argued vigorously for the family wage. In its absence, however, and without widespread unionism or social insurance, the only real alternative to persistent poverty for poor, single mothers was wage-work. Although maternalists did seek minimum wage laws for women, they remained troubled by the implications of wage-earning motherhood for family life. Defending "the American tradition that men support their families, the wives throughout life and the children at least until the fourteenth birthday," Florence Kelley mourned the emergence of a class of wage - earning adult women: "Married women immigrants from the nations of southeastern Europe . . . [add] themselves in ever-increasing proportion to the masses of young daughters of workingmen, whose youth formerly accounted for the fact that we habitually spoke, in the nineteenth century, of working *girls*, not working *women*. The Massachusetts law does not tend to check

---

[53]   Abbott to the Conference on Social Insurance, *Proceedings*, p. 834.
[54]   *Standards of Child Welfare: Report of the Children's Bureau Conferences*, p. 231.

this retrograde movement. It does not face the question: Why is the man no longer the breadwinner? It does not contribute toward conserving the family and the home with the man as its economic support."[55] During the 1920s, other reformers connected the change in the economic relationship between men and women to the disintegration of family life. Thus Sophonisba Breckinridge lamented "the increased employment of women and the consequent demoralization of the homes of irregularly employed men."[56]

Realistic about the economic necessity of wage-earning motherhood, maternalist reformers nevertheless resisted measures that would have reconciled wage work and motherhood. Though they had developed innovative day nursery programs in settlement houses, for example, maternalists worried that such programs would encourage more mothers to work outside the home. Jane Addams expressed early worries that "the day nursery is a 'double-edged implement' for doing good, which may also do a little harm," because women might be tempted to "attempt the impossible" by becoming "both wife and mother and supporter of the family."[57] Hence, unlike crêches in France, settlement day nurseries were designed to provide cultural education and recreation for immigrant children, not to support women as both mothers and workers. In fact, when a proposal for night nurseries reopened the question of child care for mothers who worked outside the home, Florence Kelley expressed horror "at the monstrous idea of having a night nursery to which women so employed might send their children."[58]

As the racial politics of the World War I period took hold, pressing the reform of mothers to the top of their agenda, maternalists abandoned the day nursery to the "child clinic," thereby rejecting the possibility that working women could be the worthy mothers

[55] Florence Kelley, "Minimum Wage Laws," *Journal of Political Economy* 20 (December 1912): 1003. Emphasis added.

[56] Sophonisba Breckinridge, "The Home Responsibilities of Women Workers and the 'Equal Wage'," *Journal of Political Economy* 31 (August 1923): 521–543.

[57] Quoted in Sonya Michel, "The Limits of Maternalism: Policies toward American Wage-Earning Mothers during the Progressive Era," in Seth Koven and Sonya Michel, eds., *Mothers of a New World: Maternalist Politics and the Origins of Welfare States* (New York, 1993), p. 291.

[58] Florence Kelley, "The Family and the Woman's Wage," National Conference of Charities and Correction *Proceedings* (1909), pp. 118–121.

of healthy children in stable homes. The maternalists' strong view that the best interests of Americanized children required full-time domestic motherhood led them to reject child care as a desirable social policy, to enforce pensioners' dependency through restrictions on wage-earning, and to track women workers into secondary labor markets through regulations on working women's hours, shifts, and types of employment.

Rather than enlarge mothers' income by expanding women's opportunities in industry, maternalists worked to uplift mothers' character by monitoring women's domestic activities. And rather than relieve wage-earning mothers' worries about untended children by developing child care systems, maternalists worked to relieve such worries through labor and pension legislation that restricted wage work altogether. Speaking to the National Consumers' League on the matter of maternity benefits for working women, Florence Kelley explained the maternalist position:

> It behooves us to get our minds quite clear as to our ideal of the American home in the future. The American home has hitherto been the most fortunate home of the working class in the civilized world, because the American workingman has been able to keep his wife much longer than he has been able to keep his young daughters in the home, and the little children in America have had their mothers with them much more than the little children in the other industrial countries have had their mothers with them. Any policy of subsidies by any branch of our Government which may tend, however slightly, to encourage the absence of mothers of little children from home and their entrance into industry should certainly not be undertaken lightly.[59]

Maternalists were not indiscriminate in their support for policies aimed at women. Like Florence Kelley, reformers in the twenties and thirties were at best generally ambivalent about maternity benefits and child care, policies that would have promoted the economic independence of women. Meanwhile, they designed, advocated, and implemented mothers' assistance, a policy aimed at the

[59] Kelley, "Proposed Sickness Insurance—Discussion," *Proceedings* of the Conference on Social Insurance, p. 610.

widowed mother who "devote[d] herself to housekeeping and the care of her children" and which thereby perpetuated women's economic dependence.[60]

Despite the reformers' commitment to mothers' pensions and the related goals of Americanization and maternal reform, the program did not reach large numbers of women. The Children's Bureau reported in 1922 that even in the most generous states only 200 children per 100,000 general population were actually assisted under mothers' pension programs. The bureau estimated in 1926 that only 37 percent of the children in need of aid actually received it.[61]

Cultural and economic impediments to eligibility, inadequate funding, weak implementation requirements, and administrative discretion all played parts in limiting the scope of pension coverage. Local option provisions created programs that were unevenly administered and distributed even within states. Within participating counties, funding constraints made for long waiting lists and eligibility rites limited the pool of recipients. In Philadelphia in 1924, for example, only one-third of the qualified applicants (needy, sane, morally fit, widowed, biological mothers of more than one child under the age of sixteen who met the residency requirement) were accepted into the program.[62]

Pensions reached only a fraction of potential beneficiaries, and benefits were meager, but the programs did serve Americanizing purposes in Northern cities, where European immigrant mothers were the majority of recipients. While instructing these women, social workers and dieticians learned important lessons that would be applied in the development of complementary social policies for maternity and infancy protection and for school reform.

Pension programs did not, on the whole, reach into African American communities. Nor were they accessible to Mexican immigrant mothers. In Los Angeles, for example, county officials

---

[60]   Abbott, "Recent Trends in Mothers' Aid," p. 191.
[61]   Cited in Lundberg, *Public Aid to Mothers with Dependent Children*, pp. 15–16.
[62]   Hall, *Mothers' Assistance in Philadelphia*, pp. 6–11, 86.

adopted a policy of refusing pensions to Mexican widows. They argued that the "feudal background" of Mexican immigrants made it difficult for them to "understand and not abuse the principle of a regular grant of money from the state."[63] Likewise deemed ineligible by stereotype, Black mothers accounted for only 3 percent of the recipient population in 1931. Half of these Blacks lived in two states, Pennsylvania and Ohio.[64] In the South, where 90 percent of the adult Black female population lived in 1920, four states did not mount pension programs at all; four other Southern and border states were among the stingiest with benefits.[65] In Houston, Texas, where Blacks comprised 21 percent of the population, not a single Black family received a mothers' pension.[66] Elsewhere, legislatures, county governments, and policy personnel made it impossible for Blacks to establish eligibility. In Illinois, where mothers' pension policy permitted wage earning by recipients after 1913, stereotyped expectations of Black women's "employability" invited discrimination against their very eligibility for benefits. Often deemed potentially "self-supporting"—as domestic workers or in other low wage jobs—African American pension applicants were dismissed by Chicago pension officials. Despite the fact that the proportion of single mothers of childbearing age was higher for African Americans than for European immigrants and despite the fact that African American mothers were disproportionately enrolled in poor relief, the mothers' pension program was not opened to them.[67]

Just as recipients' wage earning contradicted the maternalist vision of mothers' pensions, so too did racial discrimination in the administration of the program. Although maternalist settlement work and policy initiatives focused on the cultural "adjustment" of southern and eastern European immigrants, the logic of their

[63]   Mary Odem, quoting from the Department of Social Welfare of the State of California, *First Biennial Report* (1927–28), in "Single Mothers, Delinquent Daughters, and the Juvenile Court in Early-20th-Century Los Angeles," *Journal of Social History* 25 (Fall 1991): 27, 29.

[64]   Bell, *Aid to Dependent Children*, p. 9.

[65]   Missisippi, Alabama, Georgia, and South Carolina did not provide mothers' aid. Arkansas, Virginia, Texas, and Tennessee each aided fewer than 20 children per 100,000 general population. U.S. Department of Commerce, Bureau of the Census, *Population Trends in the United States, 1900–1960* (Washington, D.C., 1964), p. 231.

[66]   Ladd-Taylor, *Mother-Work*, p. 149.

[67]   Goodwin, "American Experiment," pp. 331, 335.

Americanization strategy applied to African Americans, as well. Maternalist policymakers offered conformity as the path to social incorporation to all "othered" Americans. As Hull House activist and social investigator Louise deKoven Bowen told the National Urban League in 1920, "we are not apt to think of the negro as an immigrant, but in reality he occupies the same position as does the foreigner who comes to us from other shores, except that the negro's position is more difficult."[68] Sophonisba Breckinridge and Edith Abbott acted upon this view during the 1920s, investigating, then challenging, the separate, neglectful treatment of dependent African American children.[69]

Advocacy on behalf of Black families in poverty by key progressive maternalists may have contributed to the developing discourse of racial liberalism, but it did not root out racial bias in the practical administration of mothers' pension policy. Severe and pervasive prejudice meant that single, African American mothers were assumed to be morally unfit and uneducable—by definition "unworthy." Moreover, summoning powerful negative images of African American "female loaferism" and of Black married women who "played the lady," white society defined Black mothers not as women but as workers, "fighting for their daily bread like men" and ill-suited to domestic motherhood by a long history of toil outside the home.[70] The racial specificity of the Anglo American maternal ideal held Black women outside the boundaries of domesticity, as breeders, sluts, and the caretakers of other women's homes and children.[71]

For African American single mothers who managed to qualify for allowances, as well as for immigrant recipients, racial and cul-

[68]   Mary E. Humphrey, ed., *Speeches, Addresses, and Letters of Louise deKoven Bowen*, vol. 2 (Ann Arbor, 1937), p. 630.
[69]   Sandra M. Stehno, "Public Responsibility for Dependent Black Children: The Advocacy of Edith Abbott and Sophonisba Breckinridge," *Social Service Review* 62 (September 1988): 485–503.
[70]   W. E. B. Du Bois, *Darkwater: Voices from within the Veil* (New York, 1975), pp. 179–80. See also, Evelyn Brooks Higginbotham, "African American Women's History and the Metalanguage of Race," *Signs* 17 (Winter 1992): 259–260; and Jacqueline Jones, *Labor of Love, Labor of Sorrow* (New York, 1985), pp. 58–60.
[71]   W. E. B. Du Bois, "The Black Mother," *Crisis*, December 1912, p. 78; James Weldon Johnson, "The Black Mammy," *Crisis*, August 1915, p. 17; Eileen Boris, "The Power of Motherhood: Black and White Activist Women Redefine the Political," in Koven and Michel, eds., *Mothers of a New World*, p. 217.

tural biases affected benefit levels. As noted earlier, the wage - earning potential of a recipient, as determined by local agencies, could lead to a reduced monthly stipend—some mothers were indeed expected to combine work with welfare. Supervision of home standards and the subjective determination of need by welfare workers, as well as agency discretion in establishing family budget schedules, invited variations in pension income based on the social (and racial) rank of recipients. According to the 1922 Children's Bureau Conference on Mothers' Pensions, even in states that claimed to use standard family budgets, welfare workers often assigned lower benefits to recipients from "lesser" nationalities: Czechs, Italians, Mexicans, African Americans. Mothers' pension programs thus reinforced ties between culture, race, and poverty.[72]

In different ways, the maternalists' vision of mothers' pensions and the local agencies' implementation of that vision entrenched moral and cultural distinctions among women. Monitored and managed by Anglo American professional women, mothers' assistance was a selective and conditional program targeting the "best" of the needy and demanding a behavioral and cultural return on the public's investment. The adoption by some mothers of the child-centered, Anglo American, middle-class model of gender relations and family life was the fruit of the maternalist innovation; the moral, cultural ranking of women was its yoke. Revived, nationalized, and expanded during the New Deal, mothers' pensions codified the language of cultural conformity that still dominates public discussions of motherhood and citizenship.

[72]   Conference on Mothers' Pensions *Proceedings*, p. 4.

"A BABY SAVED IS A CITIZEN GAINED"
Infancy Protection and Maternal Reform

The Italian mother can, after time, be persuaded to take off the 'fasch' which binds her new-born baby's little legs up into a tight mummy shape. The Polish mother, after patient teaching, can be induced not to give her three-months baby a taste of the cabbage, stew, or whatever else is on the family menu.

—Bessie A. Haasis, 1919

W hereas mothers' pensions reached out to single mothers according to economic and cultural "need," a second arena of maternalist policy activism—maternity policy—began as a universal effort to attenuate biological risks common to childbearing women and their infants. Conceived by Julia Lathrop and Florence Kelley, maternity policy was promoted by researchers in the U.S. Children's Bureau, shaped by literate poor and middle class women who conveyed their questions and stories in letters to the Children's Bureau, and won by organized women in an extensive lobbying campaign.[1] The nation's first maternity policy—and first health policy—the Sheppard-Towner Maternity and Infancy Protection Act offered federal assistance to states to set up educational services for expectant and new mothers. Unlike mothers' pensions, the Sheppard-Towner maternity policy did not create economic or cultural criteria for its clientele but it promised information to all women anxious to survive chilbirth and to raise healthy babies.

Maternity policy did, however, serve the cultural objectives of

---

[1] Molly Ladd-Taylor, *Mother-Work: Women, Child Welfare, and the State, 1890–1930* (Urbana, 1994), pp. 167–168; Ladd-Taylor, *Raising a Baby the Government Way: Mothers' Letters to the Children's Bureau, 1915–1932* (New Brunswick, 1986).

many progressive maternalists, central to which was the ideal of the domestic mother. Taught and monitored by visiting nurses, maternity policy standardized advice to mothers across cultures and classes and stressed cooperative, child-centered motherhood. As leading maternity reformer Dr. S. Josephine Baker recalled in her autobiography, "I became and still am a firm believer in mothering for babies . . . There is little doubt in my mind that many a baby has died for lack of it."[2] Besides encouraging mothers to conform to a class and culturally specific gender role, maternity policy addressed the choices made by mothers in the bearing and raising of children. Maternity policy favored medicalized, hospital births; asserted a partnership between women and (often male) physicians; assumed women needed to be trained for motherhood; and connected such training to the unlearning of cultural practices deemed unhealthful by reformers and physicians.

The Sheppard-Towner maternity policy culminated years of infancy protection work undertaken by the Children's Bureau at its founding in 1912. The Children's Bureau's first publication, *Prenatal Care* (1913), blamed prenatal conditions or birth injury for 70 percent of infant deaths during the first month of life. The pamphlet urged women to take better care of themselves, offering dietary, hygiene, and stress-reduction tips. The maternalist program for infancy protection expressed and imposed the class and culture biases of its proponents. On issues from breastfeeding and feeding schedules, to diet, midwifery, and the role of older siblings, maternalist appeals for more attentive, scientific mothering linked infant welfare to the Americanization of immigrant mothers. Infant hygiene work was "an entering wedge for Americanization," an opportunity, according to future Labor Secretary Frances Perkins, to mitigate the "prejudices and superstitions . . . of primitive peoples" and to "instruct foreign born women . . . in regard to diet and dietetics."[3]

[2]   S. Josephine Baker, *Fighting for Life* (New York, 1939), p. 121.
[3]   Bessie A. Haasis, "Public Health Nursing, An Agent of Americanization," Americanization Conference *Proceedings* Bureau of Education, Department of the Interior (Washington, D.C., 1919), p. 383; Frances Perkins, Maternity Center Association of New York, "Roundtable Conference in Cooperation with the National Study of Methods of Americanization," American Association for Study and Prevention of Infant Mortality *Transactions* of the Ninth Annual Meeting (December 5–7, 1918), pp. 236–239.

The principal goal of the maternalist infancy protection program was to save babies' lives, and Americanization became an important maternalist remedy for infant mortality. The United States had the highest infant mortality rate among industrializing countries: according to Molly Ladd-Taylor's review of U.S. birth registration data, in 1915, 6 women and 100 infants died for every 1,000 live births; the mortality rate was nearly twice as high for people of color.[4] As Florence Kelley revealed in her powerful story of her own mother's suffering in childbirth, all women and babies, privileged or poor, were vulnerable to maternal and infant mortality.[5] Nonetheless, Children's Bureau investigations of the causes of infant mortality made race and culture the categories of explanation. In urban and industrial areas with large immigrant populations—in the melting pot Josephine Baker described as "a huge germ culture"—maternalists drew from the diagnosis of infant mortality a prescription for cultural reform.[6] In immigrant neighborhoods, as in native white rural areas, maternal education was the reformers' strategy for infant protection. But among immigrants, this work meant not only instructing mothers in how better to cope with poverty but showing them the poverty of their cultures, as well.

At the heart of the maternalist agenda lay the assumption that improved mothering would enhance child welfare.[7] Maternalists therefore placed great stock in the quality of motherhood, measuring maternal quality in terms of mothers' assimilation of the cultural and "scientific" child care standards advocated by nurses, social workers, and dieticians. Although most maternalists identified poverty as an important, complicating context for infant mortality, an economic agenda for child health was ultimately obscured by maternalists' insistence on the primary significance of maternal reform. Maternity and infancy protection thus became an occasion for the social management of woman's "natural" vo-

[4] Molly Ladd-Taylor, " 'My Work Came Out of Agony and Grief': Mothers and the Making of the Sheppard-Towner Act," in Seth Koven and Sonya Michel, eds., *Mothers of a New World: Maternalist Politics and the Origins of Welfare States* (New York, 1993), pp. 323–324.
[5] Florence Kelley, "My Philadelphia," *Survey*, October 1, 1926, p. 50.
[6] Baker, *Fighting for Life*, p. 79.
[7] S. Josephine Baker, *Healthy Children: A Volume Devoted to the Health of the Growing Child* (Boston, 1923), pp. 24–25.

cation. Josephine Baker, the founding director of the industrial world's first Child Hygiene Bureau, summed up the maternalist program: "Our guiding principle was to start babies healthy and keep them so and, if that objective led us into far fields, all the way from the young east-side bride's diet to the habits of certain cows in Jersey, we could go right along without wondering if our procedure were orthodox."[8]

ARE YOU A 100-PERCENT MOTHER?

During the second year of U.S. participation in World War I, the Children's Bureau and the Woman's Committee of the National Council on Defense launched Children's Year "to teach mothers so to care for themselves and for their children that there would be fewer victims of preventable disease, fewer remedial defects, and fewer avoidable abnormalities amongst the children of the nation."[9] Like wartime and postwar efforts to strengthen mothers' pension programs, Children's Year and other infancy protection activities made child-centered maternal reform the template for nurturing "children fit to perpetuate this democracy."[10]

From its founding in 1912, the federal Children's Bureau worked with local maternalist allies to promote child hygiene and reduce infant mortality. In 1914, the year Congress established Mother's Day, the Children's Bureau began disseminating advice manuals on prenatal, infant, and child care to pregnant women and new mothers. Mailed at government expense and distributed by members of Congress to women in isolated rural areas, the pamphlets reached some 1.7 million women by 1918. In 1915, the bureau began a series of community studies to determine the causes of infant mortality. In 1916 and 1917, the bureau worked with the General Federation of Women's Clubs to sponsor nationwide Baby Weeks to inform women how best to ensure their babies' survival. In 1917,

---

[8]   Baker, *Fighting for Life*, pp. 108–109.
[9]   Anna E. Rude, Children's Bureau, "Child Welfare Activities in the United States: The Progress of Children's Year," American Association for Study and Prevention of Infant Mortality, *Transactions*, p. 59.
[10]   S. Josephine Baker, "The Relation of the War to the Nourishment of Children," *Woman's Medical Journal* 18 (March 1918): 52.

maternalist Jeanette Rankin of Montana, the first woman elected to Congress, introduced legislation to provide federal funds to states conducting maternity and infancy protection work in rural districts.[11]

Explicitly undertaken as a war-related activity, the mission of Children's Year was "to make plain the need for better care of young children."[12] The campaign's strategy was to enlist women's participation in the "scientific" care of children: "The most important factor in the success of the Children's Year Campaign is the co-operation of the mothers. The rest is assured."[13] The Children's Bureau's first effort to recruit mothers to save babies was a "weighing and measuring" project intended to teach the relationship between height and weight and a child's physical well-being. With the help of local women's organizations, the bureau distributed seven million height and weight record cards to mothers. Other bureau intitiatives to teach mothers infant and child hygiene included promoting development of child health demonstration centers and encouraging expansion of the corps of traveling public health nurses who could supervise maternal and infant hygiene through home visits.

Child welfare gained national attention as a result of the army's draft experience, and it became maternalists' war work for the same reason. Where xenophobes, eugenicists, and white supremacists took the army's draft data as evidence of the racial inferiority of the rejects, maternalists argued that the majority of draft rejects would have been qualified for service had they been properly cared for as children. As Children's Bureau physician Anna Rude told the Association for Study and Prevention of Infant Mortality, "Undoubtedly the draft rejections which we have seen within the past two years have helped to make clear how many physical defects we have as a nation, and the fact that at least half of these defects

[11] Anna E. Rude, Children's Bureau, "What the Children's Bureau Is Doing and Planning to Do," *American Association for Study and Prevention of Infant Mortality Transactions*, pp. 75–81. See also Richard Meckel's useful history, *Save the Babies: American Public Health Reform and the Prevention of Infant Mortality, 1850–1929* (Baltimore, 1990), chap. 5; Kevin Giles, *Flight of the Dove: The Story of Jeannette Rankin* (Beaverton, Ore., 1980).
[12] Rude, "What the Children's Bureau Is Doing," p. 79.
[13] Lois Lindsey Wynekoop, "The Woman Physician and Child Welfare in War Time," *Woman's Medical Journal* 28 (September 1918): 196.

might have been eliminated during childhood."[14] Josephine Baker, then director of Child Hygiene for New York City, explained the relationship between the war and child health:

> I think we can say, without fear of contradiction, that the future of our population depends upon the virility and vigor and health of its population. . . . The lesson we must learn from the draft will concern the future welfare of the children of this country. There has never been a time so opportune as the present for constructive health work for children. . . . While we are fighting to make the world safe for democracy, we must not be unmindful of our future citizens. Let us then build up a democracy which will result in absolute justice to all the children of the country, so that we may truly say, in this country at least, that we have made a democracy which is safe for the world.[15]

The war nationalized infant protection policy, but the content of that policy was developed during a decade of experimentation by nurses, dieticians, settlement workers, and women physicians at the local level. The most notable local program, developed by Josephine Baker in New York City, became the model for federal policy in the 1920s. Baker's program deployed nurses in homes and recruited schools into public health work, both on an unprecedented scale. While schools taught girls how to care for baby siblings in preparation for their own eventual motherhood, visiting nurses taught mothers breastfeeding, food selection and preparation, infant care, and housekeeping in order to remake the tenement into a more "American" and healthful home. "Nothing revolutionary," according to Baker, "just insistence on breast feeding, efficient ventilation, frequent bathing, the right kind of summer clothes. . . . Many of these mothers were a little flattered to have an American lady take all that trouble about little Giovanni, and were likely to go out of their way to learn and to cooperate. If the mothers were sulky or apprehensive, the nurses went again and again, wearing down their resistance,

---

[14]   Rude, "Child Welfare Activities in the United States," p. 64.
[15]   S. Josephine Baker, "Lessons from the Draft," American Association for Study and Prevention of Infant Mortality *Transactions*, pp. 181, 187–188.

establishing friendly contact, until they were ready and willing to cooperate."[16]

Baker and other maternalist health workers attributed the infant mortality problem to four practices among immigrant mothers: midwifery; artificial and irregular infant feeding; wage earning; and gamey, spicy, garlicky, or cabbage-based cooking.[17] Backed up by the anecdotal evidence of visiting nurses and by Children's Bureau research, maternalists focused their energies on mitigating these practices.[18]

Maternalists generally were resigned to midwifery, a common birthing choice among immigrants (as well as among white and Black rural women)—at least until "daughter grew up and became sufficiently Americanized" to choose doctor-assisted, hospitalized childbirth.[19] Because many "women would rather have amateur assistance from the janitor's wife . . . than submit to this outlandish American custom of having in a male doctor," midwifery was a long-term problem of assimilation.[20] In the meantime, Grace Abbott and others urged—against growing physician opposition—treating "the 'midwife' problem [as] an excellent illustration of the necessity of considering the traditions and prejudices of our immigrant population."[21] Convinced that midwives were "socially in-

[16] Baker, *Fighting for Life*, p. 86.

[17] Cabbage was at the top of the General Federation of Women's Clubs hit list of "foreign vegetables." John McClymer, "Gender and the 'American Way of Life': Women in the Americanization Movement," *Journal of American Ethnic History* 10 (Spring 1991): 12; see also Velma Phillips and Laura Howell, "Racial and Other Differences in Dietary Customs," *Journal of Home Economics* 12 (September 1920): 397; and Harvey Leverstein, *Revolution at the Table: The Transformation of the American Diet* (New York, 1988), chap. 8.

[18] The first of ten Children's Bureau studies of infant mortality was conducted by Emma Duke in Johnstown, Pennsylvania. *Infant Mortality: Results of a Field Study in Johnstown, Pa., Based on Births in One Calendar Year*, U.S. Department of Labor, Children's Bureau Publication no. 9 (Washington, D.C., 1915). Other towns studied were Manchester, N.H.; Waterbury, Conn.; Brockton and New Bedford, Mass.; Akron, Ohio; and Gary, Ind. For purposes of comparison, the bureau also studied Baltimore, Md.; Montclair, N.J.; and Saginaw, Mich. For a good discussion of these studies, see Meckel, *Save the Babies*, chap. 7. See also Richard Wertz and Dorothy Wertz, *Lying In: A History of Childbirth in America* (New York, 1977), pp. 204.

[19] Baker, *Fighting for Life*, p. 117.

[20] Ibid., p. 113; Charles V. Chapin, "The Control of Midwifery," *Standards of Child Welfare: A Report of the Children's Bureau Conferences* (Washington, D.C., 1919), pp. 157–166.

[21] Grace Abbott, "The Midwife in Chicago," *American Journal of Sociology*, 20 (March 1915): 684.

evitable" among the current generation of immigrant mothers, Baker, like Abbott, called for more rigorous training and stringent licensing of midwives and for continuing supervision of midwife deliveries by visiting nurses and health agencies.[22] Their concern was to weed out the "densely ignorant and therefore filthy, superstitious, hidebound" midwife so as to ensure a more medically acceptable grade of midwifery.[23]

In cities like New York and Chicago, maternalists secured midwife training and licensing regulations: Josephine Baker is said to have rounded up four thousand midwives for training and licensing in New York City alone.[24] Visiting nurses monitored midwife-assisted births, when they could, to prevent delivery by "witchcraft," as well as to protect the infant from blindness and infection and the mother from puerperal fever. Maternalists also appealed to women physicians to supervise home births and thereby to ease immigrant women's acculturation to obstetrical intervention by male doctors. Frances Perkins explained to the Association for Study and Prevention of Infant Mortality that "the men fly into a panic if a male physician begins to touch or do anything for the women. We have almost given up delivering women in the Polish district, through the out-patient lying-in department, and we are getting together a group of women physicians who are co-operating with us for the sake of overcoming the prejudices which Polish women have."[25]

Maternalist health reformers were less accommodating—either to custom or to necessity—when it came to infant feeding. Josephine Baker admonished "every mother [to] nurse her baby," citing the emotional and medical benefits of mothers' milk.[26] Visiting

[22]   In 1920, 20–40 percent of births in the mid-Atlantic states were delivered by midwives. The percentage was higher in cities. The writings of Josephine Baker, Grace Abbott, Frances Perkins, and Children's Bureau researchers indicate reformers strongly correlated urban midwifery with nativity. For more detailed discussion of the midwifery issue, see Molly Ladd-Taylor, "Grannies and Spinsters: Midwife Education under the Sheppard-Towner Act," *Journal of Social History* 22 (Winter 1988): 255–277; and Wertz and Wertz, *Lying In*, pp. 210–217.

[23]   S. Josephine Baker, "Schools for Midwives," American Association for Study and Prevention of Infant Mortality *Transactions* of Second Annual Meeting (1911), p. 232.

[24]   Wertz and Wertz, *Lying In*, p. 212.

[25]   Perkins, "Roundtable," p. 238.

[26]   S. Josephine Baker, *Healthy Babies: A Volume Devoted to the Health of the Expectant Mother and the Care and Welfare of the Child* (Boston, 1923), p. 81.

nurses instructed mothers on the advantages of breastfeeding and in the aseptic care of the nursing mothers' breasts.[27] Begining in Baltimore in 1916, a handful of local governments actually required breastfeeding of some (usually unwed) mothers. Meanwhile, the federal Children's Bureau reported correlations between breastfeeding and the quality of child life and between artificial feeding and infant mortality.[28]

In New York and other cities, maternalists worked to establish milk stations in immigrant neighborhoods where they offered whole milk at a slight discount for children and "for babies whose mothers had abandoned the idea of breastfeeding."[29] But in the main, maternalists encouraged mothers to breastfeed their infants with good quality mothers' milk on a regular schedule. To ensure good milk, Baker prescribed a bland diet for the nursing mother, eight hours of sleep each night, a midday nap, an hour of exercise twice a day, and avoidance of worry and excitement.[30] Backed up not only by Baker's advice but by recommendations in the widely disseminated Children's Bureau pamphlet *Infant Care* (1914), nurses insisted on feeding by the clock—not always possible for a mother in a busy household or who worked outside the home.[31]

Closely related to breastfeeding was the issue of wage earning by pregnant women and mothers. In 1908, Josephine Goldmark's research for the Brandeis Brief linked long hours of wage-earning work by women to poor maternal and infant health. Goldmark's study stressed the physical strain on women and its consequences for pregnancy, childbirth, and motherhood. Josephine Baker and other maternalist health reformers took this argument one step further, showing the irreconcilability of wage-earning and breastfeeding. A wage-earning mother could not easily follow Bakers' prescription for nourishing breast milk: she had no leisure for the required sleep, exercise, and relaxation. Even if a wage-earning

[27] Harriet L. Hartley, "The City Nurse as An Agent for the Prevention of Infant Mortality," American Association for Study and Prevention of Infant Mortality *Transactions* of the Ninth Annual Meeting, p. 125.

[28] Estelle B. Hunter, *Infant Mortality: Results of a Field Study in Waterbury, Conn.,* U.S. Department of Labor, Children's Bureau (Washington, D.C., 1918), p. 66; also *Standards of Legal Protection for Children Born Out of Wedlock, A Report of Regional Conferences Held under the Auspices of the U.S. Children's Bureau,* U.S. Department of Labor, Children's Bureau Publication no. 77 (Washington, D.C., 1921).

[29] Baker, *Fighting for Life,* pp. 124–127.

[30] Baker, *Healthy Babies,* p. 85.

[31] Meckel, *Save the Babies,* pp. 136–137.

mother wanted to nurse, she could not, according to maternalist prescriptions, assure good nourishment to her child. Although Emma Duke admitted in her study for the Children's Bureau that a mother's "own housework . . . [may be] so excessive as to affect her . . . while nursing to the extent of reacting on the health of the baby," she nevertheless concluded that "the fact is that the infant mortality rate is higher among the babies of wage-earning mothers than among others."[32] A later Children's Bureau study reinforced this claim, finding that "mothers who are obliged to work must perforce substitute artificial feeding for nursing and intrust to others the care of their infants. The result is a high mortality rate for infants of working mothers."[33]

Although Children's Bureau studies connected infant mortality to wage earning by mothers and to the artificial feeding of babies, they also explored the consequences of poverty for maternal and infant health. Emma Duke's seminal Johnstown study attributed the highest infant mortality rates to the poorest neighborhoods studied.[34] According to the study, poverty reached even the breast-fed baby, through the milk of the poorly nourished or overworked mother. The Manchester study followed the same lines, finding that low paternal wages forced mothers to abandon breastfeeding and to enter the workforce.[35] Children's Bureau data on the impact of poverty on maternal and infant health induced some maternalists to support the concept of maternity benefits for working women. Julia Lathrop, for example, initially endorsed the model sickness insurance bill of the American Association for Labor Legislation which would have provided maternity benefits to wage-earning women who earned less than $1,200 per year and who stayed home for six weeks after childbirth.[36] Reflecting the maternalists' ambivalence toward wage-earning motherhood, however, Lathrop's preferred solution to poverty-related infant mortality was the father's family wage.

[32]   Duke, *Results of a Field Study* p. 48.
[33]   Hunter, *Results of a Field Study in Waterbury, Conn.*, p. 66.
[34]   Duke, *Results of a Field Study*, p. 16.
[35]   Beatrice Sheets Duncan and Emma Duke, *Infant Mortality: Results of A Field Study in Manchester, N.H.*, U.S. Department of Labor, Children's Bureau (Washington, D.C., 1917), pp. 47–52.
[36]   Julia Lathrop, "Public Protection of Maternity," *American Labor Legislation Review* 7 (1917): 27–35.

Florence Kelley expressed the maternalist position most starkly when she explained her opposition to maternity benefits. Afraid that a maternity income subsidy might propel women into the workforce to indemnify childbirth, she told the Conference on Social Insurance: "Provisions in bills which have hitherto been introduced and submitted for discussion by the Association for Labor Legislation discriminate in favor of those husbands who send their wives into industry, and that does not commend itself to us. . . . [W]e should be exceedingly cautious how we place any premium on sending wives out into industry."[37]

Opposed to policies that would discourage domestic motherhood, maternalists sought solutions to infant mortality which would strengthen men's breadwinning role and enhance domestic mothering. Primarily a market issue to be decided by male workers, unions, and employers, the family wage—though ardently supported by maternalists—was not a focus of maternalist policy work, which sought to limit infant mortality by educating the mother. Infancy protection work brought the state into women's lives to supervise and direct the conduct of pregnancy, childbirth, and motherhood.

In mothers' homes, infant welfare workers emphasized the importance of cultural reform. They were supported in this approach by Children's Bureau evidence correlating foreign nativity and home language with high rates of infant mortality.[38] Visiting nurses taught mothers more "scientific," more "American" standards of hygiene and child care. Maternalists were particularly concerned about the immigrant diet—its nutritional value, as well as its affect on digestion and health. The fact that the leading cause of infant death was diarrhea heightened maternalist interest in reforming food habits. The Children's Bureau accordingly asked the federal Bureau of Vocational Education to sponsor cooking classes for immigrant women under the Smith-Hughes Act of 1917. Visiting nurses, dieticians, and women's groups taught immigrant mothers the dangers of spices and "foreign vegetables." They urged immigrant mothers to avoid preparations that mixed foods to-

---

[37] Florence Kelley, *Proceedings* of the Conference on Social Insurance, U.S. Department of Labor, Bureau of Labor Statistics Bulletin no. 212 (Washington, D.C., 1917), pp. 609–610.
[38] e.g., Duke, *Results of a Field Study*, pp. 16, 29, 32, 34.

gether and to select ingredients according to dieticians' advice. Josephine Baker and others prepared manuals for home visitors listing foods and food preparations mothers should be encouraged to adopt or avoid. According to Baker's manual, nursing mothers should eat bland and simple foods; babies should not be given raw fruits or vegetables, cooked or pickled cabbage, stews or solid foods; children should avoid "pork in any form, including ham and sausage, corned beef, veal, game including duck, salt fish, sauces and any highly spiced over-seasoned food, fried foods, raw celery, radishes, cucumbers, green corn, raw tomatoes, rich cakes or puddings, pastry or hot breads."[39] Though intended to promote health, these dietary interventions implicitly impugned southern and eastern European cuisines as detrimental to child health.

As a backup to work with mothers in the home and as a way of reaching children of wage-earning mothers, infancy protection advocates developed programs for young girls in the public schools. In 1910, inspired by John Spargo's Bitter Cry of the Children, Baker approached the New York City schools to set up practical courses in child hygiene: "For whether little mothers or not, most of these girls would eventually become mothers in their own right—our problem would be resolved."[40] Schools initially dismissed the idea, according to Baker, viewing child care "as natural to woman as knowing how to dress herself."[41] Once a few schools had agreed to the experiment, however, the rest of the city's schools followed suit. In the spring of 1910, Child Hygiene Bureau nurses and doctors circuited the public schools, giving lectures on infant care to "the girl child of the poor."

When school let out, Baker recruited girls into "Little Mothers' Leagues," where they received further instruction from nurses in baby feeding and baby care. Discovering that "these youngsters were among our most efficient missionaries," Baker turned the Little Mothers' Leagues into auxiliaries of her Child Hygiene Bureau.[42] She deputized the "little mothers" as volunteer aides of the department, gave them silver badges if they attended six meetings, and dispatched them to their neighborhoods to cajole "mothers of

[39]   Baker, Healthy Children, pp. 95–99.
[40]   Baker, Fighting for Life, p. 133.
[41]   Ibid., p. 133.
[42]   Ibid., p. 134.

their acquaintances into giving the baby health stations a trial" and to check "up on mothers who had backslid in attendance at the stations."[43] "Little Mothers" formed 71 leagues during the summer of 1910; 20,000 girls enrolled in 183 leagues in New York City in 1911; and 50,000 girls in 44 cities had organized Little Mothers' Leagues by 1915.

Created to reach girls often assigned care of babies and younger siblings, the leagues became an important tool of maternal reform. More welcome in immigrant homes than visiting nurses, little mothers—daughters, nieces, neighbors—taught immigrant mothers the "scientific" care of babies. Typically, the little mothers wrote and performed skits for their own mothers on subjects ranging from how best to soothe a crying baby to what to feed it. Baker recalled one of her favorites in her memoirs:

MOTHER: Baby wants something to eat.

CHILD: What?

MOTHER: I guess a piece of pineapple.

CHILD: Mother, what! Pineapple for a baby?

MOTHER: What's the matter?

CHILD: You do not mean pineapple for a baby, do you?

MOTHER: Yes, I think baby will like a piece very much.

CHILD: No matter if the baby will like it or not it is not healthy for babies.

MOTHER: Who told you that?

CHILD: I belong to the Little Mothers' League. They teach us how babies ought to be kept.

MOTHER: You did not tell me that. I would have stopped giving it to the baby a long time ago.

CHILD: I'll tell you what they taught me: how to clean bottles, how to make barley water, how the babies ought to be taken care of during the summer. You see, mamma, that the doctor in our school is very kind to take part of the Saturday to teach that to us.

MOTHER: Baby seems to be getting fatter and better every day since I stopped giving it fruit and the other things you told me were not good for the baby.

[43] Ibid.; Josephine Baker, "Why Do Our Mothers and Babies Die?" *Ladies' Home Journal,* April 1922, p. 174.

CHILD: You see that our club is of good use.

MOTHER: Thanks ought to be given to the doctor of your school.[44]

Little Mothers' Leagues were emblematic of the maternalist preoccupation with maternal reform, which operated from the premise that the social mediation of mothers' cultures, behaviors, and choices would enable poor, ethnic women and children to escape the effects of poverty. This strategy was the first step of maternalists' war on poverty; it was also their "entering wedge for Americanization."

THE SHEPPARD-TOWNER MATERNITY AND INFANCY PROTECTION ACT

Under the leadership of Children's Bureau chief Julia Lathrop, maternalists began a campaign to nationalize and standardize infancy protection policy in 1917, when Jeanette Rankin introduced into Congress a measure primarily designed for rural women. This federal maternity and infancy legislation became law in 1921. With laissez-faire resistance to federal spending and intervention temporarily eased by the wartime demographic crisis and with women's political clout temporarily strengthened by their suffrage victory, Congress enacted a version of the Rankin measure over a red-baiting and mysoginist opposition.[45] The new law, the Sheppard-Towner Act, borrowed from the experiences of settlement house workers and public health nurses like Lillian Wald; drew inspiration from the writings and speeches of Florence Kelley; found political fuel in the widespread commitment of women's organizations to public protection of infancy; and endorsed the findings and recommendations of Childrens' Bureau

[44]   Baker, *Fighting for Life*, pp. 135–136.
[45]   Sheppard-Towner proponents were denounced as "office holding spinsters," "derailed menopausics," "endocrine perverts," "bolsheviks," and "anarchists." Doris Groshen Daniels, *Always a Sister: The Feminism of Lillian D. Wald* (New York, 1989), pp. 115–116, 145–146.

studies.[46] Lending a governmental hand in defense of the republic's "maternity and infancy interests," the act codified the Lathrop-Baker model of infancy protection and designated Lathrop's Children's Bureau and such local child hygiene bureaus as Baker's as the administrative agents of federal policy.[47]

The act made few specific promises, though in its $1.9 million appropriation to support local infant welfare work, it pledged "to the mothers of the country all possible knowledge and reasonable assistance affecting their welfare in connection with all of the features of maternity and care of infants."[48] The federal appropriation took the form of matching grants to states that adopted maternity and infancy protection plans. The act created a new federal Board of Maternal and Infant Hygiene, to implement its provisions, while reserving routine administration to the Children's Bureau. Thus the act boosted infant welfare work by expressing the nation's formal commitment to "save the babies" and by authorizing the maternalists' policy network to supply meaning to the federal commitment.

The act did not, however, expressly standardize infancy protection measures. In fact, it allowed states to determine the specific content of local initiatives. A few states—Massachusetts, for example—refused to cooperate altogether. Meanwhile, some participating states emphasized demonstration clinics and prenatal centers, and others stressed the training and deployment of visiting nurses. Fourteen states designated the regulation of midwifery as their highest priority under the act.[49] In southern and border

[46] The General Federation of Women's Clubs, National Congress of Mothers, League of Women Voters, Women's Trade Union League were among the women's groups that lobbied for the bill. As examples of the maternalist case for national infancy protection policy, see: Florence Kelley, "Inaction," *Survey*, June 26, 1920, p. 452; "Why Let Children Die?" *Survey*, June 19, 1920, p. 401; "What Next?" *Suffragist*, October 20, 1920, p. 236; "Bureau of Child Hygiene," *Woman Voter*, May 1916; Josephine Goldmark, *Impatient Crusader: Florence Kelley's Life Story* (Urbana, 1953), pp. 105–109.

[47] Statement of Miss Julia C. Lathrop, Chief of the Children's Bureau, Department of Labor, Committee on Interstate and Foreign Commerce, U.S. House of Representatives, *Hearings* on Public Protection of Maternity and Infancy (H.R.2366), 67th Congress, 1st session (July 1921), p. 235.

[48] "Protection of Maternity and Infancy," Committee on Interstate and Foreign Commerce *Report*, U.S. House of Representatives, 67th Congress, 1st session, rpt. no. 467, p. 6.

[49] Wertz and Wertz, *Lying In*, p. 209.

states, infancy protection measures were developed either for whites only or on a Jim Crow basis.[50] In northern cities de facto segregation reinforced the white ethnic bias of maternalist reform. These programmatic and administrative variations notwithstanding, the network of Children's Bureau and local maternalist infancy welfare activists infused Sheppard-Towner initiatives with a common educational thrust. Maternalists seized this national opportunity to expand public health nursing, instruct and supervise midwifery, promote breastfeeding, disseminate Children's Bureau materials more broadly, set up traveling "clinics" and health demonstration centers—all toward the end of showing mothers how better to care for their children. But the maternity policy did not offer mothers and babies regular medical care or the means to secure such care. Neither did it permit clinic construction. Nor did it follow the French and German examples of maternity benefits or enforce the standards of the International Labor Organization's 1919 Maternity Protection Convention to provide maternity leaves for pregnant women workers.[51] Indeed, consistent with maternalist ambivalence toward policies legitimating mothers' work outside the home, the Sheppard-Towner maternity policy expressly prohibited the use of federal funds for "pensions, stipends, or gratuities."[52]

The maternity and infancy program provided welcome medical relief to many rural women. Traveling clinics and nurses brought needed information to women, at least in the white communities where states and localities directed most of their resources. Of particular concern to infancy protection workers in rural areas was to train and dispatch greater numbers of nurses to "educate, educate, educate" about sanitation and the need for pregnant women and

---

[50] Annie S. Veech, "For Blue Grass and Hill Babies," *Survey*, September 15, 1924, pp. 625–626. Carolyn Conant Van Blarcom laments the difficulty of reforming "backward," "superstitious," and "tribal" Black midwives in "Rat Pie among the Black Midwives of the South," *Harper's*, February 1930, pp. 322–332. For a discussion of the persistently and disproportionately high infant mortality rates among Blacks during the 1920s and 1930s, see Philip F. Williams, "Maternal Welfare and the Negro," *Journal of the American Medical Association* 132 (November 16, 1946): 611–614.

[51] Lise Vogel, *Mothers on the Job: Maternity Policy in the U.S. Workplace* (New Brunswick, 1993), pp. 34–35.

[52] "An Act for the Promotion of the Welfare and Hygiene of Maternity and Infancy," 67th Congress, 1st session, chap. 135 (Washington, D.C., 1921).

new mothers to stop work.[53] The program also brought many changes to childbirthing practices in both rural and urban America: midwifery, for example, was driven undergound in many places by licensing regulations administered by Anglo American nurses.[54]

In urban and industrial areas, infancy protection workers pursued similar goals in attempts to relieve the cultural isolation of immigrant mothers. Lathrop and Baker clearly established their model of infancy protection through Americanization in testimony on the Sheppard-Towner bill. Appearing before the House Committee on Interstate and Foreign Commerce, Baker explained the central role of education in infancy protection work: "We have induced most of the mothers who come to visit us to nurse their children. That is educational work and has been of great importance in the reduction of infant mortality. . . . If the mother needs some instruction in the home, and we have reason to believe the home surroundings are bad . . . the nurse goes to the home in the afternoon and the mother is given instruction as to the care of the baby. . . . The babies are kept under observation through the second year, and then, if possible, followed up until school age."[55]

Julia Lathrop likewise tied infancy protection to maternal reform. Assuring Congress that Sheppard-Towner proponents eschewed the concept of maternity benefits, she explained that the infant mortality problem was not subject to simple economic solution. Cash benefits were "ineffective," Lathrop maintained, and they begged the more serious issue of the family wage. Moreover, medical services—routine health care for pregant women, new mothers, and their babies—could treat illness but could not protect against it. Real protection of infants required preventive intervention, that is, the education of mothers by nurses, teachers, and social workers. Tying preventive health policy to family reform, Lathrop told the House Committee on Interstate and Foreign Com-

---

[53] Katherine M. Olmstead, "Problems of Infant and Maternal Welfare Work in Rural Communities," American Association for Study and Prevention of Infant Mortality *Transactions* of the Ninth Annual Meeting, pp. 207–214.

[54] Ladd-Taylor, " 'My Work Came out of Agony and Grief,' " p. 333. Ladd-Taylor reports that by the mid-1920s the number of midwives had droped from 6,000 to 4,339 in Virginia and from 4,209 to 3,040 in Missisippi.

[55] Statement of S. Josephine Baker, *Hearings* on the Public Protection of Maternity and Infancy, pp. 27, 19; "Bureau of Child Hygiene," *Woman Voter*, May 1916.

merce that "the problems which must be met before nursing care or medical care [can] be made effective are largely social and economic and family problems."[56]

The Sheppard-Towner Act forwarded maternalist strategies to treat "family problems" by supporting programs that disseminated advice, instruction, and supervision. Lathrop believed the act encouraged Americanization of the family. More than just a health program, Sheppard-Towner was an instrument of uplift: "[It] is not to get the Government to do things for the family. It is to create a family that can do things for itself; it is to get parents who know what their children need, who are good and wise and can secure a decent living; who know when they need a doctor and will have him; who will know when they need public health and will help to pay for it gladly; and who know what kind of a school they want their children to go to, and will help to create that and pay for that."[57]

Grace Abbott, Lathrop's successor at the helm of the Children's Bureau, reiterated the educational mission of infancy protection policy and spelled out its educational achievements when she appeared before a congressional committee in 1925. Testifying in support of extending the Sheppard-Towner Act, she enumerated the policy's objectives: first, "better infant care through the teaching of mothers"; second, "better care for mothers through education as to the need and value of skilled supervision during pregnancy, childbirth, and the lying-in period"; and third, "more widespread medical and nursing facilities so that adequate maternity and infancy supervision will be available to all who need it."[58] Describing the methods of Sheppard-Towner nurses, she discussed home visits, home demonstrations, mothers' classes, "Little Mothers" classes, and maternal and child health conferences. Echoing her predecessor's view that the linchpin of infancy protection was the mother herself, Abbott told the committee: "A maternal and infant program is, of course, not like a sanitary program where you simply

---

[56]   Statement of Miss Julia C. Lathrop, *Hearings* on the Public Protection of Maternity and Infancy, pp. 241–242.
[57]   Ibid., p. 243.
[58]   Grace Abbott to the Committee on Interstate and Foreign Commerce, U.S. House of Representatives, *Hearings* on the Extension of Public Protection of Maternity and Infancy Act (H.R.7555) 69th Congress, 1st session (Washington, D.C., 1926), pp. 8–9.

employ an expert to do the work. It has to be done by reaching every mother and the general public with a campaign of education as to what is scientific care."[59]

The passage of the Sheppard-Towner Act affirmed women's political significance and expanded Anglo American, middle-class, professional women's formal political role. Women designed and introduced the policy, campaigned for its adoption, administered its provisions, received its benefits, and bore its price. African American women, immigrant women, Latinas, and Anglo American rural and urban women shared the goals of improved maternal and infant health.[60] The rhetorical and practical content of maternity policy, however, bore the stamp of progressive maternalism. Women's first legislative achievement as political citizens, the Sheppard-Towner maternity policy was also the first national policy to tie cultural and gender-role conformity to the social welfare.

Between 1921 and 1929, when the act expired under fire from the physician lobby, infancy protection workers distributed 22 million pamphlets, convened 183,000 health conferences, set up 2,600 rural child health centers, distributed 22 million pieces of literature, and conducted 3 million home visits. By 1925, 162,000 women in 43 states had attended mothers' classes; 75,000 women had attended prenatal conferences; 600,000 babies and young children had been examined; and 4,000 Little Mothers' Leagues had been organized.[61] In its last four years, the program reached four million babies and 700,000 women.[62]

These efforts spread health information and maternity advice into remote rural areas and among urban ethnic communities and

[59] Ibid., p. 11. See also Grace Abbott, "The Federal Government in Relation to Maternity and Infancy," American Academy of Political and Social Sciences *Annals* 151 (September 1930): 92–101.

[60] For a comparison of the goals of white and Black women activists and a discussion of the common emphasis on children, see Linda Gordon, "Black and White Visions of Welfare: Women's Welfare Activism, 1890–1945," *Journal of American History* 78 (September 1991): 559–590.

[61] Wertz and Wertz, *Lying In*, p. 210; *Survey*, December 15, 1925, p. 234; Third Annual Conference of State Directors in Charge of the Local Administration of the Maternity and Infancy Act *Proceedings* (January 11–13, 1926), U.S. Department of Labor, Children's Bureau Publication no. 157 (Washington, D.C., 1926), pp. 157–163, 164–172.

[62] *The Promotion of the Welfare and Hygiene of Maternity and Infancy for the Fiscal Year Ending June 30, 1929*, U.S. Department of Labor, Children's Bureau Publication no. 203 (Washington, D.C., 1931), p. 27.

were surely appreciated by many women. But the program was also laden with class, cultural, and gender-ideological baggage: women who needed to work were admonished to stay at home and breastfeed, immigrant women were often given nutritional instructions that required them to abandon the culinary customs of their own cultures, and little girls were trained to define their futures as an idealized "American" motherhood.

Moreover, in the maternalist tradition of uplift through assimilation and reform through instruction, maternity and infancy protection policy did not socialize the infant health risks of poverty. Instead, it asked mothers to transcend the effects of poverty on maternal and infant health by improving their own behavior. This approach individualized the burden of maternity and infancy protection, hanging the infant's welfare on the assimilation and education of the mother.

MOTHER'S BARGAIN

Progressive maternalists defined the social welfare as the proximity of greater numbers of people to a common standard of Anglo American citizenship; accordingly, their reforms welded Americanism to social protection. Though maternalist policies lay the groundwork for the American welfare state by asserting the social responsibilities of government, they simultaneously imposed reciprocal behavioral and cultural responsibilities on women. Thus, even as women achieved independent citizenship during the 1920s, maternalist social welfare initiatives treated certain women—poor women—as dependent subjects of the state.

Whether through mothers' pensions or infancy protection policy, maternalist reform denied the possibility of equality under conditions of persistent diversity: the maternalist philosophy implied that inferiority and inequality inhered in cultural difference. Where white supremacists located inequality in immutable, essential race characteristics, maternalists treated inequality as a product of behavior, and their prescriptions emphasized the remediation of behavior—language, customs, home management— as the way to full political dignity and citizenship.

Maternalist efforts to universalize the quality of citizenship rested on the idea of uplift: self-improvement and transcendence of those habits and behaviors reformers correlated with poverty and a weak public spirit. Especially in the cities, with their large populations of immigrants and their children, maternalists read behavior as culture. Benevolent but hardly neutral, maternalist policy work thus proceeded from assumptions that involved ranking and judging the cultural behavior of their subjects. When maternalists introduced this idiom of uplift to American welfare discourse, they reinforced the view that cultural differences were politically significant causes and evidence of inequality.

Moreover—and notwithstanding their rejection of hereditarian notions of cultural and racial inequality—maternalists helped institutionalize stubborn gender-based ascriptive distinctions among citizens. The roots of women's inequality in the welfare state can be found in maternalist social policy, which made women's "universal" gender role the conduit for cultural reform and which conditioned social benefits on domestic motherhood. Defining motherhood as the primary role of the woman citizen and "Americanized" motherhood as the basis of a strong polity, maternalists made the imitation of a middle-class, Anglo American maternal ideal the price of woman's citizenship. They thereby embraced a gender essentialism that conferred political significance upon women's difference from men, even as they eschewed the view that all women would "naturally" pursue and excel in her vocation without social support and supervision.

As we shall see, however, the maternalist project did in fact challenge the idea of ascriptive inequality. By its faith in education, it opened the possibility that immigrants and African Americans could both earn and learn equality. And by its insistence on the distinctive value of women's citizenship, the maternalist project nurtured the possibility of difference among equals. In these ways, maternalist ideas and maternalist work forged a political path toward racial liberalism and feminism, even while making cultural and gender conformity the price of social equality.

SCHOOLING FOR MOTHERHOOD
Woman's Role and "American"
Culture in the Curriculum

Our schools should be imbedded in the home life of their communities.
—Mrs. Eva Whiting White, 1919

Most discussions of maternalist contributions to the development of the U.S. welfare state focus on the reformers' innovations in the areas of child welfare and income assistance.[1] Both mothers' pensions and maternity and infancy protection policy offer a window onto the interactions among maternalist gender claims, cultural and racial interests, and class anxieties. Together, these programs inform our understanding of the relationship between the welfare state and social inequality. Maternalist welfare work, however, reached beyond protective services: it also included an agenda for the reform of public education. This agenda reflected the American preference to offer educational opportunity as a surrogate for a social wage.[2] More important, it reinforced and elaborated the cultural strategy that lay behind the maternalists' more celebrated experiments in social protection.

Mothers' pension programs responded to the material conditions

---

[1] See, e.g., Robyn Muncy, *Creating a Female Dominion in American Reform, 1890–1935* (New York, 1991); Theda Skocpol, *Protecting Soldiers and Mothers: The Political Origins of Social Policy in the United States* (Cambridge, Mass., 1992); Linda Gordon, "Social Insurance and Public Assistance: The Influence of Gender in Welfare Thought in the United States, 1890–1935," *American Historical Review* 97 (February 1992): 19–54; Molly Ladd-Taylor, *Mother Work: Women, Child Welfare, and the State, 1890–1930* (Urbana, 1994).
[2] For a concise analysis of this preference, see Harold M. Hyman, *American Singularity: The Northwest Ordinance, the 1862 Homestead and Morrill Acts, and the 1944 G.I. Bill* (Athens, Ga., 1986).

77

in which poor widows found themselves. But, as I argued in Chapter 2, policy administrators and social workers piggybacked cultural intervention onto income support, for example, when they equated worthy motherhood with teetotaling, English-speaking domesticity. Similarly, infancy protection programs spread medical information to women whose class, cultural, or geographic isolation was believed to impede healthy pregnancy, childbirth, and infant care. Policy administrators and visiting nurses made health services a conduit for cultural reform when they defined the "American" diet as the nutritional diet, for example. School reform was no less culturally loaded, in practice, than were mothers' pension and infancy protection programs. One purpose of school reform was Americanization. By teaching foreign-born girls "American" domestic virtues and foreign-born boys "American" industrial virtues, reformed schools would turn "little aliens" into "little citizens." In the arena of school reform, in fact, the maternalist gender and cultural agendas were most fully played out.[3]

Between 1915 and 1930, maternalists supplemented their efforts to Americanize immigrant mothers through social work and social programs with efforts to Americanize their children—especially daughters—through the public schools. Joining other progressive calls for more democratic education, maternalists on local school boards, in national women's organizations, and in government helped launch nearly a half-century of debate over the significance of education to American democracy. Bringing the rhetorical weapons of the child and the home to the campaign for Americanism and vocationalism through schooling, maternalists aimed to teach young boys "the citizen's responsibilities of fatherhood" (breadwinning) and young girls the "American" mother's knowledge of domestic management and child welfare (homemaking).[4]

---

[3]   Frances Kellor, "What Is Americanization?" in Philip Davis, ed., *Immigration and Americanization* (Boston, 1920), pp. 625–626; Frances Kellor, "Americanization by Industry," *Immigrant in America Review* 2 (April 1916): 15; Louise B. More, *Wage-Earners' Budgets* (New York, 1907); Selma Berrol, "Public Schools and Immigrants: The New York City Experience," in Bernard J. Weiss, ed., *Education and the European Immigrant: 1840–1940* (Urbana, 1982), pp. 31–36; Maxine Seller, "The Education of the Immigrant Woman, 1900–1935," *Journal of Urban History* 4 (May 1978): 307–330.

[4]   Florence Kelley described the duties of manly citizenship to the New York State

Confident that ethnic children could become "American" by unlearning their cultures, Anglo American maternalist reformers argued for a universal, Americanizing curriculum in the public
schools. Uncertain that the Americanizing curriculum would in
fact be universally accessible without federal financing and standards, they further pressed for a national education policy. The
reformers' emphasis on the links between schooling, culture, and
citizenship helped transform schools into institutions of cultural
transmission and political socialization. Their insistence on the
significance of universal education to democracy helped win an unprecedented hearing for the idea of a federal role in providing education.

The gendered and cultural strategies of maternalist reform also,
however, hardened caste distinctions among citizens. The reformers' reliance on gender roles as agents of cultural transmission
turned schools into nurseries of gender inequality. The reformers'
call for cultural conformity demeaned ethnic Americans even while
the tools of that conformity (literacy, English-language skills, vocational training) opened opportunities for many ethnic Americans. Equally important, the reformers' insistence that the effects
of poverty would be mitigated by cultural reform supported development of "the culture of poverty" as a social policy idiom.

DOMESTICATING DIFFERENCE

The coincidence of industrialization, poverty, economic in-
stability, labor unrest, and immigration fanned early-twentieth-
century fears of political disorder and further economic dislocation.
Though settled, old-stock Americans responded variously to these
coinciding problems, most in one way or another identified "new"
European immigrants as the cause of America's troubles. Maternalist reformers, in this respect, fully represented the American
mainstream; they fixed their focus on the new polyglot and
multicultural populations in (mostly) northern cities. Schooled in

---

Factory Investigation Commission in 1912. See the Commission's *Preliminary Report* 3 (1912), p. 1599. For her view of the purpose of girls' education, see Kelley,
Modern Industry in Relation to the Family, Health, Education, Morality (New York,
1914), p. 97.

the settlement house tradition, however, which stressed the possibility of social harmony through social interaction and mediation, maternalists fought to incorporate the newcomers in the American political community.[5]

When the federal Dillingham Commission issued its report on the economic aspects of immigration in 1911, it armed nativists with government-approved facts about the proportions of the immigrant "menace." With the outbreak of World War I, nativists used this data, along with the army's findings of mental infirmity among new immigrant and Black recruits, to press their case for immigration restriction and nationalistic Americanization. Maternalist reformers, by contrast, eschewed nativism, countering with "remedial strategies" designed to foster national unity from cultural diversity. Domesticating Americanism, maternalists nurtured assimilation, both in settlement house projects that long preceded wartime nativist hysteria and in social policy initiatives that long outlived the mean-spirited Americanization fever of wartime and the Red Scare.[6] If the home was where maternalists treated the most immediate problems of cultural difference, the school was where they nurtured a new generation of Americans.

Grace Abbott and Frances Kellor—both settlement veterans, immigrant advocates, and skilled social researchers—played crucial roles in state-level immigration commissions, where they developed strategies to Americanize the immigrant which pivoted on the public school.[7] By 1916, they had helped organize a National Conference on Immigration and Americanization, marking the beginning of a concerted political effort to assimilate, rather than exclude, new southern and eastern European immigrant Americans.[8]

Abbott and Kellor's emphasis on education was in part supported by the Dillingham Commission's data. The commission re-

[5] Mina Carson provides a useful description of the settlement house tradition in *Settlement Folk: Social Thought and the American Settlement Movement, 1885–1930* (Chicago, 1990), especially chaps. 1 and 3.
[6] Edward George Hartmann, *The Movement to Americanize the Immigrant* (New York, 1967), pp. 258–261.
[7] On the role of the settlement in generating an agenda and a method for school reform, see Edward A. Krug, *The Shaping of the American High School* (New York, 1964), pp. 260–265; Morris Isaiah Berger, "The Settlement, The Immigrant, and the Public School" (Ph.D. diss., Columbia University, 1956), pp. 2–17; Carson, *Settlement Folk*, pp. 119–120.
[8] Hartmann, *Movement to Americanize*, pp. 70–74; Berger, "The Settlement," p. 114.

ported that 57.8 percent of school children in thirty-seven cities were children of immigrants; in New York City, 71.5 percent had immigrant fathers. Forty percent of these children were reportedly age-grade "retarded." Since fewer than a third of children were still in school by the age of sixteen, reformers worried that ethnic children were poorly prepared for work, homelife, and citizenship.[9] Nor were Abbott and Kellor alone among progressive maternalists in assigning policy priority to schooling. In numerous venues, Jane Addams argued the singular importance of education in the moral and political development of the child.[10] Sophonisba Breckinridge and Grace Abbott's sister, Edith, likewise placed special emphasis on education as an avenue for uplift.[11] All these women worried that the patent educational deficit in immigrant communities put the moral and political welfare of the nation at risk. Progressive maternalists generally feared that without the countervailing influence of education, cultural and racial solidarities would congeal into separate societies within one nation.[12] Accordingly, they stretched their welfare work to include cultural reform through the public schools.

As chief investigator for the New York Immigration Commission, founder of the Committee for Immigrants in America, and liaison between the National Americanization Committee and the federal Bureau of Education, Kellor developed programs for adult education as well as for public schooling which, through English-language and civics instruction, would produce "one language, one mind."[13] Similarly, as executive secretary of the Massachusetts Immigration Commission, Grace Abbott developed a twelve-point

[9]   John Lapp, Director of the Bureau of Legislative Information of Indiana, "National Aid for Vocational Education," National Education Association *Proceedings* (1915), pp. 322–323.
[10]   Jane Addams, "The Public School and the Immigrant Child," excerpt from the National Association of Education *Proceedings* (1908), in Ellen Condliffe Lagemann, ed., *Jane Addams on Education* (New York, 1985), pp. 136–142. See also Addams, *The Spirit of Youth and the City Streets* (New York, 1909).
[11]   Sophonisba Breckinridge and Edith Abbott, *The Delinquent Child and the Home* (New York, 1917); *Truancy and Non-Attendance in the Chicago Public Schools* (Chicago, 1917).
[12]   Frances Kellor, *Immigration and the Future* (New York, 1920), chap. 2.
[13]   Robert A. Carlson, "Americanization as an Early-Twentieth-Century Adult Education Movement," *History of Education Quarterly* 4 (Winter 1970): 448–450; John F. McClymer, "The Federal Government and the Americanization Movement," *Prologue* 10 (Spring 1978): 23–41.

program for Americanization through education which included calls for compulsory attendance in English-speaking schools that taught "American principles."[14] Breckinridge and Edith Abbott, meanwhile, worked with the Bureau of Vocational Supervision for the Chicago Public Schools in developing vocational education programs to assist immigrant children in their transition to "American" economic and social roles.

Political experience taught many social reformers the importance of education to moral and cultural uplift. As feminist Rheta Childe Dorr explained:

> What women must do, as soon as they become voters, is to survey their national situation . . . from the standpoint of experts in race improvement. The world is in a mess, and the spectacle of women trying to extricate it from the mess by applying moral mustard plasters like anti-cigarette or even anti-liquour laws, makes me tired. . . . Women should find out the essentials of reform, and let all the rest of it go. . . . Personally I believe that the first essential is more and better education . . . of the bodies and souls, as well as the minds of people, to make them understand their place in the universe as efficient, useful, productive agents.[15]

Settlement work experience gave maternalists their method for Americanizing education. Settlement house classes taught women and girls the norms of domesticity, offered civics classes and English classes to parents and their children, and inculcated "American" cuisine through lunch programs and cooking classes. This educational work provided a model for vocational programs which linked the learning of skills to the assimilation of "American" mores.

Faith in uplift through education led maternalists to join civil rights groups, mothers' clubs, domestic scientists, and educational professionals in a campaign for public school curricular reform during the 1910s. Maternalist interest in curricular reform arose from the notion that boys and girls could be inspired to "efficient man-

---

[14]   Hartmann, *Movement to Americanize*, pp. 74–75.
[15]   Rheta Childe Dorr, "What Next?" *Suffragist*, October 1920, p. 236.

hood and womanhood" with appropriate training.[16] Florence Kelley underscored the gender-socializing potential of school curricula in her 1914 critique of public schools: "The schools may truthfully be said actively to divert the little girls from homelife. . . . For the schools teach exactly those things which prepare girls to become at the earliest moment cash children and machine tenders: punctuality, regularity, attention, obedience, and a little reading and writing—excellent things in themselves, but wretched preparation either for domestic service or an alternative choice of occupations, or for homemaking a decade later on in the lives of students."[17]

Mary Simkhovitch echoed Kelley: "Every system of education must . . . relate the child to his family, his neighborhood, his state . . . as well as to . . . his prospective work."[18] But curricular reform meant more than making men and mothers of immigrant boys and girls. The public school curriculum allowed reformers to directly transform the immigrant family.[19] An enthusiastic Jane Addams, for example, explained that homemaking classes in the public schools would help immigrant girls "connect the entire family with American food and household habits."[20] For Addams as for others, girls in particular could aid their families' cultural transition if properly guided by the public schools. Addams considered the educated daughter the key to cultural reform. Through education, the immigrant's daughter could be taught to abandon "the mother's example of complaining of changed conditions," making instead "the adjustment *for her mother's entire household*." Speaking to the National Education Association in 1908, Addams previewed her vision: "We cannot tell what adjustments the girl herself will be called upon to make ten years from now; but we can give her the clue and the aptitude to adjust the family with which she is identified to the constantly changing conditions of city life. . . . I wish I had the power to place before you what seems to me is the opportunity that the immigrant colonies present to the public

[16] Paula Fass makes this point in *Outside In: Minorities and the Transformation of American Education* (New York, 1989), chap. 1.

[17] Kelley, *Modern Industry*, p. 97.

[18] Mary Simkhovitch, *The City Worker's World in America* (New York, 1917), p. 64.

[19] Mable Kittredge, "Housekeeping Centers in Settlements and Public Schools," *Survey*, May 3, 1913, p. 189.

[20] Jane Addams, *Twenty Years at Hull House* (New York, 1961), p. 253.

school: the most endearing occupation of leading the little child, who will in turn lead his family."[21]

Although their educational project was culturally intrusive, maternalist reformers warned against aggressive monoculturalism and rapid and nationalistic Americanization of immigrant children. Grace Abbott, for example, frequently invited immigrants to contribute the best aspects of their native cultures to their new American one. Edith Terry Bremer, another settlement house veteran and founder of the YWCA's International Institutes, cautioned against "compulsory assimilation" and criticized the "arrogant assumption that everything American was intrinsically superior to anything foreign."[22] In a similar vein, Ethel Bird asked the National Conference of Social Work "to question whether one human generation is not too short a period of time for a complete transfer of interests, attitudes, and mental contents; whether our Americanization haste, in such matters as language and citizenship, is not psychologically unsound . . . whether, as someone has said, we ought not to be more willing to 'leave a little to evolution' and only encourage that degree of change which is 'consciously desired' by an individual or 'socially necessary' in order to bridge the chasm between immigrant parent and American-born child which, as social workers, we are coming to recognize as fertile in social tragedy."[23]

Still, reformers, not immigrants, determined which changes were "socially necessary" and chose which cultural contributions immigrants would be encouraged to make: social workers and nutritionists discouraged "garlicky," spicy, mixed foods like spaghetti and goulash, for example, while welcoming handicrafts, pottery, and folksongs.[24]

By tempering cultural reform with cultural pluralism—however narrowly conceived—reformers distinguished themselves from the loud and visible monoculturalist Americanizers of the World

[21]   Jane Addams, "Public School and the Immigrant Child," p. 139.

[22]   Raymond Mohl, "The International Institutes and Immigrant Education, 1910–1940," in Weiss, ed., *Education and the European Immigrant*, pp. 118–119.

[23]   Ethel Bird, "Twofold Problem of Immigration," National Conference of Social Work *Proceedings*, 50th session (May 1923), p. 306.

[24]   For a fascinating treatment of the war against spaghetti and other "coarse," "overspiced," "unhealthy," and "morally dangerous" foods, see Harvey Leverstein, *Revolution at the Table: The Transformation of the American Diet* (New York, 1988).

War I period. The maternalists' cautious toleration of muted multiplicity arose from their concerns that nationalistic and culturally bigoted indoctrination of children would lead them to disrespect their immigrant parents. Grace Abbott worried that the immigrant parents' dependence on English-proficient children skewed the family relationship—especially the maternal relationship, given mothers' "peculiar isolation" in the home.[25] The potential subordination of mothers by children not only violated the reformers' family ideals but augured poorly for immigrant children's acculturation to Americanized gender relations, as well. Thus Abbott recommended "a more careful adaptation of the methods of teaching and of the course of study on the part of public school authorities in order that immigrant children would not lose respect for their parents through Americanization" and allowed that "for the sake of family life, a knowledge of that [native] language by the children is necessary."[26] Mary Hurlbutt, director of the YWCA's International Migration Service, urged social workers to understand the point of view of the immigrant mother, so that they would not even unwittingly endorse the immigrant child's "sense of queerness and increase that break between the two generations which spells the destruction of moral protection for the younger one."[27] Likewise, Jane Addams urged teachers to "know something about the lives the parents lead and . . . to reprove the hooting children who make fun of the Italian mother because she wears a kerchief on her head not only because they are rude but also because they are stupid."[28]

The maternalists' pluralism was nonetheless limited by the reformers' assumption that immigrant mores would generally impede ethnic children's ability to become productive and assimilated citizens. Rather than leave cultural adjustment to "evolution," as Ethel Bird suggested, most maternalists turned to schools for the "conscious assimilation" of children. The reformers saw the democratizing potential of education, as well, but viewed democratization less as a matter of opening opportunities than of

[25]   Grace Abbott, *The Immigrant and the Community* (New York, 1917), pp. 226–230.
[26]   Ibid., p. 230; Hartmann, *Movement to Americanize*, p. 75.
[27]   Mary Hurlbutt, "The Invisible Environment of an Immigrant," National Conference on Social Work *Proceedings* (1923), p. 311.
[28]   Jane Addams, "Public School and the Immigrant Child."

reconstructing individuals. Maternalists were not unique in this view. John Dewey, the father of educational reform, also celebrated the sifting and socializing power of the public schools in his famous treatise on democratic education:

> With the development of commerce, transportation, intercommunication, and emigration, countries like the United States are composed of a combination of different groups with different traditional customs. It is this situation which has, perhaps more than any other one cause, forced the demand for an educational institution which shall provide something like a homogeneous and balanced environment for the young. Only in this way can the centrifugal forces set up by juxtaposition of different groups within one and the same political unit be counteracted. . . . The assimilative force of the American public school is eloquent testimony to the efficacy of the common and balanced appeal.[29]

Like the maternalists, Dewey fought compulsory assimilation even as he charged the school with "creating a real unity of purpose and ideal in the youth of our country . . . of bringing together the exceedingly heterogeneous elements of our population."[30] Other educational progressives were more concerned with training boys for their appropriate economic roles in society than with spurring the acculturation of girls and thereby universalizing the quality and character of maternal citizenship. Maternalists did not have the field to themselves in education reform as they did in mothers' pensions and maternity policy, but they were nonetheless emphatic about preparing the child for her moral and political role and, with Dewey, broadened the educational reform agenda by investing vocationalism with political meaning and connecting it to family life. A blend of two sets of vocational interests, school reform brought intellectual and economic differentiation into the schools (through IQ tests, tracking, and industrial training), while turning schools into instruments of cultural remediation and homogenization (through Americanizing programs).

[29]   John Dewey, *Democracy and Education* (New York, 1916), pp. 21–22.
[30]   John Dewey, "Future Trends in the Development of Social Programs through Schools," National Conference on Social Work *Proceedings* (1923), pp. 449–450.

WOMAN'S VOCATION

Although maternalist education work began in the settlement houses early in the century, their education policy activities began in earnest when, with Florence Kelley's leadership, they signed on to lobby for passage of the Smith-Hughes Vocational Education Act in the mid 1910s. Defining "homemaking as a basic vocation for women," the 1917 act marked the federal government's first substantive intervention in elementary and secondary education. It provided funds, mainly through land grant colleges, to state and local programs for agricultural education, as well as for domestic (girls) and industrial (boys) training in the public schools and in part-time vocational classes. In so doing, the act gave legitimacy to task- and role-oriented education and staked out a political role for the central government in the education of its citizens.

The formula for distributing industrial and homemaking education funds was pegged to urban populations. The gendered schooling sponsored by the act thus favored northern and industrial states and targeted polyglot communities. Vocational programs prepared boys and girls for their industrial and domestic work lives—in the paid world of manufacture and domestic service, as well as in the unpaid world of motherhood. As school systems developed citizenship training courses within vocational programs, vocational education assumed the responsibility of instructing boys and girls in their respective spheres of citizenship.[31] At the intersection of girls' citizenship and vocational training, maternalists found their arena for cultural reform: the homemaking class.

It is not too farfetched to treat the homemaking class as the fulcrum of the maternalists' Americanization strategy. The class was not only a means of social reform—of fighting poverty, disease, and malnutrition—but was "nothing less than an effort to save our social fabric from what seems inevitable disintegration."[32] Girls learned how to cook according to nutritional standards, how to sew,

[31] "Mothercraft," *Survey*, September 24, 1921, p. 709; Thomas Woody, *A History of Women's Education in the United States* (New York, 1929).

[32] Ellen Richards, "Social Significance of the Home Economics Movement," *Journal of Home Economics* 3 (April 1911): 122.

how to manage the household, how to care for children. But homemaking classes, like Little Mothers' Leagues, did not merely prepare girls for their future vocation as mothers; they imparted skills that compensated for the ignorance of the girls' own mothers. Girls took homemaking skills home after a day's lessons, challenging mothers to adjust to "American" rules of diet, sanitation, and etiquette. Mothers were invited to participate in their daughters' development in mothers' meetings called by teachers and when daughters practiced their new skills in home projects. Moreover, home economics instruction was made available to all girls and women age fourteen and older—either in secondary schools or in part-time vocational classes—regardless of prior schooling. Thus young mothers could themselves learn "American" homemaking through extension courses sponsored under the Smith-Hughes Act. In these ways, the federal vocational education program encouraged the simultaneous domestic training of two generations of ethnic girls and women.[33]

In settlement houses and in policy venues, maternalists had long advocated schooling that would simultaneously enhance the welfare of children and the welfare of the polity. Settlement house mothers' classes, cooking classes, and lunch programs served both ends, showing immigrant girls and women how to improve their living standards through assimilation of "American" standards. Maternalists applied settlement house traditions to the public school curriculum. Other more conservative women's groups, including the National Mothers' Congress, similarly urged schools to take the lead in imparting the craft of motherhood, if not for the sake of the children then for the sake of the political order. As one spokesperson told the House Committee on Education in testimony requesting increased Smith-Hughes funding for home economics: "A large part of the rejection of men called in the recent draft could be traced to causes induced in infancy and childhood by poor health habits and home conditions largely due to the ignorance of the

[33] U.S. House of Representatives, *Hearings* on Federal Aid for Home Economics (H.R.12078), Committee on Education, 66th Congress, 3d session (Washington, D.C., 1921), pp. 48–50; Cora M. Winchell, Assistant Professor, Household Arts Education, Teachers College, Columbia University, "Homemaking as a Phase of Citizenship," *Journal of Home Economics* 14 (January 1922): 32; Adelaide Steele Baylor, Federal Agent for Home Economics, "Vocational Education in Home Economics—Part-Time Schools and Classes," *Journal of Home Economics* 12 (November 1920): 473–481.

untrained homemaker. . . . The underfed, undernourished children swell the ranks of the great army of backward, retarded, and overage children so often seen in all communities. And much of this might be prevented if the mothers were as well-trained for the business of home-making as are those who bear responsibilities in the trades and professions."[34]

The General Federation of Women's Clubs joined the appeal to public schools to institute programs in "mothercraft," tying instruction in "the duties of the efficient mother . . . [and] the application of the laws of health to the diet, bathing and sleeping, emphasizing the relationship of the clean happy home" not only to child life but to American values.[35] Meanwhile, a generation of domestic scientists was prepared to supply the substance of the girl's education for her domestic vocation. Explaining the connection between home economics and social progress, Martha Van Rensselaer, president of the American Home Economics Association, told the National Education Association in 1915: "The purpose of home economics is to improve home standards through applying the principles of art and science to home problems. Since the home is the nucleus of all social groups, home economics will more and more play a part of fundamental importance in establishing right community ideals as well as home ideals."[36]

The Smith-Hughes Act in effect gave responsibility for home-making classes to the scientific home economists of the land grant colleges. Because the land grant colleges (including Professor Van Rensselaer's School of Home Economics at Cornell University) trained home economics teachers, the home economists in those colleges enjoyed significant influence over the home economics curriculum in the public schools.[37]

The centerpiece of cultural reform through home economics was the cooking class. Home economists and social workers were of course concerned with the adequacy of vitamins and minerals in the family diet from the standpoint of child health. But because

[34]   U.S. House of Representatives, *Hearings* on Federal Aid for Home Economics, p. 30.
[35]   "Mothercraft," p. 709; Helen Varick Boswell, "Promoting Americanization," American Academy of Political and Social Science *Annals* 64 (March 1916): 205–206.
[36]   Martha Van Rensselaer to the National Education Association, *Journal of Proceedings and Addresses*, 53d Annual Meeting (Oakland, 1915), p. 821.
[37]   Leverstein, *Revolution at the Table*, pp. 96–99.

meals were important moments of family, religious, and cultural expression, reformers also saw food selection and preparation as opportunities for Americanizing cultural intervention.[38] Even when speech and appearance concealed cultural background, cuisine remained a marker of difference. Perhaps because they subscribed to the view that "you are what you eat," many Americanizers in fact believed that ethnic cooking proved the persistence of moral, social, and political difference—that immigrants would never relinquish old-country mores until they abandoned old-country cooking.[39] As one social worker noted upon her visit to an Italian household, "Still eating spaghetti, not yet Americanized."[40]

Nutritionists and social workers were careful, however, to study immigrant diets and to identify those "native traits that give good promise for rapid development under proper guidance."[41] Such sensitivity followed from the reformers' concern to foster, rather than to compel, assimilation. The influenza epidemic of 1917–1918 in New York and other cities confirmed the reformers' view that child welfare could be achieved only through the cooperative participation of immigrant mothers in the task of Americanization. Not only did child neglect by unacculturated mothers help explode the rate of infant mortality during the epidemic, but immigrant mothers' resistance to tonic foods impeded children's recovery.[42]

---

[38] As two reformers saw it, "almost their first thought on landing is something to eat, and this fact places food in the first rank of importance in our plans for Americanization." Michael M. Davis, Jr., and Bertha M. Wood, The Boston Dispensary, "The Food of the Immigrant in Relation to Health," *Journal of Home Economics* 12 (December 1920): 517.

[39] Regrettably, many Americans continue to associate ethnic food with un-American attitudes. In 1988, Crown College of the University of California, Santa Cruz, vetoed a Filipino menu planned for monthly College Night. College officials argued that it would be inappropriate to serve "Asian food" on College Night because the monthly event fell, in this case, on December 7. Needless to say, those of us who by custom sit down to miso soup and rice most nights suddenly received a harsh lesson in what it means to be an American.

[40] Leverstein, *Revolution at the Table*, p. 105, quoting from Erik Amfithreatrof, *The Children of Columbus* (Boston, 1973), p. 240. Leverstein later points out that spaghetti won a measure of toleration during World War I. Women's magazines published articles on "spaghetti, food of our ally."

[41] Lucy Gillett, New York Association for Improving the Condition of the Poor, "Factors Influencing Nutrition Work among Italians," *Journal of Home Economics* 14 (January 1922): 16.

[42] S. Josephine Baker, "Lessons from the Draft," American Association for Study

Complaining that stricken immigrant families left untouched the pots of bland but ameliorative broth social workers delivered to their homes, reformers writing in the *Journal of Home Economics* and participating in conferences on infancy protection and child welfare standards linked the immigrant's "ignorance" about diet to her community's high rates of sickness and death.

Convinced that the immigrant mother had to be recruited to adopt "American" standards as her own, maternalists identified what was nutritionally promising in her own diet while instructing her in "better" food values and recipes.[43] For example, maternalists praised Italians for their frequent use of leafy green vegetables, except when greens were used only as flavoring, but they complained repeatedly of the Italians' "strong prejudice against oatmeal and American cheese or oil," finding it incredible that an Italian would buy a small piece of parmesan cheese when she could buy three times as much American cheese for the same price. Similarly, they complained that Jewish "foods are generally over-seasoned, over rich, over sharp, or over concentrated."[44]

Curricula developed by home economists—and by maternalists like Julia Lathrop, who had founded the New England Kitchen at Hull House before heading up the Children's Bureau—applied "scientific" nutritional principles but simultaneously made the cooking class an occasion to instruct immigrant girls and women in the culinary norms of the healthy, Americanized family. Picking and choosing the salvageable elements of ethnic cuisines, reformers prepared sample menus to show girls how to substitute "better" foods for their own—potatoes for pasta, plain meats for stews, mush for breads. (Nutritionists were so concerned to promote mush consumption that they studied the "Digestibility of Rolled

---

and Prevention of Infant Mortality *Transactions* of the Ninth Annual Meeting (1918), p. 187.

[43] Frances Perkins discussed the need to sift through, rather than to reject wholesale, the immigrant diet in her remarks on the "Roundtable on the Health Problems of Foreign Born Women and Children," in ibid., p. 239.

[44] Gillett, "Factors Influencing Nutrition Work among Italians," pp. 17–18; Gillett, Chair, Social Service Section, American Dietetic Association, "The Great Need for Information on Racial Dietary Customs," *Journal of Home Economics* 14 (June 1922): 260–261. Velma Phillips and Laura Howell, "Racial Differences in Dietary Customs," *Journal of Home Economics* 12 (September 1920): 397, 411.

Oats" to determine whether oatmeal could be cooked for only twenty minutes, rather than for several hours. The worry, here, was that immigrant women's aversion to oatmeal might be due to the length of preparation).[45] Aside from the health and taste consequences of trading olive oil, parmesan cheese, and garlic for butter, American cheese, and salt, "Americanization through homemaking" exacted a heavy personal and cultural price: ethnic children and their parents were asked to trade the cultural bases of their identity for personal success, good health, and social incorporation.

Nowhere was the "Americanization through homemaking" project more comically documented than in a pamphlet of the same name by Pearl Idelia Ellis. Setting out a course of study for Mexican American girls in Southern California, Ellis observed: "Since the girls are potential mothers and homemakers, they will control, in a large measure, the destinies of their future families. The teacher of homemaking has a large field for instruction. Hers is not a mere calling but an opportunity. It is she who sounds the clarion call in the campaign for better homes."[46]

Ellis's curriculum included instruction in sewing, household budgeting, home decoration, etiquette, and mothering. She devoted special and extensive attention to the issue of food, offering the following nutritional principle: "A balanced meal is one in which there are present body regulators, builders, and energy-giving foods, and last but not least, food containing vitamines [sic]." She then applied her advice through sample menus and lessons in food preparation. Here, she substituted flour-, butter-, and sugar-based white and hard sauces for tomato-based Mexican sauces of chiles, cheeses, and nuts. For vegetables she recommended spinach boiled with bacon, creamed beets, sauerkraut or coleslaw, sweet potatoes fried with brown sugar and ham, and salads. Her salad recipes included boiled spinach served with mayonnaise, shredded cabbage with French dressing, mixed fruits and mayonnaise, a cherry-topped banana with mayonnaise, and, perhaps as a conces-

---

[45] Mary Swartz Rose, "Some Experiments on the Digestibility of Rolled Oats Prepared in Various Ways," *Journal of Home Economics* 14 (January 1922): 9–14.

[46] Pearl Idelia Ellis, Department of Americanization and Homemaking, Covina City Elementary Schools, *Americanization through Homemaking* (Los Angeles, 1929).

sion to the tropical fruit industry, "pineapple and avocado salad with mayonnaise to carry out a green and yellow color scheme." Ellis strongly recommended lettuce garnishes for her salads, but worried that "Mexican girls need to be trained in the use of lettuce. As one was heard to say, 'Lettuce is for cows and horses to eat.'" She also provided menus for school lunches appropriate to the average Mexican laborer's family budget: "One glass milk; one cheese sandwich; one lettuce sandwich; one graham cracker sandwich; one apple or pear; one cooky [sic]." Finally, Ellis prescribed proper table service: clean white table cloth or doilies; silverware, rightly placed; an "exactly centered" centerpiece; pleasant and noncontroversial conversation. Throughout, Ellis asserted the relationship between food and social order:

> The old adage, 'As a man thinketh so is he,' might easily be translated to, 'As a man eateth, so is he,' for his thinking is controlled to a greater extent than we are wont to realize by his eating and digestive processes. . . . Employers maintain that the man with a home and family is more dependable and less revolutionary in his tendencies. Thus the influence of the home extends to labor problems and to many other problems in the social regime. The homekeeper creates the atmosphere, whether it be one of harmony and cooperation or of dissatisfaction and revolt. It is to be remembered that the dispositions, once angelic, become very much marred with incorrect diet and resultant digestive disturbances.[47]

In many cities, school lunch programs reinforced homemaking lessons girls received in courses like those of Pearl Ellis. Settlement workers, nutritionists, and mothers' clubs developed lunch programs to ameliorate malnutrition among immigrant school children, but they also used the programs to apply "American" culinary principles in the daily life of children. School lunch programs weaned immigrant children from their home cuisine by habituating them to "American" food. Premised on the theory that school lunches would change children's tastes, reformers anticipated that the new food preferences of children would induce mothers to mod-

[47]   Ibid., p. 21, 22, 28, 27, 33–35, 31.

ify their home cuisine. School lunches typically substituted dietetically preferable "American" lunches for customary foods such as breads and cheese and encouraged the liberal use of milk. At the Stuyvesant Neighborhood House on the Lower East Side of New York, for example, nutritionists offered oatmeal mush, bread and butter, graham crackers and stewed prunes for Wednesday lunch. Few concessions to home cuisine were made.[48]

Other services reinforced girls' homemaking lessons, as well. With the aid of extension funds for parent education under the Smith-Hughes Act, school boards developed Home Teacher programs to connect the lessons learned by girls in schools to the practices of mothers in the home. Stimulated by women's reform groups in Boston and New York in 1906 and popular in twenty-six states by the 1920s, the programs dispatched homemaking teachers to "go into the home and teach the mother."[49] The value of the program, according to one reformer, was that the teacher "goes naturally to the mother from the child," thus bringing the school into the family to assist "in all of its needs."[50]

Visiting teachers taught immigrant mothers the standards and techniques of "American" homemaking—menu substitutions for ethnic food, etiquette, sanitation and hygiene, rudimentary domestic English ("I sew, you cook, she cleans.")[51] Home teacher programs were explicitly designed to Americanize hard-to-reach immigrants—mothers isolated in the home. According to California's *Manual for Home Teachers*: "The home teacher, as we conceive her purpose, seeks not primarily the special child, though that will often open the door to her, and afford her a quick opportunity for friendly help, but the home as such, and especially the mother who makes it. This discrimination as to aim and purpose

[48]   Mary Swartz Rose and Gertrude Gates Mudge, "A Nutrition Class," *Journal of Home Economics* 12 (February 1920): 49–58; Leverstein, *Revolution at the Table*, p. 118.
[49]   Harriet P. Dow, "Home Classes for Foreign-Born Women," Americanization Conference *Proceedings*, U.S. Department of the Interior, Bureau of Education (Washington, D.C., 1919), p. 135.
[50]   Miss E. Richardson, California State Immigration Commission, in ibid., p. 137.
[51]   Judith Rafferty, "Progressivism Moves into the Schools: Los Angeles, 1905–1918," *California History* 66 (June 1987): 94–103; Howard Nudd, "The History and Present Status of the Visiting-Teacher Movement," National Conference of Social Work *Proceedings*, 50th session (1923), pp. 422–423; Emma G. Case, "A Day with the Visiting Teacher," National Conference of Social Work *Proceedings* (1923), p. 429.

cannot be too much emphasized, or too consistently maintained; for the care of abnormal children, important as it is, can by no means take the place of the endeavor to Americanize the families of the community."[52]

Although promising as a method of integrating the school and the community with the home, visiting teacher programs did not excite great allegiance among immigrant mothers. The pioneering California program suffered an 80 percent dropout rate, for example. Nor did immigrant mothers attend mothers' meetings and mothers' classes in large numbers. Though many followed home economists' advice (substituting cocoa for coffee as a child's beverage, for example) immigrant mothers generally resisted the extension into their homes of culturally remedial school services, particularly those intrusive and judgmental services aimed at subverting the "unfavorable social attitudes, ideals, and habits" of the alien population by teaching "new ideals and new habits . . . and the American standard of living."[53] They may not have welcomed home teachers, but immigrant mothers nevertheless received the teachers' lessons through their daughters.

ENGENDERING AMERICAN CITIZENSHIP

Although maternalists expressed broad sympathy for immigrants, avowed sensitivity to the social importance of the child's relationship to her parents and heritage, and warned against reckless, rapid, and nationalistic Americanization, their writings and reforms asserted a poor fit between cultural pluralism and American democracy.[54] Anxious to blur "the differentiation that marks off one group from another," reformers like Mary Simkhovitch

---

[52] Quoted in Frank V. Thompson, *Schooling of the Immigrant* (New York, 1920), p. 110.

[53] Seller, "Education of the Immigrant Woman," pp. 317–319; Albert Shiels, *Americanization* (District of Los Angeles Public Schools, 1919), p. 29; Julius John Oppenheimer, *The Visiting Teacher Movement* (New York, 1925); William H. Maxwell, *A Quarter Century of Public School Development* (New York, 1912).

[54] E.g., Lillian Wald, "Qualifications and Training for Service with Children in a Crowded City Neighborhood," in Sophonisba Breckinridge, ed., *The Child and the City* (Chicago, 1912); Simkhovitch, *City Worker's World*, pp. 7, 61, 64; and Abbott, *Immigrant and the Community*, pp. 224, 225, 236.

sought to impart "American" ideals and standards to the child, her mother, and her neighborhood.[55] "Imbedded in the home life of the community," the school was a powerful tool for assimilation. Drawing from the settlement house model of integration under the guidance of assimilating institutions, maternalists made public school the center of mother and child's social life.[56] The reformers hoped that education—in mothers' classes or by home teachers or through home economics courses—would nurture the "common point of view" they considered the predicate to democracy. By raising children and mothers to a "higher," more Anglo American standard of family life, they hoped, too, to improve children's welfare.[57] Maternalists yearned to enrich the life chances of the child, but their fears of unmanaged multiplicity fixed their emphasis on the child not for her own sake, but for her role in the social mediation of cultural difference.

[55]   Simkhovitch, *City Worker's World.*
[56]   John Dewey explored the nexus between education and community life in *The School and Society* (New York, 1915): "When the school introduces and trains each child of society into membership within such a little community, saturating him with the spirit of service, and providing him with the instruments of effective self-direction, we shall have the deepest and best guarantee of a larger society which is worthy, lovely, and harmonious" (p. 29).
[57]   Mary Simkhovitch, "The Enlarged Function of the Public School," National Conference of Charities and Correction *Proceedings* (1904).

CULTURAL REFORM ACROSS
THE COLOR LINE
Maternalists and the Politics
of Educational Provision

Considerable efforts are directed toward 'Americanizing' all groups of alien origin. But in regard to the colored peoples, the American policy is the reverse. They are excluded from assimilation.
—Gunnar Myrdal, 1944

Progressive pedagogy and federal vocational education funds supported local curricular innovations that changed schooling but did not automatically accomplish assimilationist goals The decentralized structure of public education meant that the availability and the quality of the new curriculum varied across school districts. Discrepancies among compulsory school attendance laws in different states meant that students were not offered a universal standard of instruction based on a nationally uniform school day or school year. Meanwhile, family poverty imposed countervailing pressures on parents and children, often discouraging school participation. The economic welfare of poor families often depended on older children's wage contributions to the family income, and the needs of young siblings or sick parents often could be met only by girls who remained at home during the day.

From the maternalist point of view, students most in need of cultural training through schools were least likely to receive it. Among new European immigrants and African Americans, truancy rates were high and retention rates low. High school attendance and completion rates correlated with class, race, and culture: students from wealthier, old-stock backgrounds were more likely

97

to attend high school and to graduate than were poor Slavic, Italian, Mexican, and Asian immigrants and African Americans.[1] Despite a dramatic overall increase in high school attendance rates among girls after 1900—outpacing boys' enrollments—high school participation by non–Anglo American teenage girls in northern and eastern industrial areas remained low.[2] Throughout the South, where most Blacks lived until World War II, schooling was not an option for many Black children.[3] In southern cities, where 25 percent of the total African American population lived, more than a third of Black children received no schooling at all in 1919. In the West, the exclusion of Mexican and Asian students from schools attended by European Americans likewise limited the educational resources and opportunities available to them.

Progressive maternalists understood that the success of the Americanizing, vocational curriculum was integrally linked to improvements in educational provision. In their 1917 study of attendance problems in the Chicago public schools, Sophonisba Breckinridge and Edith Abbott argued that truancy was not the product of "willful absences" by children but was the result of weak and diverse attendance standards, feebly enforced. They urged that education be elevated to a national issue, addressed by national solutions.[4] The idea was not new: chiefly concerned by illiteracy rates among Blacks in the South, late-nineteenth-century legislators had tried repeatedly—but unsuccessfully—to federalize school standards and school financing.[5] When the Smith-Hughes

---

[1]   John L. Rury, *Education and Women's Work: Female Schooling and the Division of Labor in Urban America, 1870–1930* (Albany, 1991), pp. 93, 108; Paula Fass, *Outside In: Minorities and the Transformation of American Education* (New York, 1989), p. 63.

[2]   Rury, *Education and Women's Work*, chap. 4; Victoria Bissell Brown, "The Fear of Feminization: Los Angeles High Schools in the Progressive Era," *Feminist Studies* 16 (Fall 1990): 493–519.

[3]   Cynthia Neverdon-Morton, *Afro-American Women of the South and the Advancement of the Race, 1895–1925* (Knoxville, 1989); Neil McMillen, *Dark Journey* (Urbana, 1989), chap. 4.

[4]   Sophonisba Breckinridge and Edith Abbott, *Truancy and Non-Attendance in the Chicago Public Schools* (Chicago, 1917).

[5]   In 1870, the Hoar Bill sought to mandate school systems throughout the country, gave the president power to appoint school superintendents in laggard states, and claimed federal power to control school texts. In 1884, 1886, and 1888, the Blair Bill provided federal financial assistance to public schools based on state illiteracy rates. Sidney W. Tiedt, *The Role of the Federal Government in Education* (New York, 1966), pp. 19–21.

Act delivered the first federal investment in public schooling, it funded programs rather than schools, content rather than opportunity, and thereby both subsidized and reproduced existing disparities in educational provision.

During the 1920s, maternalists campaigned to correct inequalities in educational opportunity and so to universalize the benefits of curricular reforms. Although they were unable to convince Congress of its responsibility to fund schooling, the maternalists' educational policy initiatives were important for two reasons. First, progressive maternalist interventions in the politics of educational provision marked a significant advance in their conception of the obligations of national government. Second, this new step drew maternalist attention for the first time to the political impediments to the social incorporation of African Americans. Maternalists demanded extensive national spending and the enforcement of strict national standards for education. More important, they insisted on uniformity and equity in the distribution of educational resources. This insistence brought them to the brink of claiming universal education as an entitlement of citizenship and forced them to square off against the structure, politics, and culture of segregation in the South.

Although reformers like Sophonisba Breckinridge, Edith Abbott, Florence Kelley, Frances Kellor, and Louise de Koven Bowen had long expressed concern about anti-Black prejudice in the northern cities that were hotbeds of maternalist activity, the cultural, economic, and political condition of southern and eastern European immigrants had been their focus.[6] With the expansion of their education agenda came a wider and more complex approach to dilemmas of difference and inequality. Staunch in their defense of the universal ideal and universalizing goal of education, progressive maternalists reached beyond their region to tackle the most severe and pervasive manifestations of educational deprivation—namely, the withholding of educational opportunity from Black children in

[6] On maternalist thinking about Black-white racial issues, see, e.g., Sophonisba Breckinridge, "The Color Line in the Housing Problem," *Survey*, February 1, 1913, pp. 575–576, and Louise deKoven Bowen, *The Colored People of Chicago* (Chicago, 1913). For a good discussion of Frances Kellor's work on Black-white race relations, see Ellen Fitzpatrick, *Endless Crusade: Women Social Scientists and Progressive Reform* (New York, 1990), pp. 62–63, 133, 139. See also Steven J. Diner, "Chicago Social Workers and Blacks in the Progressive Era," *Social Service Review* 44 (December 1970): 393–410.

the South. This move forwarded the development of maternalist racial liberalism by backing up the claim that all Americans could learn equality if given government-guaranteed opportunities to learn.

Universalizing the opportunity to learn required a transformation in the organization of school financing and standards. Federal mandates and funds would bring the central government directly into the affairs of local school authorities and into conflict with local norms and biases. Until adoption of Smith-Hughes vocational education legislation in 1917, federal education initiatives had been limited to land grants to support establishment of public schools in newly admitted states and, under the Morrill Act of 1862, land grants to establish and maintain colleges of agricultural and mechanical arts. The Morrill Act stimulated development of vocational programs in colleges and secondary schools, but only upon passage of the Smith-Hughes Act did vocational education become a systematic national program, widespread in the public schools.[7] A watershed in the development of vocationalism in public schooling, the Smith-Hughes Act was also significant for asserting a federal role in determining the content of public education.

The Smith-Hughes Act provided federal support to secondary vocational education, appropriating funds for teacher salaries and teacher preparation programs in agricultural, industrial, and domestic arts. Though the act mainly funded high school programs, extension classes, and demonstration nurseries, Americanizing industrial and domestic values also found their way into the grade school curriculum. In New York, for example, domestic Americanizers introduced a grade school syllabus that included such topics as "the psychology of races—expression of the home ideal in races other than the Anglo-Saxon," "early social life of the Anglo-Saxon people," and "the home life of the Anglo-

[7]   Newton Edwards and Herman Richey, *The School in the American Social Order* (Boston, 1947), pp. 239, 717, 749.

Saxon vs. the communistic family system."[8] In addition, the act supported part-time and evening training in public programs, so that boys and girls who dropped out of high school could, in principle, continue to receive vocational training. Vocational education was aimed primarily at secondary schools, however, and therefore many target populations escaped its influence. Girls, especially, eluded capture, for home economics was not funded at the same level as industrial education. Despite its significance to the "social fabric," the cultural reform of girls was subordinated in the national budget to the training of boys for paid labor.[9]

Maternalists and other reformers reacted to gender-based disparities in educational provision with calls for equal funding for home economics.[10] They responded to class- and race-based disparities in high school participation and general school opportunities with arguments for compulsory school attendance laws, and indeed many states outside the South enacted school attendance provisions. But even among cooperating states, the standards for school attendance reproduced disparities in school participation rates among older children, for whom vocational programs were designed. These disparities, in turn, reinforced extreme variations in the level of basic academic skills learned and in the degree of exposure to the Americanizing curriculum. Pointing to the costs of illiteracy and cultural fragmentation for democracy and order, re-

[8] Quoted in Barbara Ehrenreich and Deirdre English, "The Manufacture of Housework," *Socialist Revolution* 26 (1975): 32.
[9] Industrial training programs were also made available to girls in some cities, though most high schools did not train women for industrial employment. Girls' industrial programs generally confined training to established "women's occupations"—millinery, the clothing trades, dressmaking, telephone operating. More popular in high schools were commercial arts classes that mainly prepared girls for clerical work. Old-stock, middle-class girls, who boasted the highest rates of secondary school attendance during this period, benefited most from commercial programs. The vast majority of foreign-born and second-generation immigrant women entered manufacture or domestic service, not office work. Seventy-five percent of Black women not in agriculture entered domestic service. Industrial schools for girls typically piggybacked homemaking courses onto their programs, preparing students for two vocations—worker and mother. Willystine Goodsell, *The Education of Women: Its Social Background and Its Problems* (New York, 1923), chap. 6; Rury, *Education and Women's Work*, pp. 147–155.
[10] U.S. House of Representatives, *Hearings* on Federal Aid for Home Economics (H.R.12078), Committee on Education, 66th Congress, 3d session (Washington, D.C., 1921).

formers appealed to the federal government to universalize school standards and educational access.

World War I exposed the stakes of education for citizenship and social order: low induction rates among World War I draftees called into question the quality of the male citizenry; the wartime migration of African Americans to northern cities exacerbated illiteracy rates in the northern workforce; and the growth and persistence of illiteracy among the northern poor inflamed campaigns for improved schooling. But more important, prevalent illiteracy fueled concerns about the implications of educational inequalities in the South for the nation as a whole. As one employer told a congressional committee: "Talking about illiteracy and the questions asked by some of you . . . as to how it affected New York, I would like to give an illustration of what happened during the war in Chicago. They were obliged there to bring up 20,000 negroes from the South. They are there now. They practically all stayed there. I am told by responsible people that those 20,000 negroes now practically hold the balance of voting power there. I think if that is true, and I have no reason to doubt it, that that answers the questions as to why we have an interest in the illiteracy of Mississippi, whether we live in New York, Massachusetts, or Mississippi."[11]

Among social reformers, these developments confirmed the significance of education for American democracy. Whereas reformers blamed the physical and linguistic defects of the draft rejects on home conditions, they attributed their illiteracy and "feeble-mindedness" at least in part to the inadequacies of public education. Not only was a generation of outsiders born beneath the American cultural mainstream—morally, mentally, and physically ill-prepared to fulfill the responsibilities of masculine citizenship—but this generation had not been given the tools with which to uplift itself to fully "American" standards of work and combat.

Maternalists found the "alien-baiting," "repressive measures," "intolerance," and "race antagonism" that abounded during and immediately after the war equally troubling. Frances Kellor wor-

---

[11] Statement of Mr. A. Lincoln Filene, *Hearings* on A Bill to Create a Department of Education and to Encourage the States in the Promotion and Support of Education (S.1337), Committee on Education and Labor, U.S. Senate, 68th Congress, 1st session (Washington, D.C., 1924), p. 79.

ried that the wartime draft experience had "created new racial misunderstandings." She warned, moreover, that "the American, influenced as he is by the spread of Bolshevism and by the prevalence of unrest, as well as by some spectacular evidences of disloyalty among some aliens during the war, leans more and more toward repression and intolerance of difference. The immigrant is sensitive to this change and, as he is constantly receiving messages from abroad urging him to return home, he is becoming less friendly toward America."[12] What was needed, Kellor and others argued, was an active and sympathetic assimilation program that was sensitive to the "process of Americanization" and to the distribution of opportunity.[13] School reform and adult education initiatives undertaken before the war had moved in the right direction, though too late to uplift the World War I draft generation, but these remedies needed to be strengthened and made more comprehensive. Maternalist NAACP leader Mary White Ovington echoed Kellor, arguing that "on the basis of these figures of illiteracy, taken from army camp records, a campaign should at once open for immediate national, adequate aid to education that in ten years should wipe out all illiteracy among American-born children."[14]

The maternalists' war against illiteracy was not culturally neutral. To be sure, the first aim of literacy programs was to teach reading and writing skills, but literacy instruction also afforded an opportunity to teach cultural reform. Cultural reform, in turn, provided the means to attack one of the causes of illiteracy and "feeble-mindedness" identified by maternalists—home conditions. Analytically and prescriptively, reformers thus tied illiteracy to cultural difference and literacy to cultural reform among Blacks and new immigrants alike. This cultural reading of the educational deficit was supported by both military and maternalist evidence. Army data showed that 25 percent of the draftees could not read English, Children's Bureau studies correlated age-grade retardation with the use of languages other than English in the home, and

[12] Frances Kellor, *Immigration and the Future* (New York, 1920), p. 23.

[13] See also Sophonisba P. Breckinridge, *New Homes for Old* (New York, 1921).

[14] Mary White Ovington, "Reconstruction and the Negro," *Crisis*, vol. 17, pp. 169–173. See also, Alice Barrows-Fernandez, "What Next?" *Suffragist*, December 1920, pp. 318–319.

the Women's Bureau reported massive illiteracy and English-language deficiency among immigrant women in the northern workforce. Other studies tied high truancy and low retention rates to home culture and asserted a connection between nationality, school attendance, and intelligence.[15] The correlation of illiteracy with culture extended to Blacks, as well. Scholarly studies of African American traditions and home economists' investigation of African American food habits showed Blacks to be separated from other native-born Americans not only by color but by culture.[16]

If universal literacy could also forward cultural reform, neither goal could be achieved under a regime of states' rights and local autonomy. Variations in local public spending and hegemonic white control of the southern racial order ensured inequality in both educational standards and educational access. Only national policy could break the rigid rule of discrimination.

Associating illiteracy, language barriers, and age-grade retardation with educational deprivation, maternalists called for a national education policy that would make educational opportunity universal and education itself universalizing. Florence Kelley and Mary White Ovington led the policy drive, in concert with the National Conference of Social Work, the National Mothers' Congress, the General Federation of Women's Clubs, the Women's Joint Congressional Committee, the National Education Association, the Southern Commission on Interracial Cooperation, the National Urban League, and the National Association for the Advancement of Colored People, of which Kelley and Ovington were founding members and officers.[17] Carrying the banner for universal educational provision in the 1920s, progressive maternalists called upon Congress to: establish a cabinet-level department of education; appropriate $100 million annually to public schools; fund literacy programs, including adult literacy programs; fund Americanization programs; mandate English-only instruction; fund teacher

[15]   *The Immigrant Woman and Her Job*, U.S. Department of Labor, Women's Bureau Bulletin no. 74 (Washington, D.C., 1929); Emily Palmer, *Pupils Who Leave School*, University of California Part-time Education Series, no. 17 (Berkeley, 1930).
[16]   e.g., Robert Ezra Park, *Race and Culture* (Glencoe, Ill., 1950); Lucy Gillett, "The Great Need for Information on Racial Dietary Customs," *Journal of Home Economics* 14 (June 1922): 260–261.
[17]   Jane Addams, Grace and Edith Abbott, Florence Kelley, Lillian Wald, Julia Lathrop, and Sophonisba Breckinridge were all founding members of the NAACP.

preparation programs; and set national standards for school attendance.

TOWARD UNIVERSAL EDUCATION

The maternalists' interest in the content of instruction was rooted in their experiences with the social settlement; their interest in educational opportunity derived from their goal of extending assimilating instruction to all children. Sophonisba Breckinridge and Edith Abbott, both maternalist veterans of the settlement movement, offered a blueprint for education policy in 1912 when they issued a plea for curricular innovations that would integrate the school with community life and argued for school attendance standards to ensure that all children could enjoy the benefits of public education.[18] They reiterated these views in their 1917 study, imploring the nation to attend to the problem of low school participation rates among the neediest students. Though they did not predict the need for the muscular federal intervention maternalists proposed during the 1920s, their call for universal schooling supported development of a maternalist agenda for national education policy. By the late 1910s, the agenda coalesced in Florence Kelley's work to develop federal legislation that would guarantee educational opportunity to all Americans.

First introduced in 1919, the federal aid to education bill (variously known as the Smith-Towner, Towner-Sterling, and Sterling-Reed bill) stirred debate within Congress and within the reform community. Although the measure's provisions for literacy and cultural reform enjoyed wide support, its administrative assault on the racial status quo split reformers. The racial politics of education became clear in debates over proxy issues—ascriptive industrial education, in the North, and local control, in the South. Initially united behind the Sterling Bill to provide federal assistance to public schools, the reform coalition disintegrated when specific provisions of the bill reopened questions about the meaning of democracy, the promise of equality, and the purpose of common education.

[18] Sophonisba Breckinridge and Edith Abbott, *The Delinquent Child and the Home* (New York, 1912), pp. 176–177.

Most reformers concurred with the bill's English-only, literacy, and Americanization provisions. They also agreed on the need for federally assisted school financing, on the benefits of standardized school attendance requirements, and on the political urgency of securing cabinet-level attention for education policy. But they diverged on two significant issues: occupational tracking and federal oversight of local school systems. In different ways, both issues raised the problem of discrimination. In many northern cities, occupational tracking effectively segregated new immigrant and Black children by vocational prescription into classes and schools that would restrict their opportunities in the future. In the South, segregation meant, in effect, that Black children were excluded from schooling and consequent opportunities altogether.

The Sterling Bill raised the issue of the relationship between federal and local authority in the enforcement of national mandates and in the distribution of public funds. Reformers chose sides, testing the limits of their ideas about assimilation, uplift, and social integration. Reproducing the prejudices that underlay the de facto segregation of northern reform, some reformers supported local administration in keeping with local patterns of social organization and curricular innovation. Others underscored the necessity of national standards, administered equally across administrative units. This debate revealed deep conflicts over the purpose of education: in keeping with the promise of liberal equality, should education release the individual from the social rank into which she was born?—or, in the interest of democratic order and social harmony, should education direct and contain aspiration, even while cultivating it, and thereby channel the individual towards her place and her function in society?

Among racial liberals, different readings of racial problems yielded varying strategies for reform and multiple approaches to vocationalism and segregation. Black and white southern liberals on the Council on Interracial Cooperation, including Mary McLeod Bethune, Black clubwomen like Mary Church Terrell, founder of the National Association of Colored Women, and Black women and men in the National Urban League promoted schooling as a means of social uplift for African Americans and as a means of securing racial harmony. Mobilized against inequities in educational provision but not against segregated schooling per se, clubwomen and interracialists contributed heavily to the development of private schools, colleges, and industrial training programs for Blacks. Black activists in the NAACP, most notably W. E. B. Du Bois, shared the hope that social uplift and racial harmony would follow from the education of Black children. But Du Bois, Ida B. Wells, and others worried that neither uplift nor harmony could be achieved under segregation. Anglo American leaders in the NAACP like Florence Kelley and Mary White Ovington navigated both views, arguing for equality of educational opportunity but clinging to the possibility that equality could be won without crossing the color line.

Most reformers, Black and white, placed great stock in the ameliorative power of education, both for society and for individuals. In the South, where segregation meant not lesser schools but no schools at all for many Black children, reformers like Mary McLeod Bethune subverted the southern racial status quo by founding schools for Black children.[19] Robert Moton and Mary White Ovington promoted instruction in African American history and culture, to "bring good cheer and encouragement to the young readers who have so largely the fortunes of their race in their own hands."[20] Others lobbied colleges and teacher preparation programs to adopt curricula on race relations. To help develop a pool of Black teachers, they fought to bring secondary schools to Blacks in rural areas. They built school houses when local governments would not, so

[19] Paula Giddings, *When and Where I Enter: The Impact of Black Women on Race and Sex in America* (New York, 1984), p. 101; Neverdon-Morton, *Afro-American Women of the South.*

[20] Robert Moton, Myron Pritchard, and Mary White Ovington, *The Upward Path* (New York, 1920). Compiled for children, this anthology collected the stories, poems, and essays of noted African Americans—Booker T. Washington, W. E. B. Du Bois, Frederick Douglass, James Weldon Johnson, Kelly Miller. Miller's "Oath of Afro-American Youth" closed the volume: "I will never bring disgrace upon my race by any unworthy deed or dishonorable act. I will live a clean, decent, manly life; and will ever respect and defend the virtue and honor of womanhood; I will uphold and obey the just laws of my country and of the community in which I live, and will encourage others to do likewise; I will not allow prejudice, injustice, insult or outrage to cower my spirit our sour my soul; but will ever preserve the inner freedom of heart and conscience; I will not allow myself to be overcome of evil, but will strive to overcome evil with good; I will endeavor to develop and exert the best powers within me for my own personal improvement, and will strive unceasingly to quicken the sense of racial duty and responsibility; I will in all these ways aim to uplift my race so that, to everyone bound to it by ties of blood, it shall become a bond of ennoblement and not a byword of reproach" (p. 250).

that Black children would have a place to receive instruction. These reformers were guided in all their efforts by the hope that education would encourage Blacks to enlist "in the work of individual uplift" and "to establish [a] racial personality." Though they knew the toll exacted by segregation, most of these interracial reformers were committed to "carry in peace and with justice . . . two separate races under conditions where assimilation cannot be."[21]

Leaders of the northern-based National Urban League agreed with southern interracialists that education would attenuate prejudice while "increasing the intelligence of the maligned and mistreated groups."[22] National Urban League chief E. K. Jones announced a "reconstruction program for the Negro" in 1919; at the top of his list of priorities was the academic, behavioral, and moral education of African American children. League activists believed urban racial reform and social harmony depended on education—that schooling would teach appropriate dress, language and manners, lead to wider vocational opportunities, and promote health. Equally important, the NUL expected education to identify and cultivate a cohort of African American social workers who could infiltrate cities and "organize betterment."[23]

Black leaders in the NAACP acknowledged the importance of moral and vocational curricula to African American efforts to "lift and climb." But whereas southern interracialists, NUL members, and many progressive maternalists defined a democratic education as one that promoted social harmony and molded good citizens, Blacks in the NAACP defined a democratic education as one that produced political and social equality. The civil rights community coalesced around the necessity of school reform. But whereas some pursued curricular initiatives and social goals in the interest of democratic harmony, others advocated resource redistribution and

[21]   Guichard Parris and Lester Brooks, *Blacks in the City: A History of the National Urban League* (Boston, 1971), pp. 196–198; Morton Sosna, *In Search of the Silent South* (New York, 1977), chap. 2; John B. Kirby, *Black Americans in the Roosevelt Era: Liberalism and Race* (Knoxville, 1980), chap. 1; [Ms.] George Madden Martin, "Race Cooperation," *McClure's*, October 1922, pp. 10–20; W. O. Saunders, "Where Shall Jim Crow Live?" *Collier's*, January 19, 1924, p. 16.
[22]   E. K. Jones, quoted in Parris and Brooks, *Blacks in the City*, p. 178.
[23]   Ibid., pp. 158–159; Jesse Thomas Moore, Jr., *A Search for Equality: The National Urban League, 1910–1961* (University Park, 1981), pp. 39–50; Nancy Weiss, *The National Urban League* (New York, 1974).

integrated access toward the end of releasing African American individuals from the multiple weights of social, political, and economic subordination.

W. E. B. Du Bois, the NAACP's only Black officer at its founding, moved the issue of segregation to the center of the school reform debate. Calling the maternalists' vocational goals into question, Du Bois argued that vocational education and racial separation doomed African American prospects for equality. Vocational education, he maintained, fixed Black children in a preordained social status. Even as schools were transformed by their curricula into instruments of assimilation, the tracking according to role, task class, and culture implicit in the curricula turned schools into cradles of invidious differentiation. School reformers from immigrant communities shared this worry; as Leonard Covello, school reformer from the Casa Italiana Educational Bureau, noted: "An industrial high school . . . presumes to make trade workers of our boys. It suggests that the boys of East Harlem are not capable of doing academic work."[24]

Too often vocationalism—training for maternal, martial, and industrial citizenship—led to sifting students on the basis of a priori assumptions about their roles in life. The flip side of the linguistic, cultural, and political socialization of children through schools was the enforcement of class, occupational, and aspirational distinctions among boys and between boys and girls. The language difficulties of students, the prejudice of teachers and administrators, the gender ideology behind vocationalism, and—in the new age of the IQ test—the science of intelligence were the weapons of differentiation and social ranking.[25]

In Du Bois's view, education was an ally of democracy only if it universalized opportunity. Tracking in northern schools diminished opportunity, while segregation in southern schools systems denied it altogether. Accordingly, at the core of Du Bois's educational agenda in the 1920s lay a demand for the erasure not of difference but of educational and political *differentiation*. Writing in the NAACP's journal, *The Crisis*, which he edited, Du Bois cautioned:

[24] Quoted in Fass, *Outside In*, p. 62.
[25] Paula Fass develops an illuminating discussion of these issues in ibid., chaps. 1 and 2.

Education in the public schools by races or by classes means the
perpetuation of race and class feeling throughout the land. It
means the establishment of group hostility in those tender years
of development when prejudices tend to become "natural" and "in-
stinctive" . . . [But] even where schools are mixed colored pupils
receive no inspiration or encouragement . . . We need to superin-
tend the course of colored children in the mixed public schools . . .
It is the plain duty of all true Americans who believe in democracy
and broad human development to oppose this spread of segregation in the public schools.[26]

Du Bois's call to end discrimination and segregation did not re-
sound during the 1920s, even among reformers. As the antidote to
multiplicity, school reform offered a common "American" and
Americanizing curriculum in which principles of domesticity and
industry figured prominently. Preparation for productive citizenship required training in particular tasks, including unpaid tasks
like motherhood. Designed to meet the complex and highly differ-
entiated demands of industrial life, the very curriculum that
worked to homogenize citizen attitudes, customs, and values simultaneously channeled children into separate economic, occupational, and gender paths.

   Maternalist and other school reformers pressed ahead with their
curricular agenda during the 1920s, Du Bois's warnings notwithstanding. Though such maternalists as Mary Simkhovitch and Lillian Wald realized that vocational education might reproduce class
stratification, they also believed that training in the skills and discipline of wage work and domesticity would create better breadwinners, better mothers, and better homes.[27] Many maternalists
were uncertain egalitarians—claiming a separate equality for
women and assuming for themselves the role of mother and
teacher to subaltern citizens. As one observer noted, "The representatives of settlements, for instance, took the position that the

[26] W. E. B. Du Bois, "The Tragedy of 'Jim Crow,' " *Crisis*, August 1923, pp. 170–
172; and "The Sterling Discrimination Bill," *Crisis*, March 1924, pp. 199–202.
[27] Mary Simkhovitch, *City Worker's World* (New York, 1917), p. 67; Lillian Wald,
"Qualifications and Training for Service with Children in a Crowded City Neighborhood," in Sophonisba Breckinridge, ed., *The Child and the City* (Chicago, 1912), p.
256.

immigrant must be in the position of a pupil without competent leaders or teachers except as the better schooled Americans furnish him the American standards of behavior to be accepted and adopted."[28]

However, the maternalist commitment to mitigating the political effects of diversity led several maternalist policy leaders to think seriously about the relationship between the distribution of educational opportunity and their twin goals of cultural assimilation and worthy citizenship. Though they held fast to their views of citizenship as vocation, and of vocation through training, Florence Kelley and Mary White Ovington approached Du Bois's redistributive strategy for educational provision. As they tackled the issues raised by the Sterling Bill, they confronted the fact that inequality of educational opportunity—of access to schools—defeated the political and cultural goals of their own curricular initiatives.

Studies showed that barely 10 percent of children completed high school and that only 7 percent of World War I veterans were academically prepared for college, suggesting that local reforms could not close the national educational deficit.[29] One maternalist summed up the situation: "In spite of our pretensions, America has never provided universal free education—that is education for all children. In only six states is the legal minimum school term nine months; in six states it is eight months; in ten states it is seven months; in nine states it is six months; in four states it is five months; in five states it is four months; in three states it is three months; and in six states there is no legal minimum. Five million children of school age do not go to any school—this is not merely during a war shortage of teachers, but regularly."[30] These facts fired the resolve of some maternalists to federalize education policy and brought them into collision with southerners, the National Education Association, and other groups who doubted the political wisdom and social possibility of extending the promise of assimilation to African Americans.

[28] "Uniting of Native- and Foreign-Born in America," *Survey*, May 8, 1920, p. 8.
[29] I. L. Kandel, *The Impact of War upon American Education* (Chapel Hill, 1948), p. 246.
[30] Alice Barrows-Fernandez, "What Next?" p. 318.

TOWARD RACIAL LIBERALISM

By the mid-1920s, a modified Sterling Bill received wide support among school reformers. To the National Education Association, the National Mothers' Congress (which became the PTA), the Women's Joint Congressional Committee, and the General Federation of Women's Clubs, the bill marked a victory for democratic education.[31] The bill made English the national language of instruction in all schools, both public and private; asserted federal responsibility for the education of citizens; standardized the minimum school year at twenty-four weeks; universalized school attendance requirements for children through the age of fourteen; and implied a "right to be freed from the incubus of ignorance and illiteracy."[32]

Progressive maternalists applauded the literacy, Americanization, and school attendance provisions of the Sterling Bill, but some reformers were unhappy with the bill's deference to local control. Although the bill provided resources for education, it did not impose standards on the distribution of those resources. The bill implied federal responsibility for the production of literate citizens, but in the absence of federal standards, literacy, language, and basic education might not reach communities most in need. Moreover, while claiming federal responsibility for educating the citizenry, the bill perpetuated federally supported educational deprivation of Blacks in the South—support won in 1899 from the Supreme Court, which upheld a Georgia county's right to refuse to provide a high school for Black residents.[33] W. E. B. Du Bois stated bluntly that the Sterling Bill "proposed to educate the white South, while holding the Black South in compulsory ignorance."[34]

Though Florence Kelley had helped to design early versions of the Sterling Bill, she withdrew support when the modified

---

[31]   Not all proponents of the Sterling Bill were "democrats," exactly. The Women's Ku Klux Klan, for example, supported the bill—chiefly because it believed federal aid to public schools would undermine parochial education. Kathleen Blee, *Women of the Klan* (Berkeley, 1990), p. 39.

[32]   Statement of Mrs. Cora Wilson Steward, National Chairman (sic), Illiteracy Commission of the National Education Association, *Hearings* on S. 1337, pp. 220–225; Statement of Mrs. Frederick P. Bagley, General Federation of Women's Clubs, in ibid., pp. 206–211.

[33]   *Cummings v. County Board of Education*, 175 U.S. 528 (1899).

[34]   Du Bois, "The Sterling Discrimination Bill," p. 199.

measure deferred to localities that had long denied Blacks schooling, while using their "compulsory ignorance" to disfranchise them.[35] In Kelley's view, the bill "legalize[d] discrimination against equal public education for negroes in the fifteen Southern States which are the home of negro illiteracy. It back[d] that discrimination with a federal law and one hundred million federal dollars a year."[36] Her words were not hyperbole. Studies revealed gross disparities in the distribution of education throughout the South at this time. In Georgia, for example, where Blacks and whites approached population parity, only 15 percent of county school board properties was invested in Black schools, the property value of those schools was one-eleventh that of white schools, school attendance among Blacks was one-fourth that of whites, and the average salary of Black teachers was half that of whites.[37]

Kelley's objections turned on the bill's failure to require states to fund Black and white schools equally. The bill was not merely silent on the distribution of funds: it guaranteed local discretion over the use of federal moneys, prohibiting authoritative supervision by the Department of Education. It specified that states retained autonomy over the conduct and management of their school systems, notwithstanding federal mandates for school attendance. It further forbade expenditures of federal money for school construction. Finally, the bill gave statutory legitimacy to Jim Crow, expressly promising funds to states whose constitutions required segregation and disfranchisement.

Kelley condemned these provisions on moral and practical grounds. Not only did the bill make the central government a partner in the reproduction of the southern racial order, it eviscerated its own guarantee of universal schooling. If states and localities refused to build schools for Black children, school attendance standards were meaningless. If the federal government did not provide for school construction where there were no schools for Black children then the promise of a common education was an empty one.[38]

[35] On the politics of enfranchisement, education, and disfranchisement in the late-nineteenth century, see Allen J. Going, "The South and the Blair Education Bill," *Mississippi Valley Historical Review* 44 (September 1957): 267–290.
[36] Florence Kelley, "The Sterling Discrimination Bill," *Crisis*, October 1923, p. 252.
[37] Du Bois, "The Sterling Discrimination Bill," *Crisis*, p. 201; Neverdon-Morton, *Afro-American Women*, p. 81.
[38] Statement of Mrs. Florence Kelley, National Association for the Advancement of Colored People, *Hearings* on S. 1337, pp. 54–57.

Neither the claims nor the curse of the Sterling Bill ever came to pass, for Congress never enacted it. The national investment in public schooling remained channeled through vocational education programs until the 1960s. Nevertheless, the struggle over the bill marked an important step in maternalist policy thinking, both about the importance of nationalizing standards and resources and about the problem of racial inequality. Kelley's arguments for federal standards in education heralded a shift in the racial politics of maternalist reform. The two premises of progressive maternalist philosophy—the possibility of cultural uplift and the necessity of gender-role difference among political equals—did not change. But the goal of maternalist policy expanded to include the ideal of equality of opportunity, albeit within men's and women's spheres. Even though the maternalists' Americanizing reforms denied the existence of equality by demanding conformity to "better" "American" mores and customs, their concern to reach every child drew their attention to existing inequalities in the quality of and access to education.

The meaning of equal opportunity was of course narrowed by the maternalists' cultural focus and gender bias. Theirs was a conditional and purposive equality of opportunity—in fact, a precondition of uplift. Still, maternalists like Kelley saw that those most in need of uplift were denied its possibility if they lacked equal schooling. Uplift thus required the social provision of opportunity, at least in the sense of equitable funding for schools in every community. Kelley's critique of discrimination did not constitute a critique of segregation, however. The maternalist cultural analysis naturalized segregation, tying it to the resilience of separate racial solidarities. Only after the breakdown of cultural and racial identities and uplift to a common "American" culture would integration become a political objective. In keeping with the maternalist emphasis on individual remediation through cultural reform, one had to earn equality by becoming "American."

Kelley spurred the development of racial liberalism when she probed the connection between universal access to education and the substantive goals of curricular reform. The maternalist faith in the possibility of becoming "American" offered equality to Blacks and immigrants as the reward for assimilation. Now, Kelley added, assimilation was itself contingent upon equal educational opportunity.[39] This newly asserted connection between opportunity, conformity, and equality changed the racial debate in the next decade while reinforcing the separation of men's and women's citizenship. The idiom of opportunity, though imbedded in a language of conformity, would displace the idiom of racial caste at midcentury. The language of cultural conformity, however, would harden the racial geology of citizenship. For my own generation of "others," racial liberalism would pose the question, at what price equality?

SEPARATING RACE FROM CULTURE

Despite maternalist racial liberalism, the politics of school reform reinforced divisions along the color line. Maternalist and other reform efforts to manage cultural diversity assumed that with the achievement of universal Americanism group differentiation would disappear. Class distinctions would of course remain—the maternalists did not offer an economically redistributive program—but with the elimination of cultural difference, economic differentiation would be patterned by the liberal logic of individual responsibility, merit, and accomplishment. Ethnic children would thereby be freed from the destiny of the cultural groups to which they belonged, and American democracy would be spared the contradictions of caste and citizenship.

Yet the use of gender roles to instruct American values meant that gender castes were reproduced by school reform. Though they contested the political subordination of women by men, maternalists did not contest the political and social meaning ascribed to gender identities. Indeed, they hailed woman's distinctive role, winning both rights and services for women by arguing the social significance of woman's unique contribution to political order. Thus maternalists won for women the boon of vocational education—that is, the training of girls and young women for their domestic

---

[39] Kelley's convictions ran deep: "So long as provision for the education of our negro fellow citizens in the South remains so appallingly insufficient as it now is," she wrote the Phi Beta Kappa Foundation in 1927, "and so utterly disproportionate to the provision for white students, I am confining my gifts for educational purposes in the South exclusively to institutions for the colored race." Florence Kelley Papers, New York Public Library.

responsibilities. Committed to gender equity, maternalists complained when the Smith-Hughes Act funded vocational education for boys more generously than it funded home economics for girls. Maternalists did not see homemaking programs as training for woman's inequality but believed that more practical, role-oriented education for girls would prepare them for their important, special obligations as woman citizens. A girl's assimilation of a woman's role and "American" culture would entitle her to enjoy women's hard-won political rights—for if woman's equality sprang from her cultural *similarity* to other, "American" women, it also inhered in her *difference* from men.

Whereas gender tracking was in fact intended by maternalist curricular innovations, race tracking and race discrimination were not. As Florence Kelley's critique of school conditions for Blacks in the South shows, some maternalists, at least, were deeply anxious about the immutable inequalities many Americans assigned to racial and cultural groups. Race tracking and race discrimination ran counter to the aims of assimilation, hardening divisions between groups and fastening children to their parents' poverty.

While the possibility of individual improvement and social integration propelled the maternalist impulse to assimilate, so, too, did the view that these possibilities could only be fulfilled by the individual's separation from the culture into which she was born. At the core of progressive maternalist thinking about equality and opportunity was the idea that culture and poverty, difference and inequality, were two sides of the same social problem. They placed most of the burden of achieving equality on the individuals they entreated to become "American"—even as they asked the state to pay for Americanizing instruction and supervision.

This emphasis on the responsibility of "othered" Americans sometimes obscured the maternalists' own responsibility to challenge inequalities imposed by society. Thus, in northern cities, for example, the settlement movement and YWCAs reproduced the racial status quo, effectively excluding Blacks and leaving Black clubwomen, Black social workers, and such Black settlements as the Phyllis Wheatley Settlement the task of promoting welfare and acculturation in Black neighborhoods.[40] Individually, reformers'

[40] Rosalyn Terborg-Penn, "Discrimination against Afro-American Women in the

actions sometimes contradicted their stated views. Lillian Wald, for example, though a founding member of the NAACP, resisted hosting an integrated dinner at the Henry Street Settlement because of the possible reaction of white guests. Jane Addams (also a founder of the NAACP) fought lynching, yet as head of the International League for Peace and Freedom following World War I, she sponsored a petition charging Black soldiers with committing "terrible crimes against women" and calling for their removal from Germany.[41]

Ultimately, it was the maternalists' faith in the transforming potential of cultural assimilation that blinded them from the power of color in society and in their own minds. Directing their efforts toward figuring out what was wrong with disdained people, rather than why Anglo American society disdained them, maternalists conflated cultural reform with economic and racial justice. In this way, maternalists previewed the "culture of poverty" thesis that still frames debates over social equality in the late twentieth century. As Jane Addams opined, contrasting the family values of Italian immigrants and African Americans in 1930:

> Italian fathers consider it a point of honor that their daughters shall not be alone upon the street after dark, and only slowly modify their social traditions. The fathers of colored girls, on the other hand, are quite without those traditions and fail to give their daughters the resulting protection. . . . The Italian parents represent the social traditions which have been worked out during centuries. . . . The civilizations in Africa are even older than those in Italy and naturally tribal life everywhere has its own traditions and taboos which control the relations between the sexes and between parents and children. But of course these were broken up during the period of chattel slavery for very seldom were family ties permitted to stand in the way of profitable slave sales.[42]

Woman's Movement, 1830–1920," in Sharon Harley and Rosalyn Terborg-Penn, eds., *The Afro-American Woman: Struggles and Images* (Port Washington, N.Y., 1978), pp. 17–27.

[41] Giddings, *When and Where I Enter*, p. 179; Dorothy Sterling, *Black Foremothers* (Old Westbury, N.Y., 1979), pp. 107, 146.

[42] Jane Addams, *The Second Twenty Years at Hull House* (New York, 1930), pp. 397–398.

The maternalists' cultural politics—and corresponding focus on immigrants—offered white ethnics a way out of poverty and social subordination, albeit at the price of assimilation to the customs and mores of the dominant Anglo American culture. Once schooled in "American" ways, white ethnics would possess the tools for their own social incorporation. Though many would straddle the culture line—and still do—they would do so without detection: once trained to act "American," they began even to look "American." And once instilled with academic and industrial skills, white ethnics would possess at least a modest degree of the economic and social mobility associated with American-style equality.

Anti-Semitic, anti-Catholic and other cultural prejudices persist, blocking the mobility and staining the dignity of many white ethnic Americans. But although culture and behavior remain tests of equal and deserving citizenship, the maternalist enterprise eased impediments to the political and social incorporation of the "other" white America. The maternalists' support of education initiatives and insistence on the individual's ability to transcend the categor-ical characteristics of groups helped produce uplift from poverty and into unions, professions, and politics among the second and third generation of white ethnic Americans. Dramatic improvements in secondary and post–secondary school attendance and completion rates in white America between 1930 and 1940, followed by increases in military induction rates during World War II, were marks of this success.[43]

Black America did not reap a similar dividend from maternalist education work. In urban America, school completion rates for African Americans continued to lag behind those for whites. Although Blacks accounted for 14 percent of urban high school enrollments in 1934, the median school completion rate for Blacks under the age of twenty-five in Massachusetts, Illinois, and New York in 1940 was less than eight years, as compared to the median of ten years for whites. In the South, where most Blacks lived until the 1940s, Blacks accounted for only 4 percent of rural high school

---

[43]   Edwards and Richey, *School in the American Social Order*. Edwards and Richey report that high school attendance tripled between 1930 and 1940, a decade during which population growth was reasonably low. Post–secondary school attendance increased from 3 percent of 18- to 20-year-olds in 1898 to 14 percent of the same group in 1938.

enrollments, and the median school completion rate for Blacks was five years, where for whites it was ten.[44] Nationwide, only 37.8 percent of African American adults had completed seven years of schooling in 1940, as compared to 83.1 percent of whites. Meanwhile, Blacks continued to be disproportionately excluded from the vocational education programs sponsored by the Smith-Hughes Act, especially in the South, where Blacks received only 10 percent of federal funds in 1934, or less than half their proportionate share.[45] Reinforced by prejudice, the persistent educational deficit among Black Americans, along with their subordination and separation in the labor market, capped mobility and ensured inequality.[46]

The northern, immigrant focus of school reform contributed to this outcome: the overwhelming majority of African Americans lived in the South during this period, and in northern cities maternalists targeted their settlement work and policy initiatives to the foreign-born. Maternalist work among southern and eastern European immigrants marked them as assimilable—capable, under cultural and occupational guidance, of crossing the racialized cultural divide between old-stock and "ethnic" America: it prepared them to claim whiteness. The geographic isolation of most Blacks in the South deprived them of the cultural reform, vocational preparation, and related economic security extended to immigrants. Even in the North, the social separation of Blacks in schooling, housing, jobs, and reform activities limited their access to the only path to social incorporation offered by Anglo Saxon America during this period. Those northern Blacks who received cultural and occupational guidance at the margins of school reform—in vocational high schools, for example—were tracked into a segregated labor market, where Black girls were trained not for domestic motherhood but for domestic wage work. In the North and in the South, racist myths and stereotypes arrested the maternalist project at the color line. As Gunnar Myrdal explained in *An American Dilemma,* "The Negroes are set apart, together with other colored peoples, principally the Chinese and Japanese. . . .

---

[44] Doxey A. Wilkerson, *Special Problems of Negro Education,* Advisory Committee on Education Staff Study no. 12 (Washington, D.C., 1939), pp. 40–41.
[45] Ibid., pp. 91, 93, 97.
[46] Edwards and Richey, *School in the American Social Order,* pp. 696, 706.

Considerable efforts are directed toward 'Americanizing' all groups of alien origin. But in regard to the colored peoples, the American policy is the reverse. They are excluded from assimilation."[47]

If assimilation stopped at the color line, so, too, did opportunity and the promise of equality. Gertrude Stein's Rose offers a synecdochal reminder of how prejudice choked possibility: although raised by whites, Stein's Rose could not rise above "the simple, promiscuous immorality of the Black people. . . . Her white training had only made for habits, not for nature."[48] In the South, such race essentialism supported the social and political exile of Black people. In the North, maternalist racial liberalism struggled against race essentialism, contesting the inherency of both inequality and equality.[49] That struggle softened racism with liberalism while hardening the cultural criteria of democratic citizenship. Pegging equality to cultural conformity while withholding the tools and the choice of conformity from African Americans, liberal racism marked the Black mother, worker, and child as unassimilable. At the same time, it invited future anxiety about the unreformed "culture" of poverty.

[47]   Gunnar Myrdal, *An American Dilemma*, 2 vols. (New York, 1975), 1:53–54.
[48]   Gertrude Stein, "Melanctha: Each One as She May," *Three Lives* (1909), reprinted in *The Selected Writings of Gertrude Stein* (New York, 1962), p. 340.
[49]   For an example of maternalist racial liberalism, see Mary White Ovington, *Half a Man: The Status of the Negro in New York* (New York, 1911), esp. chap. 9: "If we deny full expression to a race, if we restrict its education, stifle its intellectual and aesthetic impulses, we make it impossible fairly to gauge its ability. Under these circumstances to measure its achievements with the more favored white race is unreasonable and unjust, as unreasonable as to measure against a man's a disfranchised woman's capabilities in directing the affairs of state" (pp. 220–221). See also Ovington, *The Walls Came Tumbling Down* (New York, 1947), chaps. 2 and 8, esp. p. 298.

MATERNALISM IN THE NEW DEAL
WELFARE STATE
Women's Dependency, Racial Inequality, and the Icon of Welfare Motherhood

> Employment of mothers with dependent children on WPA is to be deplored, as experience shows that unless the mothers' earnings are sufficient to enable them to employ competent assistance in the home, the children will be neglected and the mothers' health will break under the double burden of serving as wage-earners and homemakers.
> —Grace Abbott, 1937

Demographic changes and economic crisis transformed social politics in the 1930s, as nativist immigration restriction laws enacted in 1921 and 1924 and the migration of southern Blacks to northern cities changed the profile of cultural communities. The proportion of foreign-born Americans declined, and the second generation of southern and eastern European Americans reached adulthood. Resilient in their defense against Americanizing forces during the 1920s, immigrant communities also adapted variously. Workers increasingly cooperated across cultural lines, and the children of immigrants imbibed ever more acculturating lessons as school attendance and high school completion rates improved: the homogenizing messages of mass culture were reaching their audience.[1]

Mostly left out of Anglo America's efforts to incorporate outsiders on its own terms, African Americans, meanwhile, achieved greater visibility as a subordinated people. The expansion of the Black pop-

---

[1] Lizabeth Cohen describes the textured interplay of cultural loyalties and working-class unity during the 1920s and 1930s, showing the social origins of the New Deal, in *Making a New Deal: Industrial Workers in Chicago, 1919–1939* (New York, 1990).

ulation in urban centers outside the South forced northern liberals
to confront Black-white racial inequality as their own problem.
Civil rights litigation and policy interventions exposed the indelible connections between race, poverty, and inequality, connections
that were further highlighted by the racially disparate distribution
of misery during the Great Depression. These developments kindled racial liberalism, awakening maternalists, in particular, to
the necessity of carrying their agenda forward to advance the uplift
of Black America.

Although cultural politics still provided the template for maternalist reform, the economic crisis upset the maternalist paradigm.
Whereas poverty had once been explained and treated in cultural
terms, the sheer scale of the Depression revealed clearly the structural, economic causes of poverty. Joblessness, wage cuts, business
losses, the collapse of whole industries, and the emphatic protests
by the dispossessed commanded government attention to material,
rather than cultural, politics. And indeed, with the election of a
new Democratic majority in 1932 and the political ascent of urban
liberalism, the policy terrain changed. Economic anxieties over-
whelmed cultural politics, riveting the attention of reformers on
the citizen's security in the economic order and, albeit only temporarily, displacing concerns about the quality of citizenship.

Maternalist reformers seized the opportunities opened by economic depression and political possibility. Charting a place for
women in the New Deal economic program, maternalists brought
the gender consciousness and racial liberalism that had ripened
during leaner political times to debates about economic security
and employment policies in the new Democratic order. New Deal
policy barons ratified the gender, cultural, and racial policy lega-
cies forged by maternalists during the 1910s and 1920s—mothers'
pensions, maternity and infancy protection, and education reform.
The Social Security Act, pillar of the New Deal welfare state, fed-
eralized mothers' pensions and revived the Sheppard-Towner
maternity policy. The first principle of maternalist policy was education, and whether as a condition for receiving welfare benefits,
a method of maternity policy, or a social priority in its own right,
it became a central strategy in such New Deal programs as the
Works Progress Administration and the National Youth Administration. In both programs, the idea of vocationalism thrived, as

it continued to do under the George-Deen Vocational Education Act of 1936, which directed its efforts to public schools.

New Dealers also welcomed maternalist reformers themselves into the policy fray: Grace Abbott, director of the Children's Bureau until 1934 and member of the Advisory Council on Economic Security; Molly Dewson, protective labor legislation advocate during the 1920s, and a member of the Advisory Council on Economic Security; Katharine Lenroot, Abbott's successor at the Children's Bureau; Mary Anderson, chief of the Women's Bureau from its founding until the 1940s; Frances Perkins, former settlement worker and secretary of labor under FDR; and, of course, former settlement teacher Eleanor Roosevelt.[2]

During the 1930s and early 1940s, maternalists accommodated the economic emphasis of the New Deal by foregrounding the gender prescriptions that most strongly characterized their strategy for cultural reform. Long-standing maternalist efforts to discourage working motherhood fitted readily with New Deal strategies to promote wage-earning manhood. Although maternalist policy initiatives had been woman-directed and child-centered, the maternalist vision had always been ideologically gendered, not about women only. The nub of maternalist thinking was the child; her welfare required not only a competent domestic mother but "a living wage for the father."[3] Viewing the economic situation as a crisis in men's employment, maternalists signed on for the struggle to rehabilitate men's jobs, wages, and savings, thus to promote child welfare. Interpreting the economic situation also as a crisis for child welfare, maternalists intensified their reform initiatives aimed at rehabilitating mothers and home conditions. Coincidentally, the crisis in men's employment supported maternalist appeals to mothers to stay at home. Maternalists rewarded domestic mothers by nationalizing and expanding old policies to mitigate women's dependency and by supporting new ones to deliver social benefits to the wives and widows of wage-earning men.

[2] On the important role played by women reformers who developed their policy insights and expertise during the Progressive Era, see Susan Ware, *Holding Their Own: American Women in the 1930s* (Boston, 1982), pp. 89–93; and Ware, *Partner and I: Molly Dewson, Feminism, and New Deal Politics* (New Haven, 1987), pp. 95, 176, 189, 209–210.

[3] Katharine F. Lenroot, "Child Welfare 1930–1940," American Academy of Political and Social Science *Annals* 212 (November 1940): 1–11.

Pre–New Deal maternalist policies defined motherhood as the axis of women's citizenship; wage-earning, martial vigor as men's. These policies assumed women's dependence on men and the state, while prescribing men's responsibility for women and children. In the 1910s and 1920s, social policy had formed around the notion of dependent motherhood and in the interest of the Americanized child. Reflecting masculinist assumptions, gender conventions, and maternalist achievement, the New Deal reproduced social policies contingent on maternal dependence, tying women's economic security to men's wages, aid to dependent children, and widows' benefits.[4]

What was new about the New Deal was that it also developed paternal social policies that tied men's economic security to fair wages, unions, and social insurance. By its attention to men's work-based entitlement to income security, the New Deal made the modern welfare state home to men and women both. Meanwhile, by routing women and men toward economic security differently, the New Deal entrenched separate, gendered citizenships.

The economic crisis made working men's welfare the priority for New Deal policymakers. Articulated in conceptually genderless and race-neutral terms, work-based social innovations (the Wagner Act, the Fair Labor Standards Act, unemployment insurance, and old age pensions) were brokered chiefly by businessmen, urban liberals, unions, and Dixiecrats.[5] With the exception of Frances Perkins, who as labor secretary played a crucial role, maternalists were primarily supporters and allies of the men who designed the work-based welfare state in 1935. Maternalists did, however, wield considerable influence in the development of policies for dependent families. They fought for gender equity, in both relief and social

---

[4]   On the direct descent of the Aid to Dependent Children program (Title IV of the Social Security Act) from mothers' pensions, see Jane M. Hoey, "Aid to Families with Dependent Children," American Academy of Political and Social Science *Annals* 202 (March 1939): 74–75.

[5]   See, e.g., G. William Domhoff, *The Power Elite and the State: How Policy Is Made in America* (New York, 1990) chaps. 3 and 4; Michael Goldfield, "Worker Insurgency, Radical Organization, and New Deal Labor Legislation," *American Political Science Review* 83 (1989): 1257–1282; Jill Quadagno, "Welfare Capitalism and the Social Security Act of 1935," *American Sociological Review* 49 (1984): 632–647; and Quadagno, *The Transformation of Old Age Security* (Chicago, 1988).

insurance, arguing for socially provided income parity among categorical public assistance groups and lobbying for secondary social insurance for the dependent survivors of wage-earning men.

To the extent that the "welfare state breakthrough" of the New Deal hangs on the development of national social insurance, we can say that the modern U.S. welfare state was crafted (mostly) by men—for men, capitalism, and democracy. But to the extent that the modern welfare crisis springs from contradictions among work, race, and motherhood, we must credit maternalist New Dealers for helping implant these distinctions in the women's and children's provisions of the Social Security Act.[6] The Social Security Act rewarded (men's) work, succored (mothers') dependency, and treated working women collectively as an anomaly and individually as in transition to mature, domestic, maternal citizenship. Thus, for example, unemployment insurance and old age pensions based entitlements on (white) masculine employment categories and patterns—primarily full-time, preferably unionized, continuous, industrial, breadwining work. Mothers' pensions (Aid to Dependent Children) based entitlements on the maternal ideal of full-time domesticity. Meanwhile, occupational exemptions in the work based economic security provisions—especially the exclusion of domestic workers—along with the differential treatment of insured women workers in the old age and survivors' pension system denied wage-earning women the social rights of citizenship.[7] I argue that taken together, provisions for men and mothers, together with discrimination against wage-earning women, ensured women's dependence upon and inequality within the welfare state. I argue further that these policies tilled the soil of a racialized gender politics of dependency.[8]

[6]   Lois Scharf, *To Work and to Wed: Female Employment, Feminism, and the Great Depression* (Westport, Conn., 1980), esp. p. 129. Ware, *Holding Their Own;* Winifred Wandersee, "A New Deal for Women: Government Programs, 1933–1940," in Wilbur J. Cohen, ed., *The Roosevelt New Deal: A Program Assessment Fifty Years After* (Austin, 1986), p. 191.

[7]   Retail, clerical, educational, hospital, domestic, seasonal, and "casual" work were among the occupations excluded from the economic security package.

[8]   On gendered inequality in the New Deal welfare state, see, e.g., Virginia Sapiro, "The Gender Basis of American Social Policy," in Linda Gordon, ed., *Women, the State, and Welfare* (Madison, 1990), pp. 36–55; Helena Znaniecka Lopata and Henry P. Brehm, *Widows and Dependent Wives: From Social Problem to Federal Program*

WAGE-EARNING MOTHERHOOD AND FAMILY SECURITY

Themselves women who worked outside the home, maternalists drew categorical distinctions among women—between working-class women and professional women, on the one hand, and between mothers and single or childless women, on the other. For unmarried and childless working-class and professional women, maternalists sought equal employment opportunities and rewards, with the caveat that women work within their proper sphere. Thus Mary Anderson of the Women's Bureau opposed gender-based wage differentials in NRA codes, for example, and saw to it that the Fair Labor Standards Act guaranteed the minimum wage regardless of gender (though not regardless of occupation).[9] Similarly, following a 1937 study of 12,500 unemployed, "unattached," "nonfamily" women in Chicago (44.8 percent of whom were Black) the Women's Bureau called for rehabilitative, retraining programs for these "employable" women and for an expansion of unemployment insurance to include domestic workers.[10] Maternalists also argued for wider opportunities for women in work relief projects, "while remaining mindful that women should keep out of the competitive fields, and that they are not suitable for mass projects where large groups of men are deployed."[11] Others, including Eleanor Roosevelt, worked to remove prohibitions on married women's employment contained in the married persons' clause of President Hoover's Economy Act of 1932 and in various local initiatives.[12]

But whereas maternalists defended a woman's right to work for

---

(New York, 1986), pp. 71–75; Scharf, *To Work and to Wed*, pp. 128–129; Sylvia Law, "Women, Work, Welfare, and the Preservation of Patriarchy," *University of Pennsylvania Law Review*, 131, no. 6 (1983).

[9] Mary Anderson, *Woman at Work: The Autobiography of Mary Anderson as Told to Mary N. Winslow* (Minneapolis, 1951), pp. 146–147.

[10] Harriet A. Byrne and Cecile Hillyer, *Unattached Women on Relief in Chicago, 1937*, U.S. Department of Labor, Women's Bureau Bulletin no. 158 (Washington, D.C., 1938), pp. 1, 6, 8, 18–19.

[11] Federal Emergency Relief Administration, *Proceedings of the Conference of Emergency Needs of Women* (Washington, D.C., November 20, 1935), p. 11.

[12] In her July 24, 1937, column "My Day," Eleanor Roosevelt wrote: "Who is to say whether a woman needs to work outside her home for the good of her own soul?" Rochelle Chadakoff, ed., *Eleanor Roosevelt's My Day: Her Acclaimed Columns, 1936–1945* (New York, 1989), p. 66.

fair wages, they treated a woman's labor rights as contingent and ephemeral. In the maternalists' view, the strength a of woman's labor rights faded as she approached marriage and motherhood. The child, as always, came first, and once a mother, a woman must balance her right to employment against her obligation to her child and her home. According to maternalists like Grace Abbott, women who could afford domestic assistance and thus share the double burden of employment and motherhood should be unfettered in pursuit of professional achievement. For most mothers, however, such assistance was unaffordable, and "the mother's services are worth more in the home than they are in the outside labor market."[13] Meanwhile, since most women would become mothers, maternalists treated wage earning as a step along the woman's way to her own home and defined the model woman worker as at least childless, if not unmarried.

The policy consequences of these views were twofold. First, as I suggest in Chapter 7, if the model wage-earning woman was childless, then neither child care nor the double burden of home and work was a labor issue or a social responsibility. Second, if the model mother was child- and home-centered, and if most women became mothers, then women's economic security was a matter of social concern because of children, and not a matter of rights attached to woman's citizenship. Moreover, because the model family included a breadwinning father, family security could be ensured through a paternal wage, through social protection of men's income, and, only in men's absence, through direct material assistance from the state.

Just as the New Deal took the potentially poor working man as the norm for primary social insurance, it took the potentially dependent domestic mother as the norm for aid to dependent families, whether through public assistance or secondary social insurance benefits. Further, against growing evidence of wage-earning motherhood (the 1930 census identified 3.75 million "employed homemakers"—33 percent of all women workers, 10 percent of white homemakers, and 40 percent of Black homemakers)[14] the

[13]   Grace Abbott, *From Relief to Social Security* (New York, 1966), p. 211.
[14]   Mary Elizabeth Pidgeon, *The Employed Woman Homemaker in the United States: Her Responsibility for Family Support*, U.S. Department of Labor, Women's Bureau, Bulletin no. 148 (Washington, D.C., 1936), pp. 1–3; Viva Boothe, "Gainfully

Social Security Act rendered working women invisible as productive citizens, unprotected against interruptions to their work lives, and unequal in old age and death.

The Social Security Act of 1935 extended protections to women in four ways. First, retired women workers in occupations covered by the act were insured under the old age security program provided they met the same work history requirements as men. Most women workers, however, were not reached by this provision, for most were in exempted jobs: clerical and sales work (28 percent), teaching and nursing (10.9 percent), and domestic and personal service (29.2 percent) accounted for more than two-thirds of women workers.[15] Second, the act offered health services to eligible pregnant women or mothers of eligible children. Third, the act provided a lump-sum death benefit to the survivor (usually the widow) of an insured worker (usually a wage-earning male). Fourth, the act offered public assistance to needy children under the age of sixteen who were deprived of breadwinning parental support and who continued to live with a relative engaged in their full-time care. Aside from the minority of women workers employed in covered occupations, the benefits of the 1935 act accrued to women through husbands or through children. As in politics before suffrage, so in the New Deal welfare state were women only virtually represented.

Despite women's invisibility in most of the Social Security Act, maternalists championed the maternal and child health measure and, more significantly, the Aid to Dependent Children program as women's policies. Even though the 'Mothers' Aid Act' of the Social Security bill was "not aids for mothers—[but] aids for children," maternalists appearing before congressional hearings did discuss the measure as a woman's program.[16] And although the provision extended eligibility to children raised by a close relative

Employed Women in the Family," American Academy of Political and Social Science *Annals* 160 (March 1932): 75–85.

[15] Janet Hooks, *Women's Occupations through Seven Decades*, U.S. Department of Labor, Women's Bureau Bulletin no.218 (Washington, D.C., 1951), p. 18; Pidgeon, *The Employed Woman Homemaker*.

[16] Statement of Miss Grace Abbott, Editor *Social Service Review* and Professor of Public Welfare, University of Chicago, Economic Security Act *Hearings* (S. 1130), U.S. Senate, Committee on Finance, 74th Congress, 1st session (Washington, D.C., 1935), p. 1083.

other than a parent, maternalists interpreted the program to Congress and to the public as a mothers' program. Like mothers' pension programs of the preceding two decades, Aid to Dependent Children conditioned social provision to children on the domesticity of mothers. Maternalist New Dealers appealed for passage of the dependent children's provision by arguing not only the economic necessity of grants to the needy child but also the social and cultural necessity of the full-time domestic services of her mother.

Staking the maternalist claim to the development of mothers' pensions, Katharine Lenroot, Grace Abbott's successor at the U.S. Children's Bureau, recalled the long-standing activism of the bureau in welfare policy and spoke proudly of the bureau's role as consultant to the Committee on Economic Security, which designed the Social Security Act. Reiterating the maternalist philosophy of mothers' pensions, Jane Hoey explained the guiding assumptions of the Aid to Dependent Children program to the readers of the Children's Bureau's monthly magazine: "Even where individual grants are small . . . the mother can feel that in doing a good job with her children she is making a genuine contribution to society."[17] Reflecting the program's roots in maternalist innovations, Grace Abbott told the House Ways and Means Committee, "the whole idea of mothers' pensions is that it should be enough to care for the children adequately, to keep the mother at home and thus to give some security in the home."[18] Explaining the need for socially-supported domesticity, Abbott described Aid to Dependent Children (ADC) as a working-class mothers' program, for if the mother "belongs *not to the highest paid but to the lower income group* . . . she cannot possibly carry both the burden of supporting the children and of caring for the children."[19]

When Secretary of Labor Frances Perkins went before the Sen-

---

[17] Jane M. Hoey, Director, Bureau of Public Assistance, Social Security Board, "The Social Security Program for Children: Aid to Dependent Children under the Social Security Act," *Child*, vol. 1, September 1936, p. 5.

[18] Statement of Miss Grace Abbott, Member, Advisory Council on Economic Security, Economic Security Act *Hearings* (H.R. 4120), U.S. House of Representatives, Committee on Ways and Means, 74th Congress, 1st session (Washington, D.C., 1935), p. 495.

[19] Ibid., p. 1084. Writing in *Social Service Review* one year earlier, Abbott argued: "In other words, unless she belongs to the highskilled or professional group, a mother's contribution in the home is greater than her earnings can purchase for the home." "Recent Trends in Mothers' Aid," *Social Service Review* 8 (June 1934): 193.

ate Finance Committee in 1935 to defend the Economic Security Bill, she, too, explained the separate, role-based treatment of women under the act in distinctly maternalist terms. Speaking on behalf of the mothers' pensions provision (ADC) she told the committee "You take the mother of a large family, she may be ablebodied and all that, but we classify her as unemployable because if she works the children have got to go to an orphan asylum."[20]

Meanwhile, in its *Report to the President*, the Committee on Economic Security revealed the influence of maternalist thinking in the development of the women's and children's provisions of the legislation. Clarifying the meaning of "mothers' pensions" (a term widely used to describe the provision, though it was formally titled "Aid to Dependent Children" in the act), the report cautioned "These are not primarily aids to mothers but defense measures for children. They are designed to release from the wage-earning role the person whose natural function is to give her children the physical and affectionate guardianship necessary not alone to keep them from falling into social misfortune, but more affirmatively to rear them into citizens capable of contributing to society."[21]

Though generally pleased with the incorporation of maternalist policy traditions in the federal economic security package, maternalist leaders and their allies were not fully satisfied. Because of the Children's Bureau's long involvement in the development, study, and administration of mothers' pensions, Lenroot, Abbott, and Sophonisba Breckinridge preferred that the Children's Bureau, rather than the Social Security Board, have administrative authority over the ADC program.[22] Because of the need to treat women's dependency comprehensively, other maternalists objected to the exclusions of women workers in women's jobs from work-based social insurance provisions. For example, Molly Dewson, a member of the Social Security Board, called for old age insurance protection for workers in educational and philanthropic organizations, as well as for domestic and agricultural workers.[23] Women who could purchase household help were legitimate par-

[20]   Statement of Frances Perkins, Secretary of Labor, S. 1130 *Hearings*, U.S. Senate, p. 139.
[21]   Committee on Economic Security, *Report to the President* (Washington, D.C., 1935), p. 36.
[22]   Abbott, S. 1130 *Hearings*, p. 1085; Lenroot, in ibid., pp. 342–343.
[23]   Mary W. Dewson, "Next Steps in Social Security Legislation," *Social Service Review* 12 (March 1938): 23–24.

ticipants in the work force. Uninsured under the 1935 act, these women workers were headed for relief in widowhood unless they had minor children who could qualify for ADC. Women who were other women's household help (domestic workers) were, moreover, "employable" if not mothers of young children, but they received no protections against old age dependency and unemployment. These women, disproportionate numbers of whom were African American, swelled the relief rolls throughout the Depression: 43 percent of the women seeking relief in Chicago in 1933 were Black; 55 percent of Black women were unemployed according to the 1931 unemployment census, as compared to 16.9 percent of native-born white women and 12 percent of foreign-born white women; and 57 percent of "unattached" Black women on relief in Chicago in 1937 had been domestic workers.[24] These working women included one-third of all married women workers and many who were, in the words of the Women's Bureau, "unattached" to men and families. They would become a dependent caste if not integrated into the social insurance system.[25]

Many reformers criticized occupational "exclusions unrelated to need for protection."[26] But of greater concern to most maternalists, however, were the shallow security net provided to dependent mothers and children in the ADC program and the failure to provide any security net at all to aging dependent widows in the old age insurance program. In the main, the maternalist critique of the 1935 act became a call to make the economic security of women and families a priority in the welfare state. Beginning in 1936, maternalists campaigned for social security reform that would insure women's and children's dependency more generously and so promote family security.

The League of Women Voters organized public meetings to ex-

---

[24] Harriet Byrne, *Women Unemployed Seeking Relief in 1933*, U.S. Department of Labor, Women's Bureau Bulletin no. 139 (Washington, D.C., 1936), pp. 4–6; E. Franklin Frazier, "Some Effects of the Depression on the Negro in Northern Cities," *Science and Society* 2 (Fall 1938): 489–499.

[25] Frazier found that the proportion of two-parent families among Black families on relief in Chicago, Detroit, New York, and Philadelphia in 1934 was never higher than 50 percent; that 20–25 percent of Black families on relief were headed by females; and that a "relatively larger" number of Black relief dependents than white dependents were "unattached" women. Frazier concluded: "It is because of this fact that the FERA views the rehabilitation of Negroes as less a problem of the aged than a problem of female dependency often involving children" (p. 494).

[26] Evaline M. Burns, *The American Social Security System* (Boston, 1949), p. 76.

pose the plight of elderly wives, widows, and dependent children under the 1935 act. The Women's Trade Union League and Women's Joint Congressional Committee followed suit, lobbying strenuously for liberalized provisions for women and children.[27] These women's organizations were joined by policy analysts and reformers, who specifically criticized ADC as scattershot and incomplete and who urged more generous and more standardized protections for widowed mothers and their children.[28] Katharine Lenroot foreshadowed such criticism in her congressional testimony in 1935, when she urged equalization of minimum benefits across political subdivisions, pointing to the wide variation in effectiveness and adequacy among local mothers' pension programs inherited by the New Deal.[29]

Though neither Lenroot nor other maternalist social security reformers took great issue with the ADC program's local structure, they called for uniform eligibility standards at the state level and strict state level supervision of locally administered funds. More emphatically, they expressed the need for more generous federal funding and for a proportionally greater federal investment in the program. Complaining that ADC failed to assure "either that all eligible persons in the state will receive pensions or that those on the pension rolls will receive adequate minimum amounts," reformers pressed for increased benefits (the 1935 act provided a standard maximum monthly benefit of $18 for a mother and one child) and an increase in the federal matching share from one-third to one-half of benefits.[30] Noting that widows and children were not treated equitably under the act as compared to the blind and aged needy (the standard maximum grant to a needy aged individual

[27]   Lopata and Brehm, *Widows and Dependent Wives*, p. 73.

[28]   Frederick Dewhurst and Margaret Grant Schneider, Committee on Social Security, Social Science Research Council, "Objectives and Social Effects of the Public Assistance and Old Age Provisions of the Social Security Act," National Conference of Social Work *Proceedings*, 63d annual session (Chicago, 1936), pp. 392–403; "Delay in Acceptance of Federal Old Age and Mothers' Aid Grants-in-Aid," *Social Service Review* 10 (June 1936): 346–348.

[29]   Lenroot, S. 1130 *Hearings*, pp. 339–341.

[30]   Dewhurst and Schneider, "Objectives and Social Effects of the Social Security Act," pp. 394–395; Statement of Mrs. Harris T. Baldwin, First Vice-President, National League of Women Voters, Social Security Act Amendments of 1939 *Hearings* (H.R. 6635), U.S. House of Representatives, Committee on Ways and Means, 76th Congress, 1st session (Washington, D.C., 1939), p. 1377.

was $30), reformers reminded the nation of the social importance of the domestic mother to family security. Concerned that inadequate benefits would propel mothers into the workforce, Grace Abbott's *Social Service Review*, for example, reminded readers that "employment of the widow with dependent children is recognized as economically and socially undesirable."[31]

Maternalist agitation for social security reform coincided with other political and administrative pressures to strengthen and clarify policy. The combination of competitive interpretations and criticism of policy inadequacies began to produce results in 1936. The Democratic Party's presidential platform that year pledged "protection of the family and the home." By 1939, both Congress and president were prepared to make family protection a principle of social security.[32] The Social Security Act Amendments of 1939 proposed an increase in the federal funding responsibility for ADC and raised the maximum age of eligible ADC children to eighteen, for youth who regularly attended school.[33] But the amendments did not reconcile inequalities in public assistance between the aged and blind, on the one hand, and dependent women and children, on the other hand.[34] More significant, the amendments created new inequalities among women. These new inequalities turned in part on class, continuing distinctions implicit in the Social Security Act and explicit in maternalist discourse about it between "professional and highly skilled" mothers who could afford to work and poor mothers who ought to stay at home. Primarily, however, these new inequalities arose in women's relationship to men and in the different social statuses among husbands in the work-based welfare state.

The 1939 act promoted family security by bringing the insured male worker's family under the umbrella of social insurance. The

[31]   "Delay in Acceptance of Grants-in-Aid," p. 348.

[32]   See Jerry R. Cates, *Insuring Inequality: Administrative Leadership in Social Security, 1935–1954* (Ann Arbor, 1983), chaps. 3–5, for a discussion of the external policy competition that influenced the development and revision of public assistance between 1935 and 1940, especially for the aged.

[33]   U.S. House of Representatives, *Report* no. 728, Social Security Act Amendments of 1939, Committee on Ways and Means, 76th Congress, 1st session (Washington, D.C., 1939), pp. 28–29.

[34]   White House Conference on Children in a Democracy, *Final Report* (Washington, D.C., 1940), p. 141.

amended act provided benefits to wives, elderly widows, and dependent survivors of covered male workers. These benefits included an old age pension for the retiree's wife to supplement the family income by 50 percent, an aged widow's benefit equal to three-fourths of her husband's benefit, surviving children's benefits equal to one-half of the insured father's benefit, and a benefit to the non-aged widowed mother of minor children equal to three-fourths of the deceased father's entitlement provided she was living with her husband at the time of his death and did not remarry. While offering protections to young widowed mothers and unemployable elderly widows, the new measure also discriminated against those women workers in covered occupations who met the same work history and contributory requirements as their male counterparts. For example, an eligible wage-earning woman was treated as a wife, rather than as a worker, if her own pension benefit was less than 50 percent of her husband's. In addition, the act established a family benefit limit, so that if the combined benefits of the eligible wife and husband exceeded that limit, the wife's benefit would be reduced to accommodate the limit. Finally, an eligible working mother could not protect her surviving children unless they were not living with their father at the time of her death and unless the fatherless children could prove that their mother had been the sole breadwinner for the family. An eligible working woman could not provide at all for her husband in retirement or death, as the act did not speak of husband's benefits.[35]

Though the original Social Security Act was clearly gendered, it was only indirectly so in its social insurance provisions—through the exclusion of what were effectively women's occupations, for example. By directing protection to wives, elderly widows, and widowed mothers of minor children and by confining spousal and survivors' protection to the families of covered male workers only, the 1939 amendments spelled out the gendered basis of social insurance and spread gender bias throughout the welfare state for the first time.

By singling out the widows and surviving children of insured male wage earners for the more generous family protection benefits of social insurance, the 1939 act also drew a stark distinction

[35] United States Senate, *Report on the Social Security Act Amendments of 1939*, 76th Congress, 1st session (Washington, D.C., 1939), pp. 41–45; U.S. House of Representatives, *Report* no. 728, pp. 35–38.

between types of dependent families. Widowed mothers, always the principle clientele of mothers' pensions, were uplifted from the means-tested relief of ADC and provided income security as a matter of right under social insurance—if, that is, their husbands had been insured workers. Widows, then, generally were to be treated differently and better than deserted, divorced, or unwed mothers. Among other things, the widowed mother of an insured worker's dependent children received her own benefit, unlike the mother of dependent children under ADC who received income support only through grants to her children. It also meant that even among widows, social provision would be contingent upon the status of husbands within the social insurance system. Given the disproportionate exclusion of men of color from social insurance protections—as a result of the exclusion of personal service, casual, and agricultural workers—the new provisions for widowed mothers would have a disparate racial impact.[36]

Finally, by tying survivors' income support either to the age of the widow (sixty-five years) or to the widow's care and custody of children, the act codified women's dependency and fastened women's social rights to dependent motherhood. As the Senate report read: "The purpose of (widows' benefits) is to extend financial protection to the widow regardless of her age, while she has in her care a child of the deceased husband entitled to a child's insurance benefits."[37] About women but not for us, the 1939 act left the younger dependent widow—childless, perhaps, or the mother of grown children, or a worker in an excluded occupation—altogether unprotected by the family security measure. Recalling child-centered variations in women's ascribed relationships to the workforce, the Social Security Administration explained, "Normally, young widows without children can be expected to enter gainful employment."[38]

---

[36] Of the 5.5 million African American workers, approximately 2 million were in agriculture. Another 1.5 million were in domestic service. Statement of Charles H. Houston, Representing the National Association for the Advancement of Colored People, *Hearings* on S. 1130, p. 644. For other discussions of the impact of social insurance exclusions on African Americans, see George Edmund Haynes, "Lily-White Social Security," *Crisis*, March 1935, pp. 85–86; John P. Davis, "A Black Inventory of the New Deal," *Crisis*, May 1935, pp. 141–142; Abraham Epstein, "The Social Security Act," *Crisis*, November 1935, pp. 333–334; and Statement of John P. Davis, National Negro Congress, *Hearings* on H.R. 6635, p. 1542.

[37] Senate *Report on Social Security Act Amendments*, p. 45.

[38] Social Security Administration Testimony, H.R. 6635 *Hearings*, p. 6.

Maternalist policy leaders and women's organizations did not contest the discriminations against insured women workers in the family security package.[39] They did not challenge the presumption that the childless young widow was employable and therefore ineligible for any portion of her husband's benefits. Nor did they resist the introduction of a two-tiered concept of mothers' pensions. But they did continue to call for the development of ADC to its "full possibilities."[40] In social work and in the Children's Bureau, maternalists worked for improved services and protections for poor mothers. With the worthy widows of deserving male wage earners now channeled through social insurance, ADC reformers began to fix their gaze on the family "broken" by wage-earning motherhood, "illegitimacy," and race discrimination.[41]

GENDER, RACE, AND WELFARE REFORM

Well into the 1940s, maternalists pressed for more universal protection for dependent families through the social insurance system.[42] At Children's Bureau and social work conferences and in journals, bureau reports, and publications, they called for the incorporation of excluded occupations—chiefly agriculture and domestic work—into the old age and unemployment provisions of the Social Security Act. They further emphasized the critical role played by survivors' insurance in family security. Most significantly, they devoted considerable attention to the Aid to Dependent Children program. Although the Children's Bureau had no control over ADC, the bureau's investigative authority allowed maternalists to monitor, analyze, and recommend improvement in the development of the program. Here the Children's Bureau was

[39]   Scharf, *To Work and to Wed*, p. 129; Scharf, " 'The Forgotten Woman': Working Women, the New Deal, and Women's Organizations," in Lois Scharf and Joan Jenson, eds., *Decades of Discontent* (Westport, Conn.,1983), pp. 249, 253; Wandersee, "A New Deal for Women."
[40]   White House Conference on Children in a Democracy, p. 141.
[41]   The percentage of widows on ADC declined from 43 percent in 1937 to 7.7 percent in 1961.
[42]   E.g., "Agenda for a New Decade," *Child*, vol. 4, March 1940, p. 229; Emma O. Lundberg, "Security for Children in Post-War Years," *Child*, vol. 8, July 1943, p. 8.

joined by social workers and local child advocates; together, they identified avenues for ADC reform.

The maternalists' interest in ADC was not surprising, given the policy's roots in mothers' pension programs and its role in protecting child welfare. More important to reform because less generous than survivors' benefits, ADC held maternalist attention as an essential defense against wage-earning motherhood.[43] Once the widows of better-paid, more unionized, insured wage-earning men were siphoned into a separate program, ADC became the repository of mothers most likely to seek wages. Mothers applied for ADC because of extreme poverty: it was a need-based, means-tested program. Women's Bureau studies showed that women were in the work force because of need.[44] Low and uneven ADC benefits, residency requirements, and eligibility rules reinforced the single mother's need to work and thus ran counter to the spirit of mothers' pensions and the interests of the child. Concerned to keep mothers at home to provide care for dependent children, maternalists worked to make adequate welfare more available to poor women.

The maternalists' goals for ADC were twofold: improved coverage and more effective remediation of family life. As during the 1920s, maternalists argued for higher, more consistent grant levels, for family budgeting to demonstrate variations of need, for services to meet household, dietary, and health needs, and for casework to treat the family relationship.[45] Maternalists discovered several impediments to these goals beginning in 1940. During the debate over the 1939 amendments, congressional reports con-

---

[43] Into the World War II period, maternalists treated ADC as the proper place for mothers who needed to work: "Mothers who apply for day care for their children are often in need of some other kind of help. It may sometimes be a question of assistance to the family, through 'aid to dependent children' or some other form of aid by public or private agencies, so that the mother may be able to remain at home and care for her children." Emma O. Lundberg, "Counseling Service in a Day-Care Program," *Child,* vol. 7, September 1942, p. 32.

[44] Viva Boothe, "Gainfully Employed Women in the Family"; Gwendolyn Hughes Berry, "Mothers in Industry," American Academy of Political and Social Science *Annals* 143 (May 1929): 315–323; Emily C. Brown, *A Study of Two Groups of Married Women Applying for Jobs,* U.S. Department of Labor, Women's Bureau Bulletin no. 77 (Washington, D.C., 1929); Agnes L. Peterson, *What the Wage-Earning Woman Contributes to Family Support,* U.S. Department of Labor, Women's Bureau Bulletin no. 75 (Washington, D.C., 1929).

[45] Katharine Lenroot, "Children of the Depression: A Study of 259 Families in Selected Areas of Five Cities," *Social Service Review* 9 (June 1935): 241–242.

firmed that three times as many needy aged as needy children received grants and that only a fraction of dependent children in need of assistance were actually receiving it. Congress tried to cover more children by increasing the age of the dependent child's eligibility to eighteen, but this revision did not address the heart of the matter: low standard grants and the state option. At the White House Conference for Children in a Democracy in 1940, which featured a spectrum of child-welfare advocates from the Children's Bureau and other quarters, maternalists suggested revising the rate of the federal contribution, removing rigid limits on the amounts of grants, adjusting federal assistance to local economic conditions, and equalizing benefit levels across categories of public assistance.

Later studies would show, however, that persistent deference to states blocked the possibility of universal coverage for poor dependent families. For one thing, states were not required to participate in the ADC program at all: as late as 1943, Texas, for example, had not appropriated funds for dependent children.[46] Within participating states, residency requirements sometimes deprived dependent families of eligibility, especially where nonwhite migrant populations were large. Equally important, although participating states were required to develop statewide plans and provide statewide administrative oversight, local determination of need and fitness permitted variations in grant levels and exclusion on moral grounds of families otherwise eligible.

As specialists in the Children's Bureau and participants in the National Conference of Social Work began to explore these problems, they learned that Charles Houston's description of social insurance applied to ADC, as well: "From a Negro's point of view, it looks like a sieve with the holes just big enough for the majority of Negroes to fall through."[47] Although Children's Bureau and other studies reported the highest unemployment rates among Black women during the Depression, the highest relief rates among Black families, and high rates of families headed by mothers

---

[46] Amber Arthun Warburton, Helen Wood, and Marian M. Crane, *The Work and Welfare of Children of Agricultural Laborers in Hidalgo County, Texas*, U.S. Department of Labor, Children's Bureau Publication no. 298 (Washington, D.C., 1943), pp. 18–19.

[47] Charles Houston, *Hearings* on S. 1130, p. 641.

among Blacks (20–25 percent), the recipients of ADC in 1939 were overwhelmingly (89 percent) white. And although the Federal Emergency Relief Administration concluded that "the rehabilitation of Negroes (is) less a problem of the aged than a problem of female dependency, often involving children," African American dependent mothers and children were poorly integrated into New Deal family security policy.[48]

Just as inequalities in educational provision had elicited maternalist calls for national standards of school reform during the 1920s, inequalities in the treatment of dependent families by ADC produced concerted maternalist efforts to reform welfare during the 1930s and 1940s. The consequences of educational inequality for assimilation, vocation, and citizenship had led Florence Kelley to insist on funding equity for Black children's schools. Likewise, the consequences of race discrimination in welfare pushed maternalist New Dealers to fight the rules and prejudices that barred dependent Black mothers and their children from economic assistance under ADC. In both cases, maternalists pinned social recovery on the assimilation of African American men, mothers, and children. Race discrimination in welfare not only denied economic security to dependent Black families but perpetuated their isolation from the gender and cultural norms of the white American mainstream. Whereas maternalists generally embraced the New Deal's emphasis on economic reform, then, they insisted that such reform could not be accomplished without full provision of gender and cultural services to the most economically and socially subordinated groups.[49]

Mothers' pensions, the centerpiece of maternalist social provision since the Progressive Era, linked the amelioration of the dependent family's economic circumstances to the cultural remediation of family life. A vindication of maternalist innovations when it was grafted onto the Social Security Act, mothers' pensions sustained maternalists' attention as they discovered loopholes that

---

[48] Byrne, *Women Unemployed Seeking Relief*, pp. 4–9; E. Franklin Frazier, "Some Effects of the Depression on the Negro," pp. 490–494. Robert C. Weaver, "Giving the Children a Chance," *Crisis*, March 1940, pp. 74 75, 94.

[49] For a contrasting view of the subordination of the race question to economic reform during the New Deal, see John Kirby, *Black Americans in the Roosevelt Era* (Knoxville, 1980), pp. 79–92.

omitted some groups. The Children's Bureau led the maternalist drive to close loopholes in ADC, chiefly by investigating the various ways in which race posed an impediment to participation in the program. These studies revealed three familiar discriminatory mechanisms within ADC: race-based disparities in benefits, race-based determination of a dependent mother's employability, and the exclusion of children born to unmarried mothers.[50]

One reason for variations in benefit levels was that local social welfare agencies exercised discretionary authority in assessing a family's need. Often, local agencies determined that the Black family's needs were fewer and cheaper than that of white families. This assessment resulted in grant levels so low that the African American ADC mother could not possibly obey the program's work prohibition and still assure her own and her children's survival. Annie Lee Davis, an African American social worker and the Children's Bureau's consultant on minority groups, explained: "Because the majority of persons in minority groups are also generally in the lowest income groups it is sometimes presumed that their needs are less and that naturally they are able to live on less money. Although there are standard budgets which vary from State to State, the application of the budget to specific families is influenced by the attitudes, concern, and conviction of state and local administrators and the community.[51]

Another reason for inequity was racially ascribed variation in expectations of women's "employability." Long overrepresented in the female labor force, first as slaves, then as paid domestic and agricultural workers, Black women were often viewed as a distinct class of womanhood to which the ideal of domesticity did not apply. The presumption of employability that applied to childless white women was imposed upon African American women as a whole.[52] The presumption of unemployability that applied to white moth-

---

[50]   Joanne Goodwin discusses these mechanisms in the context of mothers' pensions in "An American Experiment in Paid Motherhood: The Implementation of Mothers' Pensions in Early-Twentieth-Century Chicago," *Gender and History* 4 (Autumn 1992): 330.

[51]   Annie Lee Davis, "Attitudes toward Minority Groups: Their Effect on Social Services for Unmarried Mothers," *Child*, vol. 13, (December 1948), p. 83.

[52]   For a discussion of state level welfare rules that singled out African American women as "employable," see Martha Davis, *Brutal Need: Lawyers and the Welfare Rights Movement, 1960–1973* (New Haven, 1993), pp. 9, 62.

ers—a presumption developed and defended by Abbott, Perkins, and Lenroot during the Social Security debates—was frequently denied to Black mothers of dependent children. One ADC field supervisor reasoned: "The number of Negro cases are few due to the unanimous feeling on the part of staff and board that there are more work opportunities for Negro women and to their intense desire not to interfere with local labor conditions. . . . There is a hesitancy on the part of the lay boards to advance too rapidly over the thinking of their own communities which see no reason why the employable Negro mother should not continue her usually sketchy seasonal labor or indefinite domestic service rather than receive a public assistance grant."[53]

Yet another source of racial bias in ADC were state-level prohibitions against, or regulations of, "illegitimacy." The Social Security Act defined the dependent child as one who had lost her breadwinner and required care from one of a specified set of relatives. Unlike most previous mothers' pensions programs, the ADC provision was silent about the marital status of the child's parents. The federal program neither established marital criteria for recipients nor prohibited their establishment by states. This murkiness allowed states to transpose eligibility standards developed under their mothers' aid laws to the ADC program, including standards restricting the eligibility of children born out of wedlock.[54] It also allowed states to invent "illegitimacy" rules to limit access to the ADC program. Under the original ADC program, few children of unmarried parents counted among recipients.[55] Indeed, before 1940, when the Social Security Act Amendments took effect, ADC, like mothers' pensions, was primarily a widows' program. It was, moreover, unmistakably a mothers' program, even though legislation allowed a stepfather or a grandparent or an uncle to serve as the guardian of the dependent child: in 1942, nine out of ten ADC children lived with their mothers.[56] When the 1939 amendments placed wives and children of insured men in the survivors'

[53] Quoted in Mary S. Larbee, "Unmarried Parenthood under the Social Security Act," National Conference of Social Work *Proceedings* (New York, 1939), p. 454.
[54] Ibid., pp. 447–448.
[55] Ibid.; Maud Morlock, "Establishment of Paternity," National Conference of Social Work *Proceedings* (New York, 1940), p. 367. Morlock was the director of the Social Service Division of the Children's Bureau.
[56] Burns, *American Social Security System*, p. 321.

insurance system, it reduced widows' participation in ADC and correspondingly increased the proportion of divorced, deserted, and never-married mothers. Coinciding with a sharp increase in reported births to unmarried mothers after 1940, this policy shift foregrounded the issue of recipients' marital status and sexual behavior.[57]

Legislative proposals in several states urged welfare agencies to monitor unmarried mothers' homes more aggressively. Especially in southern states, legislators asked for more frequent and more intensive supervision of "questionable" homes as well as the removal of children from "undesirable" ones. Nationwide, half the states restricted ADC eligibility of children born to unmarried mothers; five southern states denied aid on the basis of the child's birth status alone. While maternalists fully supported local efforts to improve recipients' homemaking, child-raising, and morality, they criticized provisions excluding illegitimate children. They argued that such provisions violated the very spirit of mothers' pensions by subverting the goal of keeping children in their own homes. Moreover, maternalists warned, not only was birth status too punitive a basis for determining ADC eligibility, it was too convenient a proxy for race-based exclusion in many areas. The disproportionate exclusion of Black women and children from ADC in the most restrictive states heightened the reformers' concerns about "illegitimacy" rules and the nexus among race, "illegitimacy," and access to welfare.[58]

At the National Conference of Social Work annual meetings in 1939 and 1940, several reformers, including Maud Morlock of the Children's Bureau, presented papers on unmarried parenthood. At the 1939 meetings, Mary S. Larbee reviewed the ADC status of children of unwed mothers and examined state ADC rules govern-

[57]   U.S. Department of Health, Education and Welfare, National Office of Vital Statistics, *Illegitimate Births, 1938–1947: Vital Statistics—Special Reports, Selected Studies* (Washington, D.C., 1950). The birthrate per 1,000 unmarried women in 1940 was 7.1, and the birth ratio per 1,000 live births was 19.5 for white births, 168.3 for nonwhite births. In 1950, the out-of-wedlock birthrate rose to 14.2, with a birth ratio of 17.5 for whites and 179.6 for nonwhites. By 1957, the unmarried birthrate hit 20.9, and the birth ratio returned to 19.6 for whites and rose to 206.7 for nonwhites. It should be noted that birth registration improved during this period.

[58]   Michael Brown explores the administrative and policy consequences of illegitimacy debates in "Divergent Fates: Race, Gender, and the Legacy of New Deal Social Policy," paper presented to the Third Women's Policy Research Conference, Institute for Women's Policy Research (May 14–15, 1992), pp. 35–42.

ing "illegitimacy." She found that in 1939 (before the Social Security Act Amendments went into force) five states did not accept any children born out of wedlock into ADC, while in each of eleven other states fewer than 50 such children were accepted. Asking whether an "illegitimate family" is a family, Larbee found that according to some states it was, while in other states the answer depended on how many children a mother had borne outside of marriage. Wondering whether the unwed mother was a "fit" mother, she reported variations in state responses ranging from no, to yes, to yes, *if* the mother responds to service from the social welfare agency and makes her home acceptable.[59] She reflected, finally, on "the problems of race as they affect public service to unmarried mothers." Worried that "illegitimacy" was becoming a proxy for race-based exclusion from ADC, Larbee warned: "The states with the most concentrated racial problems are those with large Negro populations, among whom the illegitimacy birth rate is much higher than for the white race. There is, perhaps, in no other area such a wide divergence of policy and practice as in the granting of assistance to unmarried Negro mothers. It must be recalled that legal marriage has been available to this group for only seventy years."[60]

Maternalists explored the problem of "illegitimacy" throughout the 1940s. Their concern was the welfare of the child, which pivoted, in their view, on the child's relationship with her mother.[61] Against growing popular perceptions that the higher rate of "illegitimacy" among Black children was a sign of Black women's "racial misbehavior," of irremediable biological inferiority, and of the subordination of motherhood to sexuality among Black women, maternalists insisted that the relationship between the Black mother and her child was as basic to child welfare as the mother-child relationship in white families.[62] Consequently, maternalists

---

[59]   Larbee, "Unmarried Parenthood under the Social Security Act," pp. 447–449.

[60]   Ibid., p. 453.

[61]   The maternalists' interest in illegitimacy dates back to the Progressive Era. The Children's Bureau held a Conference on Standards of Legal Protection for Children Born Out of Wedlock in 1920, and recommended, among other things, that "the parents should not be permitted to surrender a child for adoption, or to transfer guardianship, or to place it out permanently for care, without order of the court or state department, made after investigation." Katharine Lenroot, "Social Responsibility for the Protection of Children Handicapped by Illegitimate Birth," American Academy of Political and Social Science *Annals* 98 (November 1921): 120–128.

[62]   On the racializing of single pregnancy in white political and social thinking, see

abjured punitive measures aimed at denying assistance to children of unwed mothers.[63] They worked to establish maternity homes for Black women. They deplored state policies requiring the unwed mother to take court action against the father before she could qualify for ADC. And they cautioned against paternity suits as a solution to child dependency. One reformer, a colleague of Florence Kelley before her death in 1932, even warned of the dangers of mandating child support from unwed fathers, arguing that a cash relationship "between biological father and mother recalls prostitution . . . traditionally men expect to pay in cash for illicet [sic] sex affairs."[64]

The maternalists' commitment to improve provisions for dependent families led them to counsel tolerance for "illegitimacy": "much as it may be regretted by society—it is not a crime," wrote Maud Morlock. But although many reformers wanted the federal law's neutrality toward unmarried parenthood to apply to state ADC programs, they were not culturally or morally neutral in their assessment of the problem. To Morlock, who, as director of Social Services for the Children's Bureau monitored services for unwed mothers, "illegitimacy" was "one manifestation of behavior." The province of social workers, behavior could be changed if "approached by the social worker with objectivity and understanding."[65] Other reformers called for better services for dependent families and more efficient supervision of home conditions, for "sociologically, at least, we have in the illegitimate family a survival of an outgrown and therefore destructive form of family organization—the mother and child, biologic unit—in a culture which is striving to bring in the third member into responsible intimacy."[66]

Rickie Solinger, *Wake Up Little Susie: Single Pregnancy and Race before Roe v. Wade* (New York, 1992), chap. 2.

[63]   Maud Morlock and Hilary Campbell, *Maternity Homes for Unmarried Mothers: A Community Service*, U.S. Department of Labor, Children's Bureau Publication no. 309 (Washington, D.C., 1946).

[64]   Marguerite Marsh, "Common Attitudes toward the Unmarried Father," National Conference of Social Work *Proceedings* (New York, 1940), pp. 378–379; Morlock, "Establishment of Paternity," p. 368. Marsh and Kelley worked together for protective labor legislation for women. See, e.g., Florence Kelley and Marguerite Marsh, "Nightwork in Industry," *Social Work Yearbook, 1929* (New York, 1930), pp. 289–291.

[65]   Morlock, "Establishment of Paternity," p. 376.

[66]   Mary S. Brisley, "Parent-Child Relationships in Unmarried Parenthood," National Conference of Social Work *Proceedings* (New York, 1939), p. 443.

The maternalists' efforts to integrate ADC during the 1940s required diligent efforts to root out race discrimination in the program, including proxy discriminations against unwed mothers. Behind these efforts lay three abiding maternalist principles: first, that racial difference could be explained by culture, not biology; second, that culture, though habitual, was learned and could therefore be changed; and third, that the mother's first obligation was to provide full-time, quality care of her child. As Annie Lee Davis put it: "Too often when we think of culture, we view it as something that is innate with certain groups of people; rather than viewing culture as the result of the interaction of people and the social forces with which they are surrounded."[67] To Davis, Morlock, and other maternalists, the social origins of cultural difference permitted social mediation of that difference. At the front line of the mediation of culture stood mothers who drew from their biological role the social gift and responsibility of ensuring family welfare and nurturing good citizens.

Maternalists had tried and savored the woman-directed, child-centered cultural re-education of immigrants during the 1910s and 1920s. As they had for immigrants before the New Deal, maternalists now sought to provide for the welfare of the Black mother's child while encouraging the Black mother's cultural reform. Reform required supervision—through case-work and counseling. It further required social support to ease poverty, thus to mitigate the cultural environment. More important, reform required understanding the conditions that produced single pregnancy and developing sympathetic prescriptions to prevent it. Social workers accordingly examined the social bases of unwed motherhood among African Americans. They interpreted the problem in ways to deter the application of punitive rules against unwed applicants for ADC. In both their findings and in their analyses, they made culture the category of explanation and thereby strengthened their case against punishing individual women from cultures that had not yet been reformed. One Smith College study, for example, concluded that although African American attitudes toward "illegitimacy" varied sharply depending on class, unwed pregnancy rates among African American women revealed cultural difference: "The analysis of the case re-

---

[67] Quoted in Solinger, *Wake Up Little Susie*, p. 62.

cords used in this study suggested that Negro unmarried mothers tend to have norms in respect to "illegitimacy" that are different from those generally accepted by the white community. Over three-quarters of the total group more or less accepted "illegitimacy" so far as its moral implications were concerned, while less than a quarter felt that they had violated a rigid moral prohibition. These differing attitudes were influenced more by culture than by psychological factors."[68]

Maternalist racial liberals treated the Black mother's exclusion from ADC both as the product of racism and as evidence of the need for the cultural integration of African Americans. Echoing E. Franklin Frazier's pathbreaking work *The Negro Family in the United States*, maternalists disputed the assumption of the "inherent moral degeneracy of the Negro" and worked to denude the political significance of African American "manifestation of behavior." Working with women and for children, they elaborated the gender implications and remedies implicit in Frazier's analysis more fully.

At the Conference on Services for Negro Children convened by the Children's Bureau in 1944, maternalists mapped out a plan to confront the problem of race for child welfare, maternal citizenship, and the political community. Like the Conference on Children in a Democracy four years earlier, this meeting urged vigorous federal and state oversight of local ADC and other child welfare programs, so that African American mothers and children who had qualified for assistance would receive equitable benefits. The conference further recommended that the Children's Bureau strengthen and extend its services to Black children and mothers, especially Black wage-earning mothers "whose children are not receiving adequate care and protection." To foster understanding, facilitate casework, and mitigate racial bias, the bureau called for the deployment of greater numbers of Black staff in public assistance programs, for more consistent guidance to Black families, and for training in race relations for white personnel in the Children's Bureau, social welfare agencies, and schools "in order that Negro and white children who are under the guidance and protec-

[68] Patricia Knapp and Sophie T. Cambria, "The Attitudes of Negro Unmarried Mothers toward Illegitimacy," *Smith College Studies in Social Work* 17 (1946–1947): 202.

tion of these workers may receive understanding and sympathetic direction."[69]

THE CULTURE OF MOTHERHOOD

Maternalists' efforts to reform welfare followed from their commitment to the child and from their long-standing goal of political reproduction through the cultural remediation of mothers. As they fought race discrimination in the application of the new federal policy, they fought the behaviors and social conditions that marked one group off from another. An uphill battle marshaled chiefly by Maud Morlock and Annie Lee Davis of the Children's Bureau, it pitted the tradition of uplift against a resilient racism that became more furious in its assault on African American women as "immorality" and "illegitimacy" entered its discourse. By 1960, maternalists had lost their campaign to develop ADC to its "full possibilities." Whereas maternalists had promoted "suitable home" provisions early in the century to improve home life, such provisions had become mechanisms for breaking up homes and for classifying some women's homes as inherently beyond repair. Although African American participation in ADC increased after 1940—to 42.2 percent of ADC families in 1958—in twenty-four states, "suitable home" laws, most of which assumed the unwed mother to be "unfit" and her home to be "unsuitable," worked to limit Black women's access to ADC.[70]

Still, the maternalists' policy struggle was problematic not only for its failure, but on its own terms, as well. It reflected the maternalist alchemy of racism and liberalism, which, while it demanded equal treatment regardless of race or culture, nevertheless calibrated group differences and measured the social rank of groups according to their distance from the dominant culture's family norms. Moreover, although maternalists used cultural dif-

[69] "Recommendations Adopted by Children's Bureau Conference on Services for Negro Children," *Child*, vol. 8, January 1944, pp. 106–107.

[70] Mimi Abramovitz, *Regulating the Lives of Women: Social Welfare Policy from Colonial Times to the Present* (Boston, 1988), p. 323; Social Security Administration, Bureau of Public Assistance, *Illegitimacy and Its Impact on the Aid to Dependent Children Program* (Washington, D.C., 1960), pp. 72–76.

ferences among groups to explain variations among individual women's choices and behaviors, maternalist reform prescribed cultural reform through the rehabilitation of individual mothers. This emphasis hung future social equality among groups on the individual achievements and failures of mothers, marrying poverty and inequality to culture in ways that in a later political context would invite scrutiny of individual and family manifestations of "racial misbehavior" and would support efforts to break the cultural "cycle of poverty" by individualizing responsibility for poverty and inequality.[71]

Rooted in idealized, middle-class gender norms and family forms, Anglo American maternalist reform assumed that conformity to the maternalists' own domestic, conjugal, and behavioral practices would assure uplift to equality. Bound to the notion that the individual could fix her behavior and transcend her culture, it assumed that the problems of discrimination, poverty, and inequality were as much a problem with the Black mother as a problem with society. It assumed, too, that the wellspring of family security and the sign of "American" family values was the husband. And, finally, this reform assumed that publicly assisted domesticity was the next best route to worthy motherhood for all single mothers who could not afford a nanny.

[71] See, e.g., *The Negro Family: The Case for National Action*, U.S. Department of Labor, Office of Policy Planning and Research (Washington, D.C., 1965), and Edward D. Berkowitz, *America's Welfare State: From Roosevelt to Reagan* (Baltimore, 1991), introduction and pt. 2.

WAGE EARNING OR MOTHERHOOD
*Maternalist Labor Policy
during World War II*

> In this time of crisis it is important to remember that mothers of
> young children can make no finer contribution to the strength of the
> Nation and its vitality and effectiveness in the future than to assure
> their children the security of home, individual care, and affection.
> Except as a last resort, the Nation should not recruit for industrial
> production the services of women with such home responsibilities.
> —Frances Perkins, 1942

In both social insurance and welfare, the New Deal assumed that men paid for their families while women raised them. Taking the breadwinning male worker as the norm, social insurance institutionalized women's economic dependence on men and made socially protected income for the male worker and his family the unconditional dividend of wage-earning masculine citizenship. Prescribing domestic motherhood as the mainstay of family welfare, Aid to Dependent Children transferred women's economic protection from men to the state, where men were absent or uninsured, and made socially provided income for the dependent family contingent on the mother's full-time care of children and on social supervision of the mother's home. In the socially insured family, the wage-earning mother was a gender anomaly; in the publicly assisted dependent family, a wage-earning mother was an impossibility.

If social insurance treated the working mother as inconceivable, ADC treated her as incompatible with family welfare. The idea that working motherhood was the bane of children's interests did not, however, apply only to poor, mother-headed families. As maternalists made clear during the social security debates, most mothers were "worth more" in the home as the custodians of child welfare. Only mothers who could afford to work because they could afford to hire household assistance were permitted the luxury of work outside the home. Because the preponderance of women workers did not meet this criterion—most were low-wage workers in industry, domestic service, offices, and shops—maternalists developed labor policies to redirect wage-earning mothers to domesticity. Maternalists did not invent the gender conventions that assigned women to the home, of course, but during the Progressive Era and throughout the 1930s and early 1940s, they designed policies to discourage wage earning by mothers through welfare stipulations, labor regulations, training for domesticity, and counseling. As the approaching U.S. involvement in World War II pulled greater numbers of women into the labor force, maternalists met their Waterloo. They met the challenge with strenuous appeals to women's patriotic duty to domestic motherhood.

Throughout the economic emergency of the 1930s and into the war mobilization of the early 1940s, maternalists defended women's general right to work but cautioned against the employment of mothers. Increasingly "feminist" by their own description, maternalists did not doubt women's ability to participate in the productive life of the nation.[1] Nor did they doubt women's right to enter jobs of their own choosing. But they did doubt that women with families worked because they wanted to.[2] They doubted that wage-earning women were in the work force to stay, and they accordingly doubted that transient women workers could wield power on their own to win working conditions consistent with the health and economic needs of motherhood.[3] Most important, they

[1] Eleanor Roosevelt defined feminism at a press conference in 1935: "The fundamental purpose of feminism is that women should have equal opportunity and equal rights with every other citizen." Quoted (ironically), in the National Women's Party's *Equal Rights*, June 1, 1935, p. 3.
[2] Mary Elizabeth Pidgeon, *The Employed Woman Homemaker in the United States: Her Responsibility for Family Support*, U.S. Department of Labor, Women's Bureau, Bulletin no. 148 (Washington, D.C., 1936); Eleanor Roosevelt, "My Day," *Ladies' Home Journal*, June 16, 1939.
[3] Mary Anderson, "Labor Legislation for Women," *Social Work Yearbook, 1929* (New York, 1930), p. 290; Sharon Hartman Strom, "Challenging 'Woman's Place': Feminism, the Left, and Industrial Unionism in the 1930s," *Feminist Studies* 9 (Summer 1983): 359–386.

doubted that women with children could work outside the home without cost to child welfare and family life. Mary Anderson summarized the problem in her reflections on more than twenty years at the helm of the Women's Bureau: "The ten hours in the factory, plus the time needed to get there and home again, did not leave any extra time for all the work at home that is almost invariably the woman's responsibility. It was bad for health and very bad for family life to have the women so worn out at the end of a day's work that they had no strength or energy left for anything else."[4]

Maternalists' efforts to encourage full-time motherhood emphasized their appreciation for the work mothers performed in the home and proceeded from their understanding of motherhood as work. These efforts addressed the oppressive dual weight of wage earning and domesticity for women with children by deterring women's movement into the labor force. Rather than alleviate the burdens shouldered by women at the intersection of wage work and motherhood—through child-care programs or through a reassessment of the father's family role—maternalists sought to regulate the conditions of wage work for most women and to discourage wage earning by mothers in order to stoke mothers' activities in the home. The only wage-earning women to escape maternalist labor standards were women of color, for labor standards did not apply to agriculture and domestic work.

From 1900 until World War II, protective regulation of women's working conditions was an important prong of maternalist reform. Maternalists sought protective laws to defend women against unscrupulous employers, ease the burden of women's double day, guard family life, and thereby preserve "the interest of the race."[5] By 1924, they had secured hours limitations in forty-three states, and in many of those states had won safety standards, maternity protections, and prohibitions against night work by women. Though maternalists welcomed enactment of national wages and hours standards for both women and men during the New Deal, they sought separate labor standards for women in local initiatives

---

[4] Mary Anderson, *Woman at Work: The Autobiography of Mary Anderson as Told to Mary N. Winslow* (Minneapolis, 1951), p. 71.
[5] Anderson, "Labor Legislation for Women," p. 240; Kelley and Marsh, "Night Work in Industry," p. 290.

and prohibitions against industrial homework and night work by women under the Fair Labor Standards Act.[6]

Labor regulations impeded women's movement into certain industries and confined women to low positions in others. Night work laws banished women from the newspaper industry, for example, while assigning women to less remunerative day shifts in the restaurant industry. Labor regulations thus capped opportunities and rewards for wage-earning women, even as they safeguarded women's terms of employment. But they did not promote domestic motherhood among wage-earning women, except by indirection. To encourage women to choose full-time motherhood, maternalists educated women to meet their maternal responsibilities. During the Progressive Era, mothers' pension and maternal health programs, mothers' classes in settlement houses, and homemaking instruction for girls had been venues for teaching domesticity; during the 1930s and 1940s, welfare, emergency education projects, and mobilization for war provided occasions for maternalists to teach mothers how best to serve child and family welfare.

The Aid to Dependent Children program was an important pillar of maternalist labor policy during the New Deal, at least for mothers without husbands. Maternalists and Works Progress Administration officials encouraged unemployed single mothers who could qualify for work-relief to enroll in ADC and remain outside the labor market.[7] The Children's Bureau and Women's Bureau advised mothers in industry and in industrial homework to consider public assistance.[8] Expressing a clear maternalist preference for welfare motherhood over wage-earning by mothers, Emma Lundberg, the Children's Bureau's consultant for child welfare, wrote: "Mothers who apply for day care for their children are often

---

[6] Louise Stitt, "The Present Status of Minimum Wage Legislation in the United States," *Social Service Review* 10 (March 1936): 110–116; "Law or Public Opinion?" *Equal Rights*, August 1, 1938, p. 298; "Working Women Again Threatened with Restriction," *Equal Rights*, August 15, 1937, p. 115; "Philadelphian Writes Mrs. Roosevelt," *Equal Rights*, January 15, 1937, p. 5; Ruth White, "Industrial Home Work in Chicago," *Social Service Review* 10 (March 1936): 23–58; Louise Stitt, "Government Regulation of Wages and Hours," National Conference of Social Work *Proceedings* (New York, 1939), pp. 191–199. Stitt was the director of the Women's Bureau's Division of Minimum Wage.

[7] Lois Scharf, *To Work and to Wed: Female Employment, Feminism, and the Great Depression* (Westport, Conn., 1980), p. 129.

[8] Anderson, *Woman at Work*, p. 244.

in need of some other kind of help. It may sometimes be a question of assistance to the family, through 'aid to dependent children' or some other form of aid by public or private agencies, so that the mother may be able to remain at home and care for her children."[9]

For mothers with husbands, maternalists championed the paternal wage as the antidote to wage-earning motherhood.[10] But rather than await the evolution of the effects of improved male wages on the family under the Wagner Act and Fair Labor Standards Act, maternalists prescribed domesticity to unemployed women in vocational programs that trained women for housekeeping and parenting. When the war moved husbands from industry into the army, diminishing the possibility of full-time motherhood in many families, maternalists voiced resounding opposition to the employment of mothers as surrogate workers. Ever flexible, they countered the seemingly irreversible movement of women into industry not with bars on women's employment but with counseling services for mothers tempted to work outside the home and with the supervision of wage-earning mothers' families. To compensate for the working mother's absence from the home, maternalists proposed visits to nursery children's homes and socially-provided wives for working mothers.

Maternalists stressed the primacy of mothers' domesticity but recognized many mothers' need to work during World War II, recognized industry's need for women workers. They did not want to coerce full-time motherhood but to induce mothers to choose it. Though they worked to deflect mothers from industry, they also advocated protections for mothers in industry—with fair wages, hours regulations, and provisions for pregnant women workers.[11]

---

[9] Emma O. Lundberg, "Counseling Service in a Day-Care Program," *Child*, vol. 7, September 1942, p. 32; Doris Campbell, "Counseling Service in the Day Nursery," *Family*, vol. 24, (March 1943), p. 29.

[10] Mary Anderson drummed home this point in her autobiography: "I think the whole thing could be taken care of if the provider for the family got sufficient wages. Then married women would not be obliged to go to work to supplement an inadequate income for their families and could make their own choice as to what they should do." *Woman at Work*, p. 157.

[11] In 1942, the Women's Bureau and Children's Bureau issued a joint statement on Standards for Maternity Care and Employment of Mothers in Industry. They called for workplace facilities for prenatal care; night work prohibitions; a maximum eight-hour day; two rest periods between each shift; transfer from hazardous jobs; six weeks' pregnancy leave before delivery and at least two months' leave after de-

Still, though maternalist labor policy was multidimensional and responsive to the differing practical circumstances confronted by real women, it nevertheless pitted wage earning against motherhood in indelible opposition. One consequence was that maternalists tabled consideration of policies aimed at reconciling work with family life. In turn, they deferred the possiblity of women's economic independence and with it women's full and equal citizenship in the New Deal welfare state.

TEACHING WOMEN'S WORK

Maternalists did not wish to disadvantage women workers, only to protect actual or potential motherhood against the ravages of work and to encourage a different occupational choice among wage-earning mothers. For professional women, for childless working-class women, and even for mothers who needed to work, maternalists demanded job opportunities and wage equity, disputed the idea that women work for "pin money," and worried over employer discriminations against women. Even while they defended regulations of women's shifts, breaks, and loads as socially decided "labor standards from the standpoint of child [and community] welfare," they opposed autonomous employer decisions to exclude women from certain types of jobs or to treat married women as secondary wage earners, potentially pregnant, and therefore unemployable.[12] Likewise, they contested discrimination

---

livery—all without jeopardy to the pregnant workers' job or seniority. Charlotte Silverman, "Maternity Policies in Industry," *Child*, vol. 8, August 1943, p. 20.

[12] *Conference on Day Care of Children of Working Mothers (July 31 and August 1, 1941)*, U.S. Department of Labor, Children's Bureau Publication no. 281 (Washington, D.C., 1942), pp. 20–27; Anderson, *Woman at Work*, pp. 96–99. In uncommon solidarity across the divide of equality and difference, the National Woman's Party (NWP) and maternalists fought discriminations against married women. Upon the repeal of the married persons' provision of the 1932 Economic Recovery Act, the NWP newspaper remarked: "I wonder if any of you realize just how important July 8, 1937, was to women. The House passed overwhelmingly the repeal of Section 213, yes—but something of much greater significance and far-reaching importance than that took place that day. For the first time in the history of our country, the women members of Congress worked side by side for legislation affecting women, disregarding party lines. They demonstrated how splendid women working together for women can be." Edwina Austin Avery, "And So the Bill Was Passed," *Equal Rights*, August 1, 1937, p. 109.

against women in the male-oriented emergency relief measures of the New Deal. The Women's Bureau, joined by the League of Women Voters and the Women's Trade Union League, condemned sex-based wage differentials, occupational exclusions, and hours violations under the National Industrial Recovery Act, and Eleanor Roosevelt spearheaded criticism of the omission of work and education projects for unemployed women from the Federal Emergency Relief Administration (FERA).[13]

By 1934, maternalist efforts won a place for women in the Civilian Conservation Corps in Camp Jane Addams and some seventy-four other residential centers that handled 8,000 to 10,000 women before the camps were closed in 1937. First managed by the FERA, then by the National Youth Administration, the camps stressed domestic training for most young women and preparation for domestic service for others. Mimicking the homemaking lessons maternalists had imparted to girls and women during the Progressive Era, camp projects taught cooking, nutrition, and table setting, as well as sewing and personal hygiene. One graduate recalled to Hilda Smith, a former settlement teacher who ran the program: "Most of us got the impression that they wanted to teach us something useful if we got married immediately and that that was the only proper thing to do."[14]

Maternalists also developed women's projects in the Works Progress Administration, which was generally more receptive to women than the construction-oriented work-relief agencies like the Public Works Administration and FERA. The WPA served unemployed adults, or, rather, unemployed breadwinners. The majority of the 3.5 million women who were unemployed in 1937 were not reached by the program, for it admitted only one worker per family and an applicant had to prove that she had been the primary wage-earner in the family. Some local agencies took the presence of an employable husband as proof that the woman applicant was not the family breadwinner and accordingly denied her work relief.

---

[13] Lois Scharf, "'The Forgotten Woman: Working Women, the New Deal, and Women's Organizations," in Lois Scharf and Joan Jenson, eds., *Decades of Discontent: The Woman's Movement, 1920–1940* (Westport, Conn., 1983), pp. 242–259; Joyce L. Kornbluh, *A New Deal for Workers' Education: The Workers' Service Program, 1933–1942* (Urbana, 1987), pp. 79–81.

[14] Quoted in Kornbluh, *New Deal for Workers' Education*, p. 87.

Others directed mothers without employable husbands to ADC. Although women accounted for 24 percent of the labor force and were unemployed at rates comparable to men, eligibility rules restricted women's participation in the WPA to only 17.5 percent of all participants. Nonetheless, by December 1938, some 400,000 women workers were enrolled in WPA projects.[15]

Maternalists carried on their tradition of vocationalized homemaking in WPA education projects developed to meet "the special needs of women." Far from teaching unemployed women to stretch their ambitions in the world of wage work, maternalist education projects refocused women's attention on home life, home conditions, and child welfare. These projects fit well with the larger aim of the WPA's emergency education activities: to restore political order through Americanization, literacy, and a strong family life.

If New Dealers worried that one-third of the nation was "ill-clothed, ill-housed, ill-fed," they also worried that one-third of the nation was either foreign born or of foreign parentage. More than 14 million immigrants and 26 million second-generation children, speaking thirty-six different languages, were reported by the 1930 census. Repeating hoary fears that immigrants were ideologically unsocialized and therefore were gullible to radical appeals, New Dealers like Harry Hopkins devised emergency education initiatives to teach "the benefits of freedom and democracy," to promote literacy ("Illiterates are dangerous to a democracy . . . They are easy prey to propaganda and exploitation"), and to instill the values of Americanized home life.[16] New Dealers also worried that dependency came "rather too easily" to male immigrants who were not well integrated into the political and economic order.[17] In ad-

---

[15]   Winifred Wandersee, "A New Deal for Women: Government Programs, 1933–1940," in Wilbur Cohen, ed., *The Roosevelt New Deal: A Program Assessment Fifty Years After* (Austin, 1986), pp. 189–190; Winifred D. Wandersee Bolin, "American Women and the Twentieth-Century Work Force: The Depression Experience," in Mary Kelley, ed., *Woman's Being, Woman's Place: Female Identity and Vocation in American History* (Boston, 1979), p. 304; Scharf, " 'The Forgotten Woman,' " p. 247.
[16]   Harry Hopkins quoted in Kornbluh, *New Deal for Workers' Education*, p. 29.
[17]   See, e.g., Lilian Brandt, *An Impressionistic View of the Winter of 1930–31 in New York City* (New York, 1932), p. 24. Brandt described dependency as a "mental infection" and warned of the uppity attitudes it produces: "After the initial embarrassment of a first recourse to charity is overcome, it is easy to ask a second time, to drop efforts to find work, accept a position of dependence, rely on the agency, and criticize its methods. . . . [as] whole neighborhoods became dependent, most of these people

dition, they worried that widespread unemployment stoked prejudice against immigrants, especially against immigrant men seeking jobs: in 1935, eighteen states either prohibited the employment of aliens on public works projects or required preference be given to citizens.[18]

Works Progress Administration education programs imparted vocational skills to all enrollees, but gave priority to educating immigrants. Teachers set up classes in literacy, citizenship, naturalization, and cultural training to encourage immigrants to move off relief and into the American mainstream.[19] Although most of the classes prepared immigrant men to re-enter the labor market as breadwinners and citizens, some courses prepared women to re-enter the home as mothers and housewives. Unemployed teachers set up nursery schools, "not as a convenience for the relief of parents . . . but [as] an educational institution, including in its routine proper nutrition, health service, supervised play, and training in good habits of personal care and behavior."[20] They offered courses in homemaking, teaching cooking, nutrition, child care, and consumer skills. They provided instruction in parenting through courses on child guidance, child behavior, home health, food preparation, and "wholesome adult living."[21] They also supervised home life through home visits to mothers enrolled in parent education. Rehearsing the justification for a long tradition of maternalist intervention in the home, a WPA teacher explained: "Unless one sees conditions under which these people live, it would be hard

---

seemed to feel that it was all in the course of events, and to accept assistance as their natural due."

[18] "Immigrants and Their Children," *Social Work Yearbook, 1935* (New York, 1935), p. 205.

[19] Doak S. Campbell, Frederick H. Bair, and Oswald L. Harvey, *Educational Activities of the Works Progress Administration* (Washington, D.C., 1939), p. 28. Civilian Conservation Corps education programs also served some of these objectives. See Howard W. Oxley, Director, C.C.C. Camp Education, U.S. Department of the Interior, Office of Education, "Objectives of the C.C.C. Educational Program," National Conference of Social Work *Proceedings*, 63d annual meeting (Chicago, 1936), pp. 261–269.

[20] Campbell, et al, *Educational Activities of the Works Progress Administration*, pp. 107–108.

[21] Muriel W. Brown, Parent Education Consultant, Federal Emergency Relief Administration, "Trends in Parent Education," American Academy of Political and Social Science *Annals* 182 (November 1935): 73–81; Katharine Lenroot, "Twenty-fifth Anniversary of the Children's Bureau," *Child*, vol. 1, March–April 1937, p. 6.

to appreciate how badly they need parent education. It would make one think that the time may come when it will be compulsory to attend parent education classes."[22]

Directed toward women, lessons in "American" family values, and more particularly in "American" maternal skills, engaged 25 percent of WPA personnel and reached 16 percent of regular enrollees and another 5.5 percent of occasional ones. Students in more general courses also received these lessons, as parenting and homemaking education penetrated literacy, naturalization, and leisure training. As Doak S. Campbell concluded in his report for the Office of Education, "The combined parent and homemaking education program is perhaps the most social and democratic of all of the emergency education activities. Possibly its greatest strength lies in the fact that the underprivileged constitute its field of application."[23]

Better known as a work-relief program, WPA education programs put many unemployed professional women to work. In fact, although they had been only 14.5 percent of the female workforce in 1940, professional women (nurses, teachers, librarians) accounted for 25 percent of the women on work relief.[24] But the WPA also offered employment and training to jobless working-class women. Typically, women on work projects were engaged in sewing, canning, and preparing school lunches; some 56 percent of WPA women worked in sewing rooms. In addition, the Division of Women's and Professional Projects, coordinated by maternalists under the direction of Ellen Woodward, set up a Household Service Demonstration Project in July 1937 to train women for domestic wage work.[25] Where homemaking and parenting education prepared women to manage their own families' lives, the Household Service Project taught young women how to cook, serve food, care for children, wash, iron, and market so that they might better serve

[22]   Quoted in Sonya Michel, "Children's Interests/Mothers' Rights: Women, Professionals, and the American Family, 1920–1945" (Ph.D. diss. Brown University, 1986), p. 204.
[23]   Campbell, et al, *Educational Activities of the Works Progress Administration*, p. 31.
[24]   Susan Ware, *Beyond Suffrage: Women in the New Deal* (Cambridge, Mass., 1981), p. 109.
[25]   Wandersee, "New Deal for Women," p. 189. Kornbluh, *New Deal for Workers' Education*, p. 12.

the families of women who hired them. Some 1,700 jobless teachers were employed under the program as home economics instructors. By December 1939, 22,000 women had passed through the program as students.

Out of the household service program maternalists developed a housekeeping aide project. Designed to promote "the employment of girls certified as qualified for private employment," the project, with five hundred local branches, secured placements for some eighteen thousand women by 1940.[26] Housekeeping aides were deployed to assist or replace mothers in practical tasks, especially where "misfortune" had made it impossible for the mother to continue to meet her home responsibilities. In most cases, housekeeping aides were offered as substitute wives and surrogate mothers to widowed fathers and their children.

The program responded to, and to some extent met, maternalist calls for improved standards for domestic work. Like mothering, housekeeping was woman's natural vocation and was essential to family welfare. But because of its social importance and because "every vocation needs training," maternalists aimed to monitor the development of homemaking skills through training programs for household workers, as well as for mothers.[27] Maternalist efforts to improve the quality of paid and unpaid domestic work were replicated in the National Youth Administration, and in vocational education programs funded by an expanded Smith-Hughes Act.[28]

Domestic training and employment in women's jobs were the norm for New Deal services for wage-earning women. Secured by maternalists like Eleanor Roosevelt and Frances Perkins, these programs brought prevailing gender conventions, cultural goals, and children's interests together under the familiar maternalist rubric of community and family welfare. Tying women's economic

[26] Marion Schmadel Goodwin, Assistant Executive Secretary, Associated Charities, Family Consultation Service, Cincinnati, "Housekeeper Service in Family Welfare," *National Conference of Social Work Proceedings*, 65th annual session (Chicago, 1938), pp. 279–287; Campbell et al., *Educational Activities of the Works Progress Administration*, p. 55.

[27] Anderson, *Woman at Work*, pp. 239–243; Amey E. Watson, "The Reorganization of Household Work," American Academy of Political and Social Science *Annals* 160 (March 1932): 165–177. Watson was a researcher for the Women's Bureau.

[28] The George-Deen Act became law in June 1936. It appropriated 4 million dollars for in-school, part-time, and evening classes in industrial and agricultural arts, in home economics, and in sales.

security to husbands, occupational fulfillment to the home, and social responsibility to children, maternalists approached the problem of unemployment among women by disputing the concept of women's unemployment altogether. Homemaking classes and parent education showed women their "true" vocation and proved that women would always have skills to learn and work to do in the home. In classes and on work projects, maternalists offered jobless women a new look at their maternal mission in hopes that they might choose to undertake it. Conceding that some women would choose work out of economic need (as opposed to men, who worked from responsibility, virility, and independence), maternalists gave self-supporting girls and women skills for employment in women's industries (garment factories, school cafeterias) and for employment in families as domestic workers. These various projects vocationalized homemaking—in woman's own home, in jobs that relied on skills women used in the home (cooking, sewing), and in the homes of other women.

SURROGATE MOTHERS

As economic emergency yielded to war emergency, maternalist prescriptions for domestic motherhood were confounded by increasing market and military demands for women to work outside the home. Not only were women needed in greater numbers in traditional "women's jobs," but they were needed in heavy industry to replace male workers who went off to war. A work force that included 11 million women in 1940 exploded by 1945 to number 19.5 million women. At least 3.5 million of these workers might not have entered the workforce without the economic and labor pressures of war. Seventy-five percent of these new women workers were married.[29] From the maternalist point of view, this development threatened the integrity of the home and the family. Accordingly, as the president, the military, and industry prepared for war, maternalists prepared to defend child welfare.

During the early 1940s, maternalists struggled against the

[29] These estimates were worked out by Alice Kessler-Harris in *Out to Work: A History of Wage-Earning Women in the United States* (Oxford, 1982), pp. 276–277.

spread of wage-earning motherhood in rhetorical appeals to women with children and in policy debates about them. Maternalists did not draw fixed battle lines in this struggle, however. Although they generalized "woman's role" from their own class and cultural location to universalize gender principles, they had never been absolutists in the application of gender prescriptions. Accordingly, though clearly engaged in a struggle *against* wage-earning motherhood during World War II, they simultaneously entertained policy adjustments to accommodate the needs of working mothers' children. They discussed day care for children, for example, and considered ways of assisting the mother with her "double day." These discussions conveyed a willingness to approach child welfare issues flexibly and pragmatically, but though sensitive to the practical needs of children whose mothers worked, maternalists encouraged mothers to remain at home even as they treated those needs.

Maternalists issued their opening salvo in the war mobilization in July 1941, when the Children's Bureau declared: "The first responsibility of women with young children, in war as in peace, is to give suitable care in their own home to their children."[30] The directive reflected a widely held view that women could best help the war effort by "doing the home job better." It became official policy of the War Manpower Commission in August 1942. Susan B. Anthony, II, summed up women's prescribed role in war in a complaint: "Lurking behind the nutrition posters, the committees and conferences, was the hoary notion that in the solemn business of winning a war women's chief contribution should come through *more* hours of cooking, *more* hours of shopping and *more* conversation about food, eat cuts, vegetables and vitamins. Naturally, no one would minimize the importance of food in war time as well as peace time; but, from the point of view of serious women's work the suggested confining of womanpower to the monotonies of nutrition seemed about as enlightened as limiting them to knitting."[31]

The Children's Bureau directive did not merely repeat social conventions. It expressed a maternalist conviction that was reaffirmed as reformers deliberated about the child welfare issues raised by

---

[30]   Quoted critically in Susan B. Anthony, II, *Out of the Kitchen—Into the War: Woman's Winning Role in the Nation's Drama* (New York, 1943), p. 130.
[31]   Ibid., p. 43.

war mobilization. Chief among these issues was the fate of motherhood. No less important was the care of children whose mothers were absent from the home. Linking the care of children to the fate of motherhood, maternalists conceded a limited need for day care services but piggybacked the counseling of mothers against wage work to those services.

The maternalist response to the emergency employment of women emerged at the Conference on Day Care of Children of Working Mothers convened by the Children's Bureau in late July 1941. In addition to Children's Bureau staff, participants included Edith Abbott; Mary Anderson; Marie Dresden Lane, director of Service Projects for the National Youth Administration; Grace Langdon, Family Life Education specialist for the WPA; Louise Moore, special assistant to the Office of Education for Women and Girls in Trade and Industrial Education; Louise Stanley, chief of the U.S. Agriculture Department's Bureau of Home Economics; and Louise Stitt, director of the Women's Bureau's Division of Minimum Wage.

Conference discussions betrayed the premises and the limits of maternalist policies toward wage-earning mothers. The social provision of child care might well have been defended as a kind of protective labor policy for women; it also could have been framed as a child welfare measure. But maternalists had never claimed labor policies for women as workers. And they always had been ambivalent toward policies that might be construed as rewarding or facilitating mothers' work outside the home. As we saw in Chapter Two, progressive pioneers like Florence Kelley and Edith Abbott opposed maternity insurance for wage-earning women because they feared it would encourage mothers to abandon the home for the workplace, while Jane Addams criticized the development of day nurseries as an alternative to care by mothers. Rather than develop policies for mothers as wage workers, maternalists had sought and won—over four decades—regulations of working conditions for women wage earners as actual or potential mothers. Fashioning mother-directed labor laws for child-centered purposes, maternalists aimed to maximize the quality of the mother's role in the home by limiting the time and energy she spent away from it. The question of child care for working mothers asked maternalists to reconsider their opposition to wage earning by mothers, to look differently at working women and their needs, and to revisit gender prescriptive labor policies to reconcile work and family life.

Fearful that policies for women as workers would encourage mothers to leave the home, maternalists answered the question of child care with old principles. Voicing opposition to congressional consideration of a federal-state wartime child care program, the Conference on Day Care urged the protection of home life and family relationships through the enforcement of women's labor standards, through counseling for working mothers, and through an expanded housekeeper aide program. The conference further resolved that "the welfare of mothers and children should be given due consideration at every point in the development of employment policies relating to national defense. Mothers who remain at home to provide care for children are performing an essential patriotic service in the defense program."[32]

A Children's Bureau bulletin reinforced the maternalist message, reminding women that "a mother's primary duty is to her home and children. This duty is one she cannot lay aside, no matter what the emergency."[33] In January 1942, the Women's Bureau followed suit, albeit with a more qualified statement of opposition to wage earning by mothers. As wage-earning women's agency in government, the Women's Bureau was generally more sympathetic than the Children's Bureau to the problems of employment discrimination and workplace injustice that confronted women. Still, like the Children's Bureau, the Women's Bureau took the protection of motherhood as its first priority and joined family welfare goals to its prescriptions for the reform of women's working conditions. The conference of the Women's Bureau Advisory Committee accordingly concluded: "Although barriers against the employment of mothers with young children should not be tolerated, such mothers should not be actively recruited as a new source of labor for either training courses or employment until other sources of labor supply in the local community have been fully utilized."[34]

Despite maternalists' resistance to the development of a child

---

[32] *Conference on Day Care*, pp. 74–75.

[33] George Martin, *Madam Secretary: Frances Perkins* (Boston, 1976), p. 458.

[34] "Policies Regarding the Employment of Mothers of Young Children."

care policy and inconclusive congressional deliberations about it, President Roosevelt allocated $400,000 in emergency funds to coordinate child care programs in August 1942. The Children's Bureau was authorized to approve plans submitted by states eligible for grants-in-aid under the allocation.[35] In a concession to the defense effort, maternalists accepted this responsibility but warned that "facilities required for the emergency should not be so permanent in structure that they cannot be changed or discontinued when the temporary need is over."[36] Pulled into the development of child care services though worried that such services would make wage earning irresistible to mothers, maternalists conceded a general need for child care while discouraging individual mothers from needing such services for their own children.

The key to the maternalist approach to child care was counseling for mothers. At the Conference on Day Care, Katharine Lenroot introduced the idea of providing counselors for women at job training recruitment centers: "We don't want to put up barriers; we don't want to get employment managers to thinking in terms of discriminating against mothers with children, because even with reference to such mothers the individual situation determines what should be done. But perhaps public employment services and possibly agencies selecting persons for training might give consideration to this question. . . . Naturally it does not relate just to what to do with preschool age children, but to the whole range of problems of school-age children who need some supervision after school and some home care."[37]

Emma Lundberg and other child welfare advocates pursued Lenroot's idea, explaining that "the mother must be helped to think through her problem and to make plans that will safeguard the health and welfare of her children."[38] Though maternalists believed that most mothers should not work, they admitted that some mothers "needed" to. Maternalists interposed counseling services between mothers and wage work to assess the individual mother's "need" for wages and the impact of her employment on her family's

[35]   "Funds for Day-Care Programs," *Child*, vol. 7, October 1942, p. 51.
[36]   Emma O. Lundberg, "A Community Program of Day Care for Children of Mothers Employed in Defense Areas," *Child*, vol. 6, January 1942, p. 153.
[37]   *Conference on Day Care*, pp. 20, 32.
[38]   Lundberg, "Community Program of Day Care," p. 157.

welfare. Day care counselors thus functioned as gatekeepers, asking mothers at the threshold of industry to "stop and think about what their working and continuing to care for their children in the present way possibly another month or two would do to them."[39]

Day care counselors advised mothers about "the practicability of . . . employment from the point of view of the welfare of the children and the stability of the home."[40] They determined whether individual children would benefit from the child care experience. They assessed whether the individual mother could work outside the home *and* be a mother "without too much disturbance to herself and to him, and, at the same time, contribute to the growth experience he is having in the nursery."[41] They routed single mothers toward the Aid to Dependent Children program. And they guided the care of children "affected by conditions arising from employment of the mother."[42]

The most important role of the counselor, however, was as the arbiter of the mother's "need" to work. Counselors determined whether the "*motives* for the mother's working" were "acceptable" and whether the family's economic situation warranted the mother's absence from the home.[43] Concerned to stifle mercenary interests among mothers, social workers urged mothers who worked outside the home because they aspired to a higher standard of living to consider the costs of seeking "such a standard in its relation to the effects of nursery care" upon children.[44] Counselors delivered information about housekeeping and budgeting; the YWCA, settlement houses, and family agencies helped mothers improve household management and spending habits to "negate the necessity for working." Turning wage-earning motherhood into a disorder, one expert insisted: "If the mother's wish for improved status, economic or otherwise, seems exaggerated and impossible

---

[39] Callman Rawley, "Case Work and Day Care," *Family*, vol. 24, March 1943, p. 22; Barbara Hewell, "The Health of the Young Child in Group Care," *Child*, vol. 7, March 1943, pp. 129-131; National Federation of Settlements, "Recommendations on Care for Children of Working Mothers," *Child*, vol. 7, April 1943, p. 151.

[40] Lundberg, "Counseling Service in a Day-Care Program," p. 31.

[41] Rawley, "Case Work and Day Care," p. 27; Doris Campbell, "Counseling Service in the Day Nursery," *Family*, vol. 24, March 1943, p. 29.

[42] Lundberg, "Counseling Service in a Day-Care Program."

[43] Rawley, "Case Work and Day Care," p. 26. Emphasis added.

[44] Campbell, "Counseling Service in the Day Nursery," p. 29.

of fulfillment, the counselor may help her to relinquish these ambitions. Often referral to an agency other than the nursery for sustained study and treatment may be helpful."[45]

Children in day care were likewise regarded by many social workers as symptoms of maternal disorder. Children's Bureau physicians and other staff asked teachers and nurses to monitor child health problems in day nurseries—especially the spread of disease, "stunted development as a result of being cooped up," and poor adjustment to "the changed family relationship."[46] Social workers supervised the nursery child's home through visits following the child's absence from day care. They further invited mothers to treat day care as an occasion for parent education: "A second aspect of the nursery setting . . . is the nature of the responsibility the parent is expected to take, always within the diagnosed limits of her capacity. . . . A certain amount of cooperation in continuing the child's training in the home may also be expected of her. What position does this put the parent in? These requirements, if wisely administered, call forth whatever strength she has within her and help to stimulate and sustain her in a mature, adult role."[47]

Counseling, home visits, and parent education mitigated the choice and effects of wage-earning motherhood, but none of these strategies answered the maternalist conundrum: how can women be at once wage earners and mothers? The answer implicit in maternalist discourse was that women could not perform both roles— at least not without detriment to the well-being of their children— because motherhood was itself a full-time job. Always troubled by the impact of wage work on motherhood and always doubtful that most women could cope with the double day, maternalists searched for policies supporting the mother care of children in their own well-managed homes. Mary Anderson expressed the maternalist reluctance to accept public child care as the best way to protect child welfare under conditions of wage-earning motherhood. She explained that even if surrogate care were provided to children while their mothers worked outside the home, it would not amount

45 Ibid.
46 Hewell, "Health of Young Children in Group Care," p. 129. Hewell was the medical adviser to the day care unit of the Children's Bureau.
47 Marcella S. Farrar and Eleanor M. Hosley, "The Day Nursery's Function in Supportive Treatment," *Family*, vol. 24, December 1943, p. 286.

to fair exchange for wage-earning mothers: "I know there are those who will say that the child is better cared for at the nursery than at home and that may be true, but the wear and tear on the mother is something to be thought of too. She cannot be a very good mother if she is so tired she is ready to drop. As a social philosophy I think that the establishment of day nurseries for the children of working mothers is only a stopgap, not a solution of anything."[48]

One proposal favored by maternalists as a counterpart to day care, if not as its alternative, was the Supervised Homemaker Service. Drawing from the example of the housekeeping aide program of the WPA, maternalists led by Lenroot at the Conference on Day Care called for an expanded and professionalized homemaker service to deploy "mother substitutes" in the homes of working mothers.[49] Conference participants described the success of the WPA program, which trained 37,000 women to serve 65,000 families each month in 1941. Most notable was the program's contribution to family "uplift": "We think the long-range value of the service is very great. In fact, sanitation standards are generally raised, nutrition standards sometimes are raised, the physical care of the children is certainly improved, and we think there is a definite improvement in family relationships because when the house is clean and the meals are prepared, obviously members of the family are going to be happier about it."[50]

Whereas the original WPA program gave priority to widowed fathers in assigning housekeeping aides, maternalists began to discuss the homemaker service as a resource for mothers as women went to work. Maternalists explained this policy shift as a way of promoting the home care of children. Moreover, as Children's Bureau analysts reasoned, providing wives to wage-earning mothers would attenuate the costs of wage earning for both mothers and children: "Such a plan would provide the maximum of assistance to the mother and the least strain on the children. The mother who accepts employment in most instances has far more household re-

---

[48] Anderson, *Woman at Work*, p. 157.
[49] *Conference on Day Care*, pp. 48, 66–70; *Supervised Homemaker Service: A Method of Child Care*, U.S. Department of Labor, Children's Bureau publication no. 296 (Washington, D.C., 1943).
[50] *Conference on Day Care*, p. 67; Marjorie H. Boggs, "Some Treatment Implications in the Use of Homemaker Service," *Family*, vol. 24, May 1943, pp. 107–112.

sponsibilities than are usually assumed by the father . . . . She not only has to arise early to prepare the children for the day but often must work late at night perhaps doing the washing, cleaning, and mending. She must buy the food and cook it. In addition she must be fresh in spirit to give her children the companionship and affection they need."[51]

Regretting that it was not fiscally feasible to place a homemaker in every working mother's home, the Children's Bureau developed criteria and priorities for the service. Treating the homemaker service as a method of supervising home life, the bureau called for the careful training of "good quality" homemakers capable of introducing nutrition to the household and of providing care to the children of mothers who might be better suited to the defense industry than to motherhood.[52] The bureau further specified that caseworkers be assigned to participating families to "make sure that family problems don't interfere with the best use of the homemaker."[53] Given limited resources, the bureau hoped that homemakers could be made available at least to sick mothers, to the sick children of working mothers, and to large families whose mothers worked outside the home.

The homemaker service did not meet the potential maternalists assigned to it. President Roosevelt liquidated the WPA in December 1942 and with it the administrative and fiscal backbone of the program. Maternalists sought a new legislative authorization for the program in 1943, but without success. When the United States went to war and mothers went into industry, maternalists lost control of child care policy to the Federal Works Agency, which administered Lanham Act funds with the explicit goal of enabling mothers to work outside the home.

SOCIAL RESPONSIBILITY AND SOCIAL EQUALITY

World War II marked the end of the maternalists' role in government and influence over policies toward women. The "great

---

[51] *Supervised Homemaker Service*, p. 3.
[52] Lenroot to the *Conference on Day Care*, p. 70; *Supervised Homemaker Service*, p. 14.
[53] *Supervised Homemaker Service*, p. 6.

ladies of Chicago" died over the course of the 1930s—Florence Kelley, Julia Lathrop, Jane Addams, Grace Abbott. Mary Anderson retired in 1944. Eleanor Roosevelt left the White House in 1945 and with her departed the maternalists' direct link to power. But the policies won by maternalists between 1917 and 1945 survived to frame the paradigm for women's work and women's welfare well into the 1960s.

Central to this paradigm was the idea that woman's social responsibility for children overrode her political and economic rights of citizenship. Maternalists struggled mightily to guide culturally and economically "needy" women toward meeting their responsibilities. By subordinating women's rights to children's welfare in policies affecting mothers, however, maternalists inscribed not only gender roles but gender inequality in the New Deal welfare state. And, by defining child welfare in terms of an Anglo American, middle-class norm, maternalists joined culture and race to women's gender in the ascriptive stratification of the welfare state.

Speaking as women and for "women's interests," maternalists in effect collaborated with masculine policymakers in closing off the only two avenues for independence in capitalist America: work and education. Approaching wage earning by mothers as a matter of "need" rather than of right, maternalists insulated women in a small sphere of the labor market, mediated women's conditions of employment, and weakened women's contract rights in relation to men's. Pitting wage earning against motherhood, maternalists codified women's secondary status as economic citizens and reinforced the presumption that a woman's worthiness as a citizen hung on her success as a domestic mother. Viewing education as an occasion to instruct mothers in how to meet their social responsibility, maternalists used teaching to secure gender and culture conformity rather than to achieve equality.

Perhaps most damaging to women's prospects for social equality was the maternalists' need-based understanding of women's wage earning.[54] Where wage-earning manhood followed from rights and expressed virtue, maternalists explained wage-earning woman-

---

[54]　On needs and rights in the gendered discourse of social reform, see Linda Gordon, "Social Insurance and Public Assistance: The Influence of Gender in Welfare Thought in the United States," *American Historical Review* 97 (February 1992): 19–54.

hood as the temporary need of the single woman to support herself before marriage and as the dysfunctional need of the mother to compensate for the absence or inadequacy of the paternal wage. Only for professional women did work approach the stature of rights and virtue in the maternalist vision—but only if professional mothers secured surrogate care for their children, and then only because professional women met a higher social responsibility to nurture the polity through teaching, nursing, and social work.

The need-based conception of women's wage earning excused the differential treatment of women in the welfare state. If women worked from need, then the welfare state did not have to indemnify women's work, whereas it should indemnify women's dependency. Diagnosing and judging women's need, maternalists pursued such policies as welfare and widow's pensions to mitigate the most common source of women's need to work: the loss of the male breadwinner. To shore up the fathers' ability to provide, they supported such policies as unemployment insurance, workmen's compensation, and old age insurance for masculine occupations. Maternalists believed women ought not to work, although sometimes they "needed" to, and therefore maternalists did not contest the omission of women from policies developed for workers. The only occupational exclusion seriously challenged by maternalists was the exclusion of domestic work under the Social Security Act. This limited defense of women as workers coincided with a long-standing, separate conception of Black women (a third of all domestic workers) as workers rather than mothers. Perhaps it also coincided with the reformers' view that for some women to work in other women's homes promoted legitimate interest in child and family welfare. Maternalists did not contest the exclusion of women's occupations under the Fair Labor Standards Act, though those exclusions denied women full protection under the act's wages and hours guarantees.

The blend of mothers' provisions and worker exclusions affecting women meant not only that women's relationship to the welfare state differed from men's but that this relationship varied among women themselves according to social rank, marital status, and economic condition. For most women, their place in the welfare state was conditional. Where men's benefits (outside of agriculture, casual labor, and personal service) flowed automatically from work and wages, women's protections depended on marriage and motherhood. Within the framework of the New Deal, women's only hope for equal social provision was in approximating (white) male employment patterns: by moving into men's jobs, securing men's wages, and adopting men's work history. Women, however, were trained for women's work, mothers were implored to stay at home, and a mother's need to work was mediated by her social responsibility for children in ways that produced distinctively female work histories characterized by low wages, part-time and temporary employment, and interrupted cycles of wage earning.[55] The child of maternalism, women's inequality in the New Deal welfare state left exacerbated dilemmas of equality and difference for the next generation of political women to resolve.

[55]   In 1990, women were the majority of involuntary part-time workers, two-thirds of temporary workers, and the majority of low-wage workers. Three out of five minimum wage workers were women. Statement of Roberta Spalter-Roth and Heidi Hartmann, Institute for Women's Policy Research, "Improving Women's Status in the Workforce: The Family Issue of the Future," paper presented to U.S. Senate, Committee on Labor and Human Resources, Subcommittee on Employment and Productivity, July 18, 1991; National Commission on Working Women, "No Way Out: Working Poor Women in the United States," unpublished report (1988).

POSTMATERNALIST
WELFARE POLITICS

The descent from maternalist welfare innovation to contemporary welfare politics has been neither linear nor automatic. Yet the maternalist idiom continues to inform political debates about poverty and social provision in the late twentieth century. At the center of these debates are struggles over women's dependency, women's inequality, and women's responsibility.

As it emerged from the New Deal, the welfare state socialized men's rights and risks at work (the Wagner, Social Security, and Fair Labor Standards Acts) and in war (the G.I. Bill)—though these were mostly limited to *white* men's rights and risks, given occupational and income exclusions biased against workers of color in New Deal measures and given racial discrimination in the military. Meanwhile, it socialized women's "needs" and dependency in the family. The New Deal welfare state mediated women's dependency by conferring residual social protections to women in marriages (social insurance) and by providing supervised social support to uninsured single mothers (welfare). A maternalist innovation, welfare met the basic needs of dependent motherhood: filling the breach left by low-wage or absent fathers, deterring mothers from work outside the home, and encouraging the uplift of home life. Expressing simultaneous and coinciding social interest in child welfare and the quality of motherhood, the maternalist wing of the welfare state substituted women's services for women's rights, anchored women's citizenship in maternal responsibility, and institutionalized social, economic, and political resistance to gender equality and women's independence.

An early version of this chapter was published as "Welfare Reform in Historical Perspective," Gwendolyn Mink, guest editor, *Women and Welfare Reform*, special issue of *Social Justice* 21 (Summer 1994): 114–131, and in *Connecticut Law Review* 26 (Spring 1994): 879–899.

The welfare politics that succeeded the New Deal reiterated the moral and cultural stigma, judgment, and anxiety from which women's social policies of the early twentieth century were spun. But whereas maternalist politics assumed that single mothers could be made worthy through supervision and education, post-maternalist welfare politics essentialized the choices and behaviors of welfare mothers and disputed their entitlement to social support. Mothers' pensions became discursively transformed into a "way of life" by the late 1960s, and the worth and rights of single mothers were displaced by the icon of the Black "welfare mother."[1]

At least four policy decisions paved the way for these changes. First, the Social Security Act of 1935 created occupational and work history requirements that excluded many women from unemployment compensation and other income protection. Second, in 1939, New Dealers adopted a two-tiered approach to mothers' pensions when they folded into the survivors' insurance system the widows and children of male workers insured under the Social Security Act. Much like social security benefits for the elderly, survivors' insurance offered widows of insured men an automatic and unsupervised income subsidy. With "the best" single mothers tracked separately into the social security system, Aid to Dependent Children became a program for the widows of uninsured men and for morally suspect mothers who were single because divorced or never married. Where widows accounted for 43 percent of the ADC case load in 1937, they accounted for only 7.7 percent by 1961.

A third policy decision came in 1950, when the ADC formula for children's benefits was amended to include a grant for mothers. A fourth policy change developed over the course of the 1960s, when the Aid to Families with Dependent Children program was expanded and barriers to eligibility (e.g., employable mother rules, residency requirements) and moral supervision (e.g., "man in the house" rules, "suitable home" tests) were eased.[2] Commentators have pointed out that the relaxation of eligibility barriers coincided with an increase in the welfare "take-up" rate for women of color. It also coincided with a wildfire of popular perception that women on welfare didn't deserve it.

[1] Rosemary L. Bray, "Growing Up on Welfare," *New York Times Magazine*, November 8, 1992.
[2] *King v. Smith* 392 U.S. (1968); *Shapiro v. Thompson* 394 U.S. (1969).

If the swift adoption of mothers' pension proposals by states after 1911 and the relatively uncontested incorporation of the mothers' pension concept into the Social Security Act are any gauge, the idea of welfare motherhood per se has not always been controversial. As long as welfare recipients were morally supervised and culturally regulated, as long as they assimilated their gender lessons, as long as they for the most part bore their children in marriages, and as long as they could "melt" into the dominant culture—in short, as long as they were white—welfare recipients were not stigmatized as such. Mothers' pensioners were stigmatized—but for their cultural deviations, not for their economic need. Today, by contrast, the stereotype of the welfare mother is Black: she cannot "melt." Equally important, today's welfare mother is stigmatized for needing it: for having children outside marriage, for not earning wages, for not choosing to depend on men. One reason for today's stigma is the deeply embedded stereotype of the Black single mother and the slurs of matriarchy, dependency, and promiscuity from which it springs.[3] Another reason are the abiding cultural images in white America that hold African American women beyond the pale of domesticity as Mammies, Jezebels, and chattel.[4] Yet another explanation is gender discomfort with the idea that women can choose not to depend on men, whether through wage work, divorce, or unmarried motherhood.

Though voting Americans have always been stingy with poor mothers, I can't quite believe that they want to deny their children food, shelter, and other rudiments of subsistence. What I do think they want is to restore the regulatory tethers that once governed welfare and thereby to reinstate old gender norms, family forms, and racial hierarchies of conduct. "Ending welfare as we know it" means forcing women to choose work outside the home or marriage after two years on AFDC. It means forcing poor mothers to sink or swim in an economy that could not provide jobs for the 9 million socially insured workers who collected unemployment compensation between 1990 and 1993. It means forcing women into some-

---

[3]   Regina Austin, "Sapphire Bound!," reprinted from the *University of Wisconsin Law Review* in Patricia Smith, ed., *Feminist Jurisprudence* (New York, 1993), p. 583.
[4]   Ibid., p. 585; Patricia Morton, *Disfigured Images* (Westport, Conn., 1991); Margaret Burnham, "An Impossible Marriage: Slave Law and Family Law," *Journal of Law and Inequality* 5 (1987).

times unwanted and dangerous relations with the fathers of their children through child support enforcement. It means forcing the poorest single mothers—women of color—into low-wage community jobs because high rates of unemployment among men of color erase the economic benefits promised by child support enforcement and marriage. It means forcing the poorest single mothers to control their fertility; it means limiting their reproductive choices.

The conservative impulse behind welfare reform is in some respects reminiscent of maternalist welfare politics. Like mothers' pensions policies of the early twentieth century, conservatives seek to use welfare policy to enforce gender ideology and racial and cultural control. Today's welfare reform is, however, discursively different. Most important, it rejects the idea that the poverty of mothers and children is a social concern and seeks to privatize economic uplift: hence the notion of coercive work requirements. Hence also the incentives to poor mothers to seek economic security through men and marriage. Reformed welfare policy will punish mothers who do not conform to legislated morality (it already does so in many states)—a shape-up-in-the-home or ship-out-to-work principle.

I don't think the apparent popularity of work requirements for welfare mothers reflects a new social consensus that all mothers should work outside the home. The work requirements are rather a response to widespread resentment that "those people" are allowed to stay at home through welfare while 50 percent of mothers with young children are to some degree or another connected to the labor market. This resentment conjures up old racial concerns of "female loaferism" in the form of the contemporary welfare myth that mothers on welfare are "unwilling" to work.[5] It feeds off stereotypes and resists facts that would explode them: for example, that 43 percent of AFDC recipients either combine work with welfare or cycle between them.[6] It ignores evidence that most recipi-

---

[5]   Jacqueline Jones, *Labor of Love, Labor of Sorrow* (New York, 1985), pp. 58–60; Evelyn Brooks Higginbotham, "African American Women's History and the Metalanguage of Race," *Signs* 17 (Winter 1992): pp. 254, 259–260; Martha Minow, "The Welfare of Single Mothers and Their Children," *Connecticut Law Review* 26 (Spring 1994): 826–841.
[6]   Heidi I. Hartmann and Roberta Spalter-Roth, "The Real Employment Opportunities of Women Participating in AFDC: What the Market Can Provide," paper presented at "Women and Welfare Reform: Women's Poverty, Women's Opportunities,

ents try to move from welfare to work, though many return intermittently to welfare because permanent jobs are declining, because they can't secure health care, and because child care arrangements break down: 56 percent of recipients are continuously enrolled on welfare for fewer than two years, while 70 percent of all people entering AFDC leave within two years, at least for a time.[7]

At bottom, work requirements, like marriage incentives, are manifestations of backlash politics: backlash against the economic necessity that drives some married mothers into the workforce to enhance their family's income; backlash against feminist insistence on equal employment opportunity; backlash against women who either by circumstance or by choice chart an independent path for themselves and their children; and backlash against the very group of women who have always been "othered" in gender ideology—women of color, workers in the fields and in other people's homes, and caretakers of other women's children.

Welfare politics has always been a discourse about gender roles and about racial and cultural order. It has always articulated hierarchies of motherhood calibrated by women's behavior. It has always entangled our social obligations to mothers and children with the social stigma we stamp upon them. But in notable ways, the late-twentieth-century welfare debate differs sharply from the debates of the maternalist period. Then, the necessity and legitimacy of mothers' pensions were assumed, and political conflict pivoted on eligibility, funding, and administrative issues. Now, policymakers question the very legitimacy of a program that enables single mothers to stay at home and thereby supports people who do not "value work" and encourages "welfare dependency" as "a way of life." Then, the worthy woman citizen was a domestic mother; now, she can be a mother and worker both. Then, social policies counseled even poor mothers not to work outside the home; now, the social politics of welfare insist that poor mothers should choose wage work over welfare. Dramatic changes in attitudes to-

and Women's Welfare—A Policy Conference to Break Myths and Create Solutions," Washington, D.C., October 23, 1993.
[7] Congressional Research Service memo, February 25, 1994; Children's Defense Fund, "Basic Facts on Welfare" (1994); "Getting Off Welfare Is Half the Job: Permanent Employment Proves a Harder Goal," *Washington Post*, November 11, 1993.

ward welfare and women's wage earning over the last fifty years notwithstanding, those attitudes are still marked by maternalist ideas about culture, race, and character.

Though marked by maternalist ideas, contemporary welfare politics also distorts those ideas. Now dominated by male policymakers from all across the political spectrum (Daniel Patrick Moynihan, Charles Murray), postmaternalist welfare politics have redefined women's dependency from a norm to a pathology. To some extent, this shift followed cynically from social and political decisions beginning in the 1960s to abate restrictions on women's participation in and remuneration from the labor market.[8] In combination with the secular increase in the proportion of women workers, these decisions fueled the impression that single mothers with economic "needs" could meet them by going to work. The idea that mothers should work if they needed to contradicted maternalist suppositions about the impact of wage-earning motherhood—especially single motherhood—on child welfare and family life. The idea nevertheless fits within the maternalist prescriptive idiom of culture and character. The question of whether one "values work," in fact, has intensified the behavioral and cultural cache of welfare politics. Where wage-earning motherhood once provoked maternalist initiatives to support and reward uplifted maternal behavior, today unemployed welfare motherhood incites initiatives "to promote positive behavior" through work requirements, automatic rotation off welfare and into the workforce, and coerced

---

[8] The crucial political decision was Title VII of the 1964 Civil Rights Act, followed by Title IX of the Education Act Amendments of 1972 and by the Pregnancy Discrimination Act of 1978. Several Supreme Court rulings gave strength to these provisions, striking down protective labor laws, formal distinctions between men's and women's work, and many employer practices that discriminated against workers on the basis of race or gender (e.g., *Griggs v. Duke Power, Corning Glass Works v. Brennan, Dothard v. Rawlinson, UAW v. Johnson Controls*). Still loyal to its maternalist heritage in 1964, the Women's Bureau initially opposed applying Title VII's prohibition on employment discrimination to women. Only *after* the sex discrimination amendment to Title VII passed the House of Representatives did the Women's Bureau sign on in support. This shift, arguably, marked the end of maternalism. See Lise Vogel, *Mothers on the Job* (New Brunswick, 1993).

school attendance.[9] As Daniel Patrick Moynihan told the Senate in 1990, in language not unfamiliar in welfare history: "The problems of children in the United States are overwhelmingly associated with the strength and stability of their families. Our problems do not reside in nature, nor yet are they fundamentally economic. *Our problems derive from behavior.*"[10] Clearly, even though attitudes toward women's wage earning have changed, the nexus between welfare and behavioral discipline of poor mothers remains taut.

Although the prescriptivity of welfare politics has not wavered since the maternalist era, the spread of popular hostility toward "welfare dependency" over the past twenty-five years proves how far beyond the maternalist framework we have moved. But the popular view that welfare mothers *should work* points disingenuously to the erosion of barriers to women's employment to explain why. Women have won greater social acceptance and legal rights as workers since the maternalist period, but women's position in the labor market remains inferior to men's: most women still do not have access to breadwinning wages.

Moreover, most women are not expected to work while they are mothers of young children. We may no longer find it remarkable that mothers work outside the home, but we do not have a normative expectation that they do so. Critics of welfare argue that single mothers should prove they "value work" by seeking wages rather than welfare. But the prevailing discourse still defends middle-class, married mothers when they choose full-time domesticity; meanwhile, political majorities still withhold social supports that would normalize wage earning by mothers—policies like child care, paid maternity leaves, and gender-sensitive unemployment insurance.

In contemporary welfare politics, the only women for whom wage

[9] "Wisconsin Makes Truancy Costly by Tying Welfare to Attendance," *New York Times*, December 11, 1989; "Ohio Welfare Bonuses Keep Teen-Age Mothers in School," *New York Times*, April 12, 1993; "Vermont Gets Approval for Welfare-Work Plan," *San Francisco Chronicle*, April 15, 1993; "Massachusetts Welfare Plan to Limit Cash Grants," *New York Times*, January 14, 1994; "Welfare Planners Struggle over Final Sticking Points," *New York Times*, March 21, 1994.
[10] Senator Moynihan, *Congressional Record* (October 3, 1990), p. S14417, quoted in Martha Fineman, "Images of Mothers in Poverty Discourses," *Duke Law Journal* 41 (April 1991): 279, emphasis added.

work is an unambivalently assigned social responsibility are welfare mothers. Compare, for example, the opprobrium we foist on welfare mothers with the recent celebration of heterosexual, married domesticity surrounding the introduction of federal legislation to permit independent retirement account tax deductions for housewives. According to Senator Diane Feinstein, who sponsored the bill with four women colleagues in the Senate and Republican Nancy Johnson in the House of Representatives, the proposal "says to every woman that's at home and takes care of the family that this is a job and is recognized as a job. It puts an imprimatur on the ability of women to take pride in being a homemaker."[11] Arguably, who welfare mothers are and what their families look like account for the differential understanding of their caretaking domesticity as pathological.

Although the idea that wage earning is the social responsibility of poor mothers marks a real break from maternalist welfare ideology, the postmaternalist language of pathology borrows heavily from maternalist rhetoric and policy. Among the more resilient features of welfare politics are the asserted causal connection between maternal poverty and women's relationship to men and the repeated prescriptive association between family welfare and the cultural/behavioral reform of mothers. The maternalist analysis of women's dependency underpins prominent contemporary strategies to overcome it. Ever since Moynihan's 1965 report on *The Negro Family*, policymakers and social commentators have emphasized welfare mothers' conjugal status, reproductive choices, and family structures as objects of reform. Contemporary exhortations against single pregnancy and for marriage and paternal child support all reflect a persistent faith that the economic security of women and children depend upon their relation to men. Where race and welfare collide, these exhortations are offered as remedies for the cultural conditions of welfare motherhood. In the icon of the Black welfare mother, old maternalist notions about cultural poverty reappear.

Although images of cultural poverty continue to fire welfare politics, the context of welfare politics has changed. Since the 1960s,

---

[11] "Bill Would Give Homemakers Bigger IRAs," *San Francisco Chronicle*, February 4, 1994. Even Merrill Lynch joined the celebration with a full-page ad in *Roll Call* that read: "Finally, a benefit program for the most important job in America."

political indictments of welfare mothers have replaced the maternalist scrutiny of motherhood. Under pressure from politically mobilized welfare recipients, from the civil rights movement, and, to a lesser extent, from rights-seeking feminism, welfare policy has relaxed its formal regulation of women's home lives as well as its racially discriminatory impediments to participation in the program. When they opened up welfare to women of color and reduced the moral and cultural supervision of motherhood, reformers at least theoretically democratized welfare. The gender basis and behavioral premises of welfare remained intact, however. If welfare workers lost the tools of moral discipline, they gained a new lever in work rules beginning in 1967. More important, even as behavioral regulation through welfare policy eased, the cultural and behavioral bias of welfare politics persisted—no, grew more intense.

The end of "man in the house" rules and other barriers to welfare coincided with an increase in eligibility rates, especially among women of color. African Americans, who accounted for nearly 95 percent of nonwhite recipients in 1960, participated in ADC in increasing numbers after the 1939 Social Security Act amendments took effect. This increase took place under conditions of strict, discretionary, and discriminating rules for recipients. Judicial decisions, legislative changes, and Social Security Administration holdings began to weaken discretion and discrimination during the 1960s. For example, the Social Security Administration argued in 1960 that "illegitimacy" was a "constitutionally obnoxious" basis for differentiating among children and families.[12] The application of such rights-based, equal protection principles began to erode discriminatory regulations and eligibility criteria, making welfare more like an entitlement and less like relief. This change racialized welfare politics. The long-standing, structural coincidence of race, gender, low wages, and poverty meant that a more accessible welfare would serve not only larger numbers of women and children, but also disproportionate numbers of women of color.[13] And it did: by 1967, a welfare caseload that had once been 86 percent white had become 46 percent nonwhite. The coexistence of racism and

---

[12] Social Security Administration, Bureau of Public Assistance, *Illegitimacy and Its Impact on the Aid to Dependent Children Program* (Washington, D.C., 1960), p. 53.
[13] Rose M. Brewer, "Black Women in Poverty: Some Comments on Female-Headed Families," *Signs* 13 (1988): 331–339.

liberalism in an idiom of cultural conformity fired a backlash against the new welfare constituency—a backlash that was encouraged by Richard Nixon and George Wallace in 1968 and 1972 but that soon took on a life of its own.[14]

The politics of backlash marked the welfare mother as Black and took her newly unregulated "dependence" on welfare as proof of her irremediable failure to assimilate the work, cultural, and family values of the American middle class.[15] From the 1960s, forward, racially coded welfare politics stamped the Black welfare mother as unworthy and culturally deprived. (Before the 1960s, of course, the presumed "unworthiness" of the Black single mother deprived her of welfare in many places.) Rooted in a priori assumptions about the Black welfare mother's character, the racial mythology of welfare suggested solutions to "welfare dependency." This mythology supported liberal ruminations about how to return (Black) single mothers to marriage: to economic security through a paternal wage and through reproductive and sexual self-control.[16] It also supported conservative admonitions that women on welfare – though not other mothers of young children—must work.

The federal government codified the impulse to teach poor women the discipline of the labor market and the ethic of self-sufficiency in the Family Support Act of 1988. The most significant revision of the welfare system since the New Deal, the Family Support Act (FSA) appropriated $1 billion annually for employment training, education, and related child care costs. This appropriation transformed AFDC, making wage work, rather than domesticity, its goal for recipients. Judging from the large numbers of recipients who are motivated to work outside the home—39 per-

---

[14]   For an explanation of this backlash, see Thomas Byrne Edsall and Mary D. Edsall, *Chain Reaction: The Impact of Race, Rights, and Taxes on American Politics* (New York, 1991). For a critique of this backlash, see Maxine Baca Zinn, "Family, Race, and Poverty in the Eighties," *Signs* 14 (1989).

[15]   Wahneema Lubiano, "Black Ladies, Welfare Queens, and State Minstrels: Ideological War by Narrative Means," in Toni Morrison, ed., *Race-ing Justice, Engendering Power: Essays on Anita Hill, Clarence Thomas, and the Construction of Social Reality* (New York, 1992), pp. 323–364; Marion Wright Edelman, *Families in Peril* (Washington, D.C., 1987), pp. 24, 25.

[16]   See, e.g., William Julius Wilson, *The Truly Disadvantaged: The Inner City, the Underclass, and Public Policy* (Chicago, 1987); David Ellwood, *Poor Support: Poverty in the American Family* (New York, 1988); Edward Berkowitz, *America's Welfare State: From Roosevelt to Reagan* (Baltimore, 1991), pt. 2.

cent, according the Institute for Women's Policy Research, either combine work and welfare or cycle between them—this new attention to poor women's wage-earning potential held promise.[17] States, however, did not fully match the federal investment as the law required them to do, child care provisions broke down, and many recipients were trained for low-wage, unstable jobs rather than for jobs offering economic security and opportunity. Moreover, though the FSA instructed women to work, it did not address the fact that women's earnings keep them poor. Nearly half of women wage earners earned less than a minimum sufficiency wage in 1991, that is, less than $6.67 per hour. Prescribing work for work's sake, the FSA thus avoided the causes of women's need for welfare.[18] In the absence of social supports, wage reforms, and full employment, this new emphasis on wage-earning motherhood intensified and expanded the behavioral lexicon of welfare politics.

REFORMING WELFARE

If maternalist reform contributed the gauge of culture and character to debates about women and welfare, it also institutionalized the subordination of *woman's* welfare to her social responsibility. The maternalists' subordination of the woman to the child, of independence to dependency, and of wages to domesticity ran to the core of their policies toward women. These policies not only gave vent to maternalist ideological formulations about gender and culture but also deepened the structures of women's inequality in both state and society. Chief among these structures are women's prescribed relationship to men, designated position in the labor market, and assigned responsibilities in the household. These structures continue to track many women toward low, part-time, or temporary wages and to mire many single mothers in poverty.

---

17   "Mothers on Aid Rolls and Payrolls," *Washington Post*, May 18, 1992.
18   "Child Care Shortage Clouds Future of Welfare Program," *New York Times*, December 12, 1989; Casey McKeever, Western Center on Law and Poverty, "Easy Targets: A Critical Analysis of Governor Wilson's Proposed Cuts to Needy Children and the Aged, Blind, and Disabled" (Sacramento, 1991); Heidi Hartmann and Roberta Spalter-Roth, Institute for Women's Policy Research, "The Labor Market, The Working Poor, and Welfare Reform: Policy Suggestions for the Clinton Administraton," (Washington, D.C., 1992).

Maternalists did raise many of the right questions when they addressed the effects of poverty on women and children. Most important, they recognized caretaking as work, and asked both why single mothers, at least, should not be supported in this work and how mothers could be expected to perform two jobs. These sorts of questions bear repeating in the contemporary context, as welfare reformers plan to compel work outside the home, even from mothers of infants and toddlers.

The prevailing wisdom among welfare reformers continues to echo the most problematic themes of welfare history. Current proposals and reform-by-waiver initiatives already under way in the states reinforce the differential legal treatment of poor mothers (other mothers are "allowed" to work, not forced to). Even more alarming is the fact that the welfare debate in recent years has provided the model for enumerating social preferences about who should be mothers and how gender relations should proceed. Liberals and conservatives alike have converged around a welfare morality that invites public adjudication of poor women's right to mother and that attaches the welfare of women and children to the presence of men in their lives.[19] Whether in Dan Quayle's attack on single mothers' lack of "family values" or in Bill Clinton's plaintive 1994 State of the Union announcement that too many children "are born outside of marriage," the message is clear: social policy must manage women's morality. At the center of the new welfare morality are two assumptions: that some women should not be mothers ("family cap" incentives) and that deserving mothers must have explicit and publicly recognizable connections to the fathers of their children (child support or marriage).

Though it recalls a discredited eugenic agenda of an earlier period, the first assumption has produced popular proposals to deny benefits to children born to mothers on AFDC. Paraphrasing Chief Justice Holmes's reasoning in *Buck vs. Bell*, many welfare reformers complain of intergenerational "welfare pathology" and seek to end it by preventing the next generation from being born. This argument has had magnetic appeal in the politics of backlash—notwithstanding government-published proof that 61 percent of

[19] "Husbands No, Babies Yes," *Newsweek*, July 26, 1993, p. 53; "The Infertility Trap: Why Do Some State Medicaid Programs Help Single Mothers Have More Babies?" *Newsweek*, April 4, 1994, pp. 30–31.

AFDC units did not bear any children while on welfare, that 72 percent of AFDC families have only one or two children, that almost 90 percent have three or fewer children, and that, counting adults, the average AFDC family has 2.9 members.[20]

In addition to family "caps" for welfare recipients, this argument has unleashed frighteningly broad calls to compel, bribe, or cajole poor women to accept long-term contraception in exchange for welfare. Lawmakers in at least thirteen states have sought measures encouraging or requiring the use of Norplant by poor women; in Tennessee and Kansas, legislators introduced proposals to pay welfare mothers $500 to receive the implant and an additional $50 each year that they keep it in.[21] Proponents of these measures view single motherhood as a stigma rather than a choice, as a sign of social depravity rather than an occasion to celebrate life. As Faye Wattleton pointed out in her response to a *Philadelphia Inquirer* editorial suggesting Norplant as a solution to welfare: "Can it be that they do not care whether pregnancy among the 'underclass' is intended or not? . . . Do the editors deem 'these women' unfit to make their own decisions about childbearing?"[22]

The public clamor to regulate single motherhood is undoubtedly inflamed by anxieties about single pregnancy, especially among teenagers. Some states have proposed requiring teenage AFDC mothers to live with their parents. Republican Congresswoman Jan Meyer has introduced federal legislation to nationalize this rule, and Democratic welfare planners have endorsed a similar provision.[23] Although single pregnancy has increased, accounting for 28 percent of all births in 1990, the most dramatic increases have been among white women, college graduates and women in professional and managerial jobs.[24] Furthermore, the icon of the

---

[20] State of California, Department of Social Services, Health and Welfare Agency, *Aid to Families with Dependent Children Characteristics Survey: Study Month of July, 1992* (Sacramento, 1993), p. 21; U.S. Department of Health and Human Services, *Characteristics and Financial Circumstances of AFDC Recipients: FY 1991* (Washington, D.C., 1993), p. 24.

[21] "In Baltimore, A Tumultuous Hearing on Norplant," *Washington Post*, February 10, 1993; Ellen Goodman, "The Politics of Norplant," *Washington Post*, February 19, 1991.

[22] Faye Wattleton, "Using Birth Control as Coercion," *Los Angeles Times*, January 13, 1991.

[23] "Clinton Advisers Urge Tough Line on Welfare," *New York Times*, March 3, 1994; "Clinton Target: Teen Pregnancy," *New York Times*, March 22, 1994.

[24] "Husbands No, Babies Yes," *Newsweek*.

teenage welfare mother rests on very thin evidence. According to data from the U.S. Department of Health and Human Services, the number of teenage mothers on welfare (11–19 years of age) was 293,443 in fiscal year 1991, or approximately 5 percent of AFDC recipients. Most of these teenagers were either 18 (33.4 percent) or 19 (47.2 percent) years old.[25]

The second assumption of contemporary welfare morality—that worthy mothers are connected to men—is equally troubling. In this view, mothers who do not choose to link themselves to fathers— because they want to avoid abusive situations for themselves or their children, or because they are lesbian, or because they haven't met the right guy—are the source of social disorder. To correct the problem, some states have enacted marriage bonuses for women on welfare. New Jersey not only rewards the welfare mother for marrying, but stipulates whom her husband should be: any man *not* the biological father of her children.[26]

At the federal level, the Clinton administration (and the Family Support Act before it) stresses child support enforcement for welfare mothers without husbands. Outside the administration, some liberals have extended the concept to a child support assurance system, whereby an automatic and predictable tax would be withheld from the noncustodial parent's income and paid out as a child support benefit.[27] Of course child support should be available and collectable for mothers who want it, whether or not they are on welfare. But child support enforcement should not be confused with welfare reform for several reasons. Most obviously, for many of the poorest mothers, the fathers of their children are poor. Though helpful to middle-class mothers, a child support system that pivots on fathers' income will not eliminate the poor single mothers' need for social provision.

Equally important, child support enforcement and assurance will bring men with whom mothers do not want contact a little too close to the family. Although the assurance payments would come from the government, they would be pegged to the individual non-

[25] U.S. Department of Health and Human Services, *Characteristics of AFDC Recipients.*

[26] Julie Kosterlitz, "Behavior Modification," *National Journal*, February 1, 1992, p. 273.

[27] Theda Skocpol and William Julius Wilson, "Welfare as We Need It," Op-ed, *New York Times*, February 9, 1994.

custodial parent's income (this is not a plan for, say, a universal child subsidy). To create a direct relationship between a father's wages and the children's economic security would suggest an exchange relationship in which a mother's right to raise her children independently is traded for the father's access to those children. The Clinton administration's proposals for welfare reform make this exchange explicit. They include establishing paternity for all births where the parents are not married, requiring women to identify their child's father as a condition for receiving welfare, and requiring mothers to let fathers visit their children.[28]

Two aspects of child support enforcement/assurance schemes are even more deeply troubling. However carefully phrased in the gender-neutral language of "custodial" and "noncustodial" parents, the scheme perpetuates women's economic subordination and designates fathers as the economic saviors of the family. Most parents on welfare are women. It is women's poverty that creates the need for welfare. The child support alternative to welfare elides this basic fact. Far from being a benign contribution from a noncustodial parent, the child support remedy enforces women's dependency by transferring it from the state to the father. As a welfare reform strategy, child support enforcement and assurance simply reiterates hoary assumptions about gender roles, begging the question of how those assumptions work to keep single mothers poor.[29]

More alarming, it restores the economic authority of the father on the basis of a fleeting biological act. Current discussions about child support enforcement are not confined to collecting contributions from fathers who leave marriages. Welfare reformers across the political spectrum have called for more vigorous and more aggressive "establishment of paternity" even when a mother has chosen to bear her child alone.[30] Though newly popular, this proposal is not new. In fact, under the Family Support Act of 1988, states are required to establish paternity for as many children born to unmarried mothers as possible. Since 1992, federal standards have

---

[28]   "Novel Idea in Welfare Plan: Helping Children by Helping Their Fathers," *New York Times*, March 30, 1994.
[29]   Nan D. Hunter, "Child Support and Policy: The Systematic Imposition of Costs on Women," *Harvard Women's Law Journal* 6 (Spring 1983): 2–27.
[30]   Congresswoman Lynn Woolsey, U.S. House of Representatives, Special Orders (C-SPAN, 7:00 P.M. PDT, March 24, 1994).

been in force for establishing paternity as a means of obtaining child support from absent fathers.[31] At least one state now requires all single mothers to participate in paternity proceedings, not just in exchange for welfare but because every child has a "legal right" to a father.[32] What does this mean for lesbian mothers? For victims of rape who choose to keep their babies? For women who become accidentally pregnant? For women who choose to conceive with a man but who learn in pregnancy that he is ill-suited for fatherhood? And what does this do to the whole legal structure of reproductive choice—to woman's right to choose when and whether to bear children? Will popular crusades against single motherhood intersect with popular campaigns against abortion to assign biological fathers a role in reproductive decision making?

SHIFTING THE AGENDA

Neither marriage nor wages will end women's "welfare dependency" if relations of gender inequality remain inscribed socially and politically in the family, in work, and in the state. Exhortations to poor women to seek economic refuge in "stable marriages" or to behave more like middle-class women will not uplift poor women to the political privilege and economic security from which independence springs. Nor will admonitions to welfare mothers to "take responsibility" for their own social location by leaving the home to work for wages end many women's need for social support. If welfare is a problem it is not *that* women use it but *why* they do. Given the deep structures of inequality in society and in the state, welfare continues to be not a choice but a necessity, not a "way of life" but a way to survive. If women turn to welfare it is because they have been denied the tools of economic security—equal access to paid labor, equitable pay, free choice of vocation, social provision for the care of children, and social policies that are sensitive to the multiple roles most women play.

Both emblem and axiom of woman's relationship to the state, welfare treats women's citizenship as contingent and conditional.

[31] Fineman, "Images of Mothers," p. 279.
[32] Ibid., p. 294.

Still culturally prescriptive—even in the postmaternalist era—
welfare policy and politics interprets and adjudicates women's
needs on behalf of women but not truly for them, scrutinizes the
terms of motherhood, and forgets that women's "dependency" is
really a metonym for women's inequality.

Real welfare reform entails rooting out the premises, prescriptions, and stigma that drive welfare policy—not modifying the behavior and restricting the choices of mothers who need welfare. A
first step would be to end welfare as recipients know it. The de-
meaning, invasive, and sometimes silly system of welfare rules
should be replaced by predictable and automatic standards of eligibility and disbursement of benefits.[33] Reuniting all single and/or
unemployed parents in a unitary program for social provision
along the model of the survivors' insurance system (under which
children currently receive over twice the benefits as do those on
AFDC)[34] would be one possibility. Another option would be to develop a system of caretaker allowances in recognition of the social
value of family work.[35] A caretaker allowance would be a social
wage for a parent who chooses to work in the home raising her
children; a parent who chooses to work outside the home could use
her allowance to purchase child care.

These changes would bring gender consciousness to social policy
without imposing gender prescriptivity. Responsive to women's
poverty and to the reality of most mothers' care-giving responsibilities, these policies would enhance women's choices in the labor
market and at home and would invite men to see family work as
a vocation. Equally important, these policies would socially affirm
child raising and household management as work. This approach
would help undermine the myth that poor women who are full-
time domestic caregivers are "too lazy" to work.

Thus might "end welfare as we know it," but the need for welfare
will not disappear. Women's "need" for welfare attests not to their

---

[33]   On the intrusiveness and unreasonableness of welfare rules, see Theresa Funi-
ciello, *Tyranny of Kindness* (New York, 1993).

[34]   Fineman, "Images of Mothers," quoting Senator Moynihan, p. 282 n.19.

[35]   Nancy Fraser develops this idea in "After the Family Wage: What Do Women
Want in Social Welfare?" paper presented at "Women and Welfare Reform—A Policy
Conference to Break Myths and Create Solutions," October 23, 1993. See also Mimi
Abramovitz, "Challenging the Myths of Welfare Reform from a Woman's Perspec-
tive," paper presented at the same conference.

"dependency" but to their economic inequality, derives not from bad behavior but from poverty. The real issue is how to lift mothers and children from poverty by enhancing their choices in and rewards from the labor market and the home, through, for example, fully funded employment training and education programs, socially provided child care, a higher minimum wage, and full employment policy. Ending women's distinctive poverty will require initiatives on many fronts: in the workplace, in the wage system, in schools, in family law, and in the welfare state.

I · N · D · E · X

Abbott, Edith: Conference on Day Care, 164; educational provision, 105; family structure, 27; family wage, 46; labor standards for women, 46; maternalist reform, 5, 13; mothers' pensions, 40, 51; school attendance, 98–99; vocational education, 81–82

Abbott, Grace: ADC, 131–132; Americanization, 80, 82, 84–85; labor standards for women, 46; maternalist reform, 5, 13; midwifery, 59–60; mothers' pensions, 29; New Deal policy-making, 125, 129; Sheppard-Towner Act, 70; wage-earning mothers, 143

Addams, Jane: day nurseries, 47, 164; education, 81, 83, 85; immigrants, 10; segregation, 117; social settlements, 13

Aid to Dependent Children (ADC): child welfare, 132, 139, 149; domestic motherhood, 3, 127, 130–132, 147, 151; employability of mothers, 142–143; funding of, 133–135, 139; grant for mothers, 175; illegitimacy, 143–149; local administration of, 134, 140–149; race discrimination, 140–150; reform of, 133–135, 138–150; remediation of family life, 139–151; Social Security Act Amendments of 1939, 137–138, 143–144; wage-earning mothers, 139, 151–152, 154–155, 158, 167; women in the welfare state, 151, 175

Aid to Families with Dependent Children (AFDC): eligibility barriers, 175, 182; expansion of program, 175;

moral supervision, 175, 182; "take-up" rate for women of color, 175, 182–183

American Home Economics Association, 89

Americanization: infant welfare, 54–55; Little Mothers' Leagues, 66, 72; maternalist reform, 12, 24, 28, 30, 80; midwifery, 59–60; mothers' pensions, 35–41, 49; school reform, 78–106, 109–120; WPA education projects, 158–160

Americanization Conference, 35

Anderson, Mary: child care, 164, 168, 169; maternalist reform, 13; New Deal policy-making, 125, 128; wage-earning mothers, 153

Association for Study and Prevention of Infant Mortality, 60

Baker, Dr. S. Josephine: Americanization, 69; breastfeeding, 60–61; democracy and child health, 58; diet manuals, 64; immigrants, 55–56; infant mortality, 59; maternity reform, 54; midwifery, 60

Bethune, Mary McLeod, 106

Bird, Ethel, 84–85

Board of Maternal and Infant Hygiene, 67

Bowen, Louise deKoven, 51, 99

breastfeeding, 54, 60–63

Breckinridge, Sophonisba: ADC, 132; educational provision, 105; family structure, 27; labor standards for women, 46; maternalist reform, 5, 13; mothers' pensions, 40, 51; school

193